Goldwater v. Carter

LANDMARK LAW CASES & AMERICAN SOCIETY

Peter Charles Hoffer
N. E. H. Hull
Founding Series Editors

RECENT TITLES IN THE SERIES

Prigg v. Pennsylvania, H. Robert Baker
The Detroit School Busing Case, Joyce A. Baugh
Lizzie Borden on Trial, Joseph A. Conforti
The Japanese American Cases, Roger Daniels
Judging the Boy Scouts of America, Richard J. Ellis
Fighting Foreclosure, John A. Fliter and Derek S. Hoff
The Passenger Cases and the Commerce Clause, Tony A. Freyer
Discrediting the Red Scare, Robert Justin Goldstein
The Great Yazoo Lands Sale, Charles F. Hobson
The Free Press Crisis of 1800, Peter Charles Hoffer
Rutgers v. Waddington, Peter Charles Hoffer
The Woman Who Dared to Vote, N. E. H. Hull
Plessy v. Ferguson, Williamjames Hull Hoffer
The Tokyo Rose Case, Yasuhide Kawashima
Gitlow v. New York, Marc Lendler
The Unusual Story of the Pocket Veto Case, 1926–1929, Jonathan Lurie
Opposing Lincoln, Thomas C. Mackey
Medellín v. Texas, Alan Mygatt-Tauber
American by Birth, abridged ed., Carol Nackenoff and Julie Novkov
The Supreme Court and Tribal Gaming, Ralph A. Rossum
The 9/11 Terror Cases, Allan A. Ryan
Obscenity Rules, Whitney Strub
On Account of Sex, Philippa Strum
Speaking Freely, Philippa Strum
The Campaign Finance Cases, Melvin I. Urofsky
Race, Sex, and the Freedom to Marry, Peter Wallenstein
Bush v. Gore, 3rd expanded ed., Charles L. Zelden

For a complete list of titles in the series go to www.kansaspress.ku.edu.

JOSHUA E. KASTENBERG

Goldwater v. Carter

Foreign Policy, China, and the Resurgence of Executive Branch Primacy

UNIVERSITY PRESS OF KANSAS

Published by the University Press of Kansas (Lawrence, Kansas 66045), which was organized by the Kansas Board of Regents and is operated and funded by Emporia State University, Fort Hays State University, Kansas State University, Pittsburg State University, the University of Kansas, and Wichita State University.

Library of Congress Cataloging-in-Publication Data
Names: Kastenberg, Joshua E., 1967–, author.
Title: Goldwater v. Carter : foreign policy, China, and the resurgence of executive branch primacy / Joshua E. Kastenberg.
Description: Lawrence : University Press of Kansas, 2023. | Series: Landmark law cases and American society
Includes index.
Identifiers: LCCN 2022061298 (print)
ISBN 978-0-7006-3546-7 (cloth) | ISBN 978-0-7006-3547-4 (paperback)
ISBN 978-0-7006-3548-1 (ebook)
Subjects: Mutual Defense Treaty between the United States of America and the Republic of China (1954 December 2) | Treaty-making power—United States. | Executive power—United States. | Treaties—Termination. | United States—Foreign relations—Treaties. | United States—Foreign relations—China. | United States—Foreign relations—Taiwan. | United States—Politics and government—1977-1981.
Classification: KF5055 .K37 2023 (print)
LC record available at https://lccn.loc.gov/2022061298.
LC ebook record available.

British Library Cataloguing-in-Publication Data is available.

Printed in the United States of America

10 9 8 7 6 5 4 3 2 1

The paper used in this publication is acid free and meets the minimum requirements of the American National Standard for Permanence of Paper for Printed Library Materials Z39.48-1992.

CONTENTS

PREFACE AND ACKNOWLEDGMENTS

Sometime in spring of 1979, my dad announced that he was going to travel to the Republic of China (Taiwan). My older brother and I were in middle school, and our knowledge of Taiwan was limited to how many hours the flight would take and whether he would be on a 747. My dad was a nuclear engineering professor at the University of California. Taiwan had obtained a nuclear reactor for the production of electricity during President Dwight Eisenhower's Atoms for Peace program, but after President James Earl Carter announced his intention to have the United States exit the Mutual Defense Treaty, the federal government determined to retrieve some of the fuel rods and replace these with uranium that would be more difficult to weaponize into warheads. My dad was ostensibly going as a consultant for Argonne National Laboratories and the Nuclear Regulatory Commission. As a result of complicated political maneuvering by both governments, his travel went through a Canadian, rather than US, program. In other words, his travel was official, without having to call it such. And, ironically, his trip occurred a week after the Three Mile Island partial meltdown incident in Pennsylvania.

I remember that when he returned home from Taiwan, he brought a small Republic of China flag on top of a paperweight. The flag stayed on his desk at the university until he retired. His Taiwanese counterparts asked of him a simple request in presenting him with their flag: "Please do not forget us." That story stuck with me through the sixth grade to the present. When I started work on this project, my dad told me that over the years some of the graduate students from the People's Republic of China would ask him about the flag, and a few of them expressed dismay he had it in the open. My dad has always, to the best of my recollection, been something of a diplomat. But he is also a fervent believer in democracy and had no difficulty in relaying—in an unclassified manner—how the flag came into his possession. And, he never wanted to forget about the people who gave him the flag or have others forget them.

The nature of this series, aptly titled Landmark Law Cases and American Society, precludes the use of footnotes or other conventional citations. There is a benefit as well as a concern with such an approach.

The twofold concern, for me, is that a scholar, pundit, or critic might seek proof that an executive branch official, legislator, or jurist actually wrote or spoke the words credited to them in this book. The archival material listed in the bibliographic essay is where all the quotes and commentary can be discovered. Most of these originate from original source material, and I maintained copies to check and recheck accuracy. Second, a reviewer might wonder if this book is largely based on readily available secondary sources. It is not, although in the bibliographic essay section at the end I stress some of the sources I relied on for background and context. The benefit to a work that has abandoned the rote citation method is, I presume, to make it more readable to the general public. It is my hope that this book accomplished just that.

The 1970s were no less complex than the present. There are many descriptions in this book of how chaotic life had become in the 1970s: stagflation, the steel crisis of 1973, Watergate and Richard Nixon's impeachment, two fuel crises that resulted in shortages and significant price increases, the fall of the Republic of Vietnam in 1975, Iran's revolution and the hostage crisis, the Three Mile Island nuclear power plant mishap, hostage taking throughout the Middle East and Europe, and the pending Soviet invasion of Afghanistan. One of my peers suggested that I put too much nonlegal history in this book. One theme of the book is a search for stability. Carter, in continuing President Richard Milhous Nixon's policy toward recognizing the People's Republic of China, sought needed stability. Senator Barry Goldwater (R-AZ) and his allies believed the price of this stability meant the retreat of democracy and the abandonment of an important ally. Therefore, they argued, the stability would be short-lived, if not illusory. These were the policy arguments undergirding the constitutional arguments to the judiciary. *Goldwater v. Carter* is best understood in this light. As to putting too many facts in the book, I responded to my peer that had I discussed Disco Demolition Night at Chicago's Comiskey Park, which incidentally occurred close in time to when Goldwater initially filed his challenge against Carter in the district court, I then might have added needless trivia.

"Might," though, requires a qualifier. Disco Demolition Night was chaotic and represented a cultural revolt between rock and roll adherents and the followers of the newer disco dance music. I have used this episode in my criminal law class to show that the difference between criminal negligence and tort negligence is sometimes a matter of prosecutorial discretion. In 1976, a right-wing newsletter accurately titled *The Right Report* claimed that President Gerald Ford had only belatedly promised to defend Taiwan in order to woo conservatives away from his Republican rival, former California governor Ronald Reagan. The author of the newsletter claimed that Ford wanted to enable Goldwater and other longtime allies to continue to support him. "Conservative Republicans no longer look to Barry Goldwater and other aging lions for leadership," the author claimed. "They are lining up with newer men." This may have been true, but it was overstated, and the legislators who signed on with Goldwater were both from the "aging lions" and much younger men such as Newt Gingrich and Dan Quayle.

A preface is supposed to be short, but it is not complete unless it contains mention that while every mistake in this book is my own, the book could not have been written without the help of friends. A scholar of American history has no better ally than the professional staff at the Library of Congress Manuscript Division. In that regard, I owe a special thanks to Ryan Reft, Edith Sandler, Bruce Kirby, Patrick Kerwin, Lewis Wyman, Lara Szypszak, Loretta Deaver, and Kerrie Cotten Williams, who enable so many researchers to write history. I have traveled to over fifty historic archives across the United States and abroad and always met helpful librarians and archivists. But, as for those at the Library of Congress, their enthusiasm for supporting the works of others is a "platinum standard" model.

I am also lucky to have friends in my profession. I thank them as well, for both their ideas and, more important, their encouragement: at High Point University in North Carolina, Frederick Schneid; at the University of Iowa School of Law, Kevin Washburn; and at the University of New Mexico School of Law, Sonia Gibson-Rankin, Maryam Ahranjani, Paul Figueroa, John Kang, Laura Spitz, Mario Occhialino, Leo Romero, Scott England, Mary Pareja, Clifford Villa, Alfred Mathewson, Camille Carey, and Sergio Pareja. The last three people on this list not only are friends but also served as deans of the law school and made possible funding for my research over the last few years. The law school is a special place. It is collegial, and it is full of life. Many of its students do want to make a difference in creating a more just world. This also propels me to turn my passion for legal history into publishing works in the hopes of preventing false and expedient narratives that may block their goals from becoming reality.

With the unprovoked and utterly brutal Russian invasion of Ukraine less than a year old and the North Atlantic Treaty Organization holding fast in its commitment to defend its member states, the importance of the alliance to freedom at home and across the ocean has been, in my estimation, proved. Whether future administrations or the Congress remains committed to the treaty, however, is another question, and when an administration, such as had occurred between 2017 and 2021, acts to cast doubt on the treaty's efficacy, there is little redress in the federal courts to stop further deleterious actions to it.

Ever since I retired from the military in 2016, I decided that my books should be dedicated to people who earlier stood by me, encouraged me, or reminded me that all of us have moral worth. I can never write enough books in the time I have left to recognize the debt that I have to people in this category. But I can batch them into groups, even if the "people" and the "batching" are unconventional. This book is dedicated to "M," "C," "A," "C," "A," and "L." At various times, and always out of love, they enriched my life and reminded me that, even on my worst days, I was luckier than many people on their best day.

Introduction

Lord Palmerston, the United Kingdom's prime minister between 1859 and 1865, once proclaimed that the British Empire had "no eternal allies"—and "no perpetual enemies." He concluded with the statement "Our interests are eternal and perpetual, and those interests it is our duty to follow." His real name, Henry John Temple, followed by his title, 3rd Viscount Palmerston, befitted the British Empire and reflected the aristocracy that once governed it. Palmerston actually made the statement in a prior capacity, when he served as Britain's secretary of state for foreign affairs and explained to the Parliament why the Royal Navy might undertake a military action against Greece. While it is perhaps odd that one might compare Palmerston, a nineteenth-century British imperialist, to President James Earl Carter, a decidedly anti-imperialist president, there was, in 1979, a point of comparison between the two. Perhaps the resemblance is quite small, but it is not insignificant. Palmerston made his statement to justify a shift in Britain's foreign policies toward past allies. In December 1978, Carter sought to cement relations with the People's Republic of China—a communist country with the largest population in the world—by renouncing a treaty with the Republic of China (Taiwan), a US ally and a post–World War II strategic bulwark against the spread of communism. The treaty had a withdrawal provision requiring one year's notice from the government that intended to terminate its treaty obligations. However, it was reasonable for the governments of Taiwan and members of the US Congress to believe there would be a role for the Senate in any decision to withdraw. And Carter's opponent, Senator Barry Goldwater of Arizona, an ardent conservative Republican, swore that he would stop Carter from doing so.

Goldwater also had similarities to Palmerston. Like Palmerston, Goldwater espoused the need for massive military strength, and he sought to maintain US influence over key areas around the world as a matter of strategy. Palmerston centered his attentions on the Mediterranean and control of sea routes to India; Goldwater insisted on maintaining the Panama Canal under US control. Of course, Palmerston was prime minister as a result of Britain's unique parliamentary system, and he owed fealty to Queen Elizabeth; Goldwater had aspired to become president in 1964, but through a direct election, unknown to the British parliamentary system. Palmerston was an imperialist who sought the expansion of the British Empire, and Goldwater—though not a proponent of European-style imperialism—advocated the maintenance of American power around the world to protect against communism, including allying with dictatorial regimes. Goldwater refused to see the Panama Canal as a symbol of American imperialism, which put him in conflict with Carter, who did. To Goldwater, the loss in of South Vietnam and Cambodia to communism in 1975 was not merely humiliating for the United States; it made the defense of Taiwan critical to stopping the spread of communism. When Carter acted to remove the United States from the Mutual Defense Treaty with Taiwan, Goldwater challenged him in the federal courts. Such a path was impossible for Palmerston's parliamentary opponents because, if for no other reason, Britain did not have a Supreme Court. But a path to challenge Carter in the federal courts was available to Goldwater. Or so it seemed.

Goldwater warned that if Carter could unilaterally act to withdraw the United States from a treaty with Taiwan, then another president could remove the country from the North Atlantic Treaty Organization (NATO). From its founding, NATO has been the preeminent bulwark against Soviet, and Russian, aggression toward Central and Western Europe. It was also instrumental in fostering democracy in Eastern and Central Europe and is now, in theory, protecting Poland, Latvia, Lithuania, and Estonia from Russian aggression. While some of Goldwater's critics claimed the threat of a NATO exit to be fanciful hyperbole, it is noteworthy that fears of the United States exiting from that treaty organization resurfaced as a result of the actions of former president Donald Trump. Goldwater and his congressional allies had more complex reasons for challenging Carter than a disagreement over foreign policy. But it is noteworthy that Goldwater was not alone in his warning about the future of NATO. On June 6, 1979, former undersecretary of state Eugene Rostow implored Congress that if Carter were permitted to unilaterally withdraw the United States from the Mutual Defense Treaty, then the United States' allies could never be assured they would be protected if an enemy state were to threaten their existence. Rostow and other Cold War Democrats such as Paul Nitze, former secretary of the navy and deputy secretary of defense in President Lyndon Johnson's administration, allied with conservatives to form political organizations such as the Committee on the Public Danger in order to curb Carter's policies. This group, not surprisingly, aligned with Goldwater on the treaty revocation, and Rostow served as Goldwater's lead counsel in the litigation over the revocation.

The study that follows is not a historical analysis of Carter's foreign policies, though an understanding of the uniqueness of these policies is important to comprehending the traverse of *Goldwater v. Carter* through the federal courts. So too is an understanding of the crises facing the United States in the last two years of Carter's presidency, if not throughout the decade of the 1970s. A domestic economy marked by rising unemployment, inflation, oil shortages, significant disagreements with European allies, an increasingly aggressive Soviet Union, and, of course, the Iranian Revolution and hostage crisis placed the Carter administration in a continual reaction mode. This book is a study of Congress's relations with the executive and judicial branches through the analysis of one of the Supreme Court's more important actions on presidential authority. (From this point forward, the singular capitalized word "Court" denotes the United States Supreme Court.) The political ideologies and conduct of the main actors are highlighted to contextualize the Court's strengthening of the executive branch in the national security and foreign policy arenas. When Carter became president, the power of the presidency was in decline in relation to Congress and the courts. This was not always the case. Since the New Deal of President Franklin Delano Roosevelt, the Oval Office had become, in the words of historian Arthur Schlesinger Jr., an "imperial presidency." After the Vietnam Conflict, Congress, with some assistance from the lower federal courts, curbed the expansion of executive branch authority. Whether by design or by accident, *Goldwater v. Carter*, along with other highlighted decisions, enabled the growth of the imperial presidency to resume.

There is another aspect to this study. Given the importance of the US government's recognition of China and its willingness to have Taiwan relegated to a status of less than a nation, to a person not fully immersed in the federal court system or the important nuances of constitutional law, it may come as a surprise that the nation's highest court did not substantively resolve an issue of presidential power or permit the lower courts to do so. But many in Congress supported the Court's decision, even if they disagreed with Carter. As one example, Senator David Boren (D-OK) informed his constituents that he believed Carter's actions imperiled the constitutional structure of government, if not the survival of democracy in the Pacific. "I will strongly support the idea that a president has no right to take unilateral action which results in the abrogation of any treaty that required Congressional approval," Boren insisted. "The precedent thus established placed an unchecked authority in the hands of the Executive Branch that could threaten the security of this nation and which goes far beyond the intent of the Constitution." Yet Boren never signed on to Goldwater's lawsuit against Carter because, as he later explained, it would enable the judicial branch to replace congressional power as well as executive authority with its own. Boren would not be alone in his worries about an empowered judicial branch, a matter that, in the previous two decades, southern segregationists had routinely claimed would occur in civil rights cases.

Why *Goldwater v. Carter*?

Goldwater v. Carter is important not simply because during the journey of the appeal and after the Court issued its decision to dismiss, dozens of law review articles analyzed the judiciary's role in foreign policy or the defining of the Constitution's allocation of powers in the arena of treaties, or because the news media covered Goldwater's challenge to a greater degree than it did for most other appeals in the later 1970s. True enough, *Goldwater v. Carter* is highlighted in several constitutional law casebooks that professors assign to first-year law students, giving the decision a prominence that many other judicial opinions do not possess. From the vantage of history, the decision is important because conservatives used Carter's policy on China and Taiwan, among other issues, to doom his reelection efforts. On the eve of the 1980 election, George Will, a young but influential commentator with the *Washington Post*, captured the essence of conservative anger at Carter in regards to Taiwan in arguing: "A nation that uses an ally such as Taiwan as a pawn for utterly unnecessary appeasement had better get used to having fewer and fewer allies of any size, and to the worldwide conviction that it is a nation with no serious convictions." While Will did not attack the Court—this makes sense since, after all, most of the justices who decided to dismiss *Goldwater* were conservative jurists—the Court did articulate an important constitutional law rule. This too establishes its importance.

The Constitution presents the signing of treaties as a shared power. A president is the voice of foreign affairs and therefore initiates the United States entering into a treaty with a foreign government. The Senate, in order to make a treaty become law—and coequal to the domestic laws—must vote in favor of the treaty by a margin of two-thirds of the sitting senators. There are other complexities to treaties, such as whether implementing legislation is necessary for a treaty to take effect. Nonetheless, a president and the Senate have the sole role in treaty making. In the 1950s, a congressional effort, known as the Bricker Amendment, to amend this construct came close to succeeding, but it has not been attempted since. The Constitution is silent on treaty termination, though one could surmise that in instances where the United States has a treaty with another country and then enters into an armed conflict with that country, the treaty is null and void. Likewise, if a foreign government were to collapse, a treaty might also be found to cease to exist. Yet, the Republic of China existed, and it contributed to the US government's policy and promise of containing communism in the Pacific.

Carter insisted on terminating the Mutual Defense Treaty with the Republic of China and without the Senate voting on it. The Constitution's plain language provides no mandate or guidance on treaty termination. The specific language of the Constitution's treaty clause reads as follows: "[The president] shall have Power, by and with the Advice and Consent of the Senate, to make Treaties, provided two-thirds of the Senators present concur." The Constitution also contains a clause, titled the supremacy clause, which places the authority of treaties high in the nation's legal structure. Indeed, that clause reads: "This Constitution, and the Laws of the United States which shall be made in Pursuance thereof; and all Treaties made, or which shall be made, under the Authority of the United States, shall be the supreme Law of the Land;

and the Judges in every State shall be bound thereby, any Thing in the Constitution or Laws of any State to the Contrary notwithstanding." In contrast, the Mutual Defense Treaty contained a termination clause that allowed one of the two signatory parties to withdraw from the treaty as long as a year's notice was given to the other signatory.

Because a treaty becomes, under the supremacy clause, the law of the United States and only Congress has the authority to terminate a law, there was an important constitutional question within the lawsuit to stop Carter. That is, would not Congress have an important role in treaty termination, just it does in the removal and replacement of laws? The Constitution's framers had never addressed that question, or at least, they left it for another day for the Congress and the federal courts, or presidential acquiescence, to determine the issue. For three days beginning on April 9, 1979, several dozen leading legal experts, including professors, former secretaries of state, State Department lawyers, and former attorney generals, debated this issue in front of the Senate Foreign Relations Committee. With such a robust debate, one might have assumed the courts, rather than the Congress or academia, would conclusively answer the issue.

The Court, however, did not rule that a president generally, or Carter specifically, had the constitutional authority to terminate a treaty. Rather, the Court issued a plurality of four justices who explicitly insisted that the lawsuit was incapable of resolution in the judicial branch. Another justice determined that the issue could have been determined in the federal courts, but only if the Senate or Congress had acted as a body, rather than a fraction of the legislators bringing suit. Two lower courts—the US District Court for the District of Columbia and the Court of Appeals for the District of Columbia, or nine judges in all—believed that the courts could resolve the question in one way or another and the courts were a proper place to do so. But, on the Court, six of the nine justices disagreed, and the Court moved the question of presidential authority in foreign affairs back into the political arena and out of the judicial. Put another way, in the words of one scholar, the Court's opinion did not involve a ruling on the merits, and "the net effect was to insulate the President's decision from judicial review, thereby increasing his power."

There were, in point of fact, four parts to the Court's order to dismiss. Justice William Rehnquist authored a lengthy explanation on the dismissal order describing why the federal courts could not, based on the political question doctrine, adjudicate suits against a presidential foreign policy decision. Chief Justice Warren Burger and Justices Potter Stewart and John Paul Stevens joined with Rehnquist. Justice Thurgood Marshall agreed with the dismissal but did not join with Rehnquist's explanation. Justice Lewis Powell authored a concurring opinion to the dismissal order, but he believed the order had unnecessarily taken from Congress an important avenue for redress in the federal courts. To Powell, if all of Congress had acted against a presidential decision and the president refused to comply, then Congress should be able to seek a remedy in the courts. He urged that while the Court's order was constitutional as it applied to Goldwater's suit, if used against a Congress that had voted against a treaty termination, the order would be unconstitutional. Justice William J. Brennan dissented from the dismissal order. He wanted the Court to issue a formal opinion stating that Congress did not have a constitutional role in treaty termination. Justices Harry Blackmun and Byron White also dissented, but unlike Brennan, they insisted that a substantive opinion on the constitutional question before the Court could resolve in favor of Congress. However, they did not actually commit a substantive answer to that position. Rather, they objected to the Court not giving "plenary consideration" to the issue. This type of objection had occurred before. During the Vietnam Conflict, in 1967, Stewart and Justice William O. Douglas, who retired from the Court in 1975, were appalled with their fellow justices not ruling on whether it was unconstitutional to send conscripted soldiers to an undeclared conflict. Yet in their objection to the Court's denial of considering the legality of the war, they did not state how they personally would vote on the appeal.

There are several ironies to the Court's actions in *Goldwater*. Senator Goldwater had run for president in 1964 as a conservative wedded to the idea that the federal government had grown too powerful and its regulatory authority had to be reduced to a level predating the New Deal, if not the Progressive Era. Rehnquist not only embraced much of Goldwater's ideology, but both men were from Arizona, and it was Goldwater who championed Rehnquist to become a justice and then, in 1987, the chief justice. Indeed, in 1971, Goldwater ceremonially "introduced" Rehnquist to the Senate after President Richard Milhous Nixon publicly announced the nomination. While Rehnquist did not denounce

Goldwater's suit—indeed, the dismissal order provided Goldwater with a political victory of a different nature than what he sought—the fact that Rehnquist dismissed a lawsuit raised by one of his key supporters does bear an ironic note. It is also ironic that the Court enabled Carter to derecognize an allied nation, the Republic of China, in order to recognize the People's Republic of China, a communist behemoth.

A fourth irony is that while Carter had been elected on a promise to integrate human rights into US foreign policy and conservatives derided him, when it came to recognizing the People's Republic of China, conservative opponents of his policies reminded the nation that China's human rights record was abysmal. Not only had millions of Chinese citizens died during the Cultural Revolution, but China had aligned with the Khmer Rouge in Cambodia and gave sanction to that genocidal regime. In contrast, when Carter tried to reduce the US military presence in South Korea and return the Panama Canal to Panama, conservatives lambasted him for showing weakness in the face of communism, notwithstanding that the South Korean government itself had been dictatorial. Aspects of these disagreements appeared in the federal courts during Carter's presidency.

Goldwater v. Carter, as the suit was captioned, presents a study of legislative-judicial relations as well as executive-judicial relations in a time of crisis. From the beginning of Carter's presidency, the Soviet Union attempted to spread communism in South and Central America, in concert with a foreign policy established by Premier Leonid Brezhnev, the general secretary of the Communist Party. The so-called Brezhnev Doctrine promised Soviet military and economic aid to socialist and communist governments confronted by internal revolt as well as to communist organizations in other countries. For most of Carter's presidential tenure, he tried to commit the United States and the Soviet Union to a second arms reduction treaty. But the second Strategic Arms Limitations Talks (SALT II) never resulted in a treaty once the Soviet Union invaded Afghanistan. And this invasion was not the most severe test of Carter's presidency.

In the second half of Carter's presidency, Iran—an American ally—convulsed in a revolution that resulted in a Shia Islamist government that was wedded to denouncing the United States as a satanic enemy, killing its own citizens, and supporting international terrorism. Its leaders, as well as its more radical revolutionaries who seized US embassy personnel as hostages, brought the United States to the brink of military conflict. The judges and justices involved in Goldwater's suit were well aware of the crisis with the Soviet Union and Iran, as well as the economic downturns and incommensurate inflation endemic to the 1970s. They were also aware that a relationship with the People's Republic of China could bring stability, at least to Asia, as well open markets to US commerce at a time when domestic US industries such as automobile production, garment manufacture, and steel and aluminum production were in severe decline.

For the Court to come to the conclusion that it did may not have been simply a matter of contemporaneous crises. Indeed, the justices might have tried to insulate themselves from world events and make their decisions in a vacuum, free from the fears of an aggressive Soviet Union and an Iranian government baiting the United States into a war. On the other hand, if détente with the Soviet Union had not been failing and had the Soviet Union not invaded Afghanistan or the Shah not been deposed, it is possible that the Court and the judges on the Court of Appeals for the District of Columbia might have had a different approach to the issue they had to decide. It is partly for this reason that *Goldwater v. Carter* cannot be viewed without the context of multiple crises to the United States. After all, the lower courts that first decided on Goldwater's suit wove, throughout their decisions, an understanding of the importance of the issue to contemporaneous events, as well as the distinct possibility of global crises in a long duration.

There is another reason that *Goldwater* is a landmark decision. In studying the resurgence of presidential power, or what Schlesinger termed the "imperial presidency," it can be seen as part of a line of Court opinions that enabled a stronger presidency. Surrounding *Goldwater* are three judicial opinions that provide significant leverage to the presidency over civil servants working in the intelligence and foreign policy arena: *Haig v. Agee*, *United States v. Snepp*, and a decision by the US Court of Appeals for the Fourth Circuit that did not make it to the Court, *United States v. Marchetti.* These opinions would place limits on the ability of civil servants to tell publicly their stories about governmental missteps in the foreign policy, national defense, and intelligence arenas. There is also the Court's opinion captioned as *Fitzgerald v. Nixon*, which solidified the doctrine of presidential immunity against civil suits for official acts, and, as noted in the next chapter, Arthur Ernest Fitzgerald was the very definition of a dedicated civil servant who uncovered fraud in the Department of Defense only to have his professional and personal life upended by a president. Finally, the Court in *Dames & Moore v. Regan* recognized a presidential authority, albeit one granted by Congress, to intrude into a category of civil suits that might, in the judgment of the president, impact foreign policy or national security. *Goldwater* resides in an elevated center position among these opinions, as well as others noted throughout this study, as it recognized the existence of a supreme presidential power, immune from judicial review. Put another way, a president who treats an ally with disregard for treaty norms, and at the same time curries favor with a foreign government long believed to harbor an aggressive expansion strategy at the expense of the ally, does not need to worry about judicial interference. This power is given greater meaning when the president is also able to intrude upon, if not violate, the legal rights of individuals working in the government who try to guide the administration back into the realm of legal conduct.

The Court and Foreign Policy Before Goldwater

While it is possible to write a multivolume treatise on the federal judiciary and foreign policy, there are four decisions—among the many listed throughout this book—that are important to reference from the start. In 1920, the Court determined, in *Missouri v. Holland*, that because a treaty is coequal to a federal statue, and the Constitution's supremacy clause places federal law above that of the states, the state of Missouri could not stop the federal protection of migratory birds. In 1918, the United States signed a treaty protecting migratory birds with the United Kingdom on behalf of its dominion, Canada. Missourians did not want to comply with the limits on bird hunting because, they argued, the Constitution did not delegate the regulation of game hunting to the federal government. That is, the Tenth Amendment reserved to the states a wide swath of authorities, including the regulation of hunting. *Holland*, it has been argued, enables an "end run" on constitutional processes and limitations, including the ability to craft federal crimes that were normally reserved to the state governments. *Holland*'s legacy as applied to Carter's actions led to an important question: If a treaty is the law of the land, then doesn't a treaty termination require Congress's approval, just as the termination of a statute would?

In 1935, in *Van Der Weyde v. Ocean Transport Co.*, the Court upheld a treaty termination that involved Congress's approval. In 1915, Congress passed a maritime act and requested the president renounce various maritime treaties in conflict with the act. The issue before the Court in 1935 had to do with a maritime injury. A Dutch sailor filed suit against a ship company that had been registered in Norway but later sold to a Japanese company. The Court observed, "We think that the question as to the authority of the Executive in the absence of congressional action, or of action by the treaty-making power, to denounce a treaty of the United States, is not here involved." Thus, instead of a definitive answer, the Court left open the possibility of judicial review of a presidential treaty termination for another day. From a historical standpoint, one might conclude that between the Constitution's ratification and 1935, the issue of treaty termination remained an open question, albeit one that did not come to the courts.

The Court's recognition of executive branch supremacy in a foreign policy arena recognized by Congress occurred in 1936 as a result of Attorney General Homer Cummings's appeal against a district court quashing a federal indictment against a corporate officer accused of illegally selling arms to a warring nation. On May 28, 1934, the House and Senate passed a joint resolution empowering Roosevelt to embargo the sale of arms to Peru and Bolivia, both of which were involved in a conflict known as the Chaco War. The joint resolution authorized a sentence of two years' imprisonment and a fine of up to $10,000, and therefore it worked as a de facto criminal statute. The same day Congress published the joint resolution, Roosevelt issued a proclamation prohibiting the sale of arms to Bolivia and Peru. Both the corporation and its corporate officer convinced a US district court that Roosevelt's proclamation was unenforceable because Congress had unconstitutionally delegated its lawmaking authority to the executive branch, and that by the time the government discovered the corporate officer's alleged offenses, the prohibition had been rescinded.

In *United States v. Curtiss-Wright Export Corp.*, a decision authored by

Justice George Sutherland, the Court overturned the district court. Sutherland first distinguished limits on presidential actions in the nation's internal affairs from the broad constitutional foreign policy authorities of the president. He then articulated several historical examples of executive branch supremacy, as well as congressional statements on the almost unimpeded authority of the president to conduct foreign policy. As a result, Sutherland concluded, the Court should not overturn a principle as old as the nation that recognized the president's broad powers to prohibit foreign commerce or enforce other aspects of foreign policy when Congress had acted to empower the president. *Curtiss-Wright* created a basis for Carter to argue that the termination of a treaty was solely within the executive branch's province. But there was a notable difference between Roosevelt's actions and Carter's in that Congress had authorized Roosevelt to prosecute the sale of arms to specified foreign nations and at no time did Congress expressly empower Carter's decision to terminate a treaty. In 2015, the Court, in *Zivotofsky v. Kerry*, upheld a president's constitutional authority to recognize a foreign country or, more particularly, which city the government recognizes as the foreign country's capital. But in doing so, the Court reminded the executive branch that *Curtiss-Wright* only decided a question of congressional delegation to a president and not the absoluteness of presidential power in foreign policy.

The fourth decision of importance did not stem directly from a foreign policy dispute at all, though it occurred in a time of armed conflict and therefore was important to a president's ability to lead the country during times of foreign crisis. On April 8, 1952, with an ongoing war in Korea and a seemingly unsolvable labor dispute between labor unions and steel mill owners, President Harry S. Truman ordered Secretary of Commerce Charles Sawyer to seize commercial steel foundries. Truman insisted that the continued production of steel was vital to the war effort in Korea. His actions were not without precedent. In 1940, Robert Jackson, while serving as attorney general, advised Roosevelt that the government had the authority to seize the nation's aviation industries in order to achieve labor peace, although in that instance the fear of communist-led strikes was at the forefront of his advice. One of the World War II property seizures, involving the Montgomery Ward Corporation, reached the Court. By the time it did so, however, the appeal was moot.

In a 1953 decision titled *Youngstown Sheet and Tube v. Sawyer* (which Rehnquist later characterized as one of the more contentious decisions in the Supreme Court's history), the Court curbed the presidential authority to take exclusive actions during crisis times, short of a declared war. At no point in the Korean War did Congress declare war on either North Korea or the People's Republic of China. *Youngstown* proved influential in the traverse of Goldwater's appeal to the Court, particularly as Goldwater would use it to argue that in matters of constitutional silence, such as treaty revocation, a federal court could not only take jurisdiction of the suit but also issue a decision contrary to a president. There were other parallels with *Youngstown* to Goldwater's suit. *Youngstown*'s history through the courts is worthy of note because Goldwater's lawsuit underwent a similar journey, albeit with a much different ending.

At a news conference on May 22, 1952, Truman not only claimed the authority to seize property without congressional approval but also hinted that he believed the judiciary did not have the jurisdiction to intervene. In one of his "give-and-take" moments with the press, he asserted, in response to a question about the Court, that "nobody can take it away from the President because it is inherent in the Constitution." He was mistaken. The steel companies had already filed for an injunction against the seizure in federal court, and the case was not dismissed. Truman may have been lulled into making his statement as a result of a district court's earlier actions as well as by Chief Justice Frederick Vinson's private unseemly assurance that the Court would rule in his favor. One month earlier, Judge Alexander Holtzoff had refused to issue a preliminary injunction against the president because, in his estimation, the Korean War constituted a national emergency and, on balance, more harm would come from the issuance of an injunction. However, this was not the end, and Holtzoff set April 24 as the date to determine the legality of Truman's actions. But Holtzoff did not preside over the merits of the case.

On April 24, Judge David A. Pine heard arguments for granting an injunction against raising wages. Justice Department lawyers argued that Truman possessed an almost unrestricted authority to manage the steel mills. As a result of the government's brief, Pine did not merely consider granting an injunction. Based on the economic injury the steel mill owners might suffer as a result of the seizure, Pine decided to assess the constitutionality of the full array of Truman's actions. Five days later, he ruled against Truman, who then appealed directly to the Supreme Court, bypassing the Court of Appeals for the District of Columbia. While the justices considered granting certiorari, Truman also appealed to the court of appeals to temporarily lift Pine's order. In a divided five-to-four vote, the appellate court voided Pine's order for two days, until the Court's grant of certiorari. Judge Elijah Prettyman, who would be gone from the appellate court by the time of Goldwater's case, recorded that the decision was contentious and that all of the judges retreated to their chambers for personal prayers before voting.

The justices heard arguments on May 12 and 13, 1952, and issued their opinions on June 2 of the same year. In conference—a term to denote the discussions of the justices—Vinson insisted that the conflict in Korea and the potential for full-scale war in Europe made it imperative that presidential authority not be narrowed. Justices Stanley Reed and Sherman Minton agreed with Vinson on this point. Minton, Justice Felix Frankfurter later recorded, became agitated and pounded the conference table, claiming, "There is an emergency. Truman seized the plants because the defense of the country required it!" Justice Hugo Black disagreed and accused Vinson and Minton of using "irrelevancies" to secure their position. Black countered with the observation that if a president possessed the quantum of authority Vinson claimed, then a president could routinely bypass Congress on other important matters affecting foreign affairs and national security. Douglas agreed with Black on this point, as did Justices Frankfurter, Robert Jackson, Tom Clark, and Harold Burton. What emerged from the conference was a fractured decision, but one that placed limits on presidential authority in times of crisis, if not during peace.

Black's insistence on a constitutional ruling took form in the first sentence of the opinion: "We are asked to decide whether the President was acting within his constitutional power when he issued an order directing the Secretary of Commerce to take possession of and operate most of the Nation's steel mills." Black emphatically dismissed the notion that because property seizures had occurred in the past, this created a constitutional precedent. Importantly, Black stated there were two means by which Truman could have lawfully seized the mills. The first was if the Constitution permitted it; the second was if Congress expressly authorized it. But Truman had acted without congressional sanction, and the Constitution does not give to a president, in express language, the power that Truman sought.

Jackson authored a concurrence that has, more than Black's decision, become an anthem for judging whether a president has overstepped his or her authority. Jackson's three-part analysis divided extraordinary presidential action into when a president acts according to a legislative grant, when a president acts in the absence of either a congressional grant or denial of authority, and when a president's acts are "incompatible with the express or implied will of Congress." Jackson clearly would have found the seizure lawful had Congress authorized Truman. The middle area—he called it a "zone of twilight"—might have enabled Truman's authority if a president enjoyed either "concurrent authority with Congress, or a combination of congressional inertia, indifference, or quiescence," coupled with the magnitude of events required the seizure to occur. But this was not the case. Many scholars argue that Jackson's concurrence has taken precedence over Black's decision. Justices Frankfurter, Burton, and Clark also concurred with Black.

Carter, Goldwater, and the federal courts relied on historic actions of the executive and legislative branches on treaty termination to support their positions. This is precisely what the steel mill owners and Truman attempted to do even though they, like the litigants in Goldwater, interpreted history differently. The lower courts also took cognizance of prior practices of property seizures in wartime. Carter and Goldwater assumed that the nation's diplomatic history regarding treaty termination would create a basis for the district and appellate courts to determine the merits of their respective positions once the issue of standing was resolved. Carter's attorneys believed they could prevail even if the court of appeals determined that the issue did not present a political question. In other words, they—like Goldwater's attorneys—believed that history was on their side. No judge serving on the appellate court, in fact, voted to dismiss Goldwater's case on the political question doctrine. In the lower courts, the history of treaty termination presented a basis for the judges believing that the issue before them was, in fact, justiciable.

Up until 1979, the United States had outright terminated forty-eight treaties, and in four instances a president had done so without express congressional authorization. In other instances, Congress took a direct role in the revocation, but in none of these instances was the judiciary involved. In 1798, Congress passed a measure, signed by President John Adams, nullifying four treaties between the United States and France. Adams did not object to the termination of the treaties, in all likelihood, because as a Federalist he believed that France, in spite of its critical support in securing American independence, had become the preeminent threat to the United States. (The Federalist Party favored Britain over France during the revolutionary France and Napoleonic eras.) Between the signing of the four treaties and Congress's action, the French monarchy had fallen and the revolutionary government pursued aims contrary to the United States' understanding of relations between the two nations. Indeed, the Court, in *Bas v. Tingy*, recognized that the United States and France were engaged in a naval conflict. Thus, at the time of the treaty termination, relations between France and the United States had reached a nadir. President Thomas Jefferson later commented that this action evidenced the requirement of a president to seek congressional approval to revoke a treaty. Yet, the treaty revocation in this instance could also stand for the principle that a treaty's duration equals the duration of the signatory government.

In 1846, Congress passed a resolution empowering President James Knox Polk to terminate the 1818 Oregon Treaty with Great Britain. This was not controversial, since Britain and the United States had already negotiated a new understanding on the division of the territory in question. However, there was a good deal of debate within Congress as to whether the House of Representatives had a formal role in treaty revocation, since it did not have a formal role in treaty approval. The issue of the House's involvement in treaty revocations remained unsettled because of the amicable settlement between the United States and Britain. In 1855, the Senate passed a resolution requesting President Franklin Pierce to terminate a commercial treaty with Denmark. In 1864, President Abraham Lincoln informed the British government of his intention to revoke the Rush-Bagot Agreement, which governed freedom of navigation in the Great Lakes. Confederate agents ran clandestine operations from Canada into the northern United States, and the Canadian authorities did little to stop this from occurring. Only after Lincoln's announcement to terminate Rush-Bagot did Congress act in favor of it.

In 1876, President Ulysses Grant informed Congress that Britain had failed to enforce an extradition provision and then requested congressional support for further action to revoke the treaty. In seeking approval, Grant urged Congress to consider that the extradition treaty was silent on the matter of diplomatic assurances, but "Her Majesty's government" had demanded assurances that would have further bound the US government. Congress complied with Grant's request. Three years later, President Rutherford Hayes vetoed a bill restricting Chinese immigration on the basis that the bill was contrary to a treaty with China, although he conceded that Congress could affirmatively vote to revoke an entire treaty. And, in 1883, a resurgent Congress affirmatively placed on President Chester Arthur a duty to rescind parts of an 1871 treaty with Britain. In 1911, the House passed a resolution demanding that President William Howard Taft rescind a commercial treaty with czarist Russia over that country's maltreatment of its Jewish population. Taft quickly complied but then asked the Senate to endorse his actions. In turn, the Senate, along with the House, issued a joint resolution supporting Taft's termination of the treaty. During debates on the League of Nations in 1919 and 1920, a consensus in the Senate was achieved that a president could not unilaterally withdraw from a treaty.

Unilateral presidential action in revoking a treaty is a rarity, and each instance prior to *Goldwater* is explainable by the surrounding circumstances. For instance, President James Madison cast doubts on the existence of a treaty with the Netherlands because that treaty had been signed in 1792, and by 1815 the Netherlands had fallen under French occupation. In 1806, Napoleon Bonaparte installed his brother Louis as the king of the Netherlands, and in 1810 Napoleon formally annexed the Netherlands into France. As a result, there was a question as to whether the United States was bound by treaty to a country that, in all practicality, had ceased to exist. In 1899, President William McKinley revoked some of the provisions of an 1850 trade treaty with Switzerland. However, he did so in response to a legal conflict between a federal statute and the treaty. In 1913, in *Charlton v. Kelly*, the Supreme Court suggested that a president could ignore treaty obligations—at least in terms of extradition agreements—when the other signatory country had failed to comply with the treaty's terms. In 1933, President Franklin Roosevelt unilaterally rescinded an extradition treaty with Greece after that nation shielded a US citizen accused of fraud from extradition. Three years later, Roosevelt renounced a treaty with Italy for similar reasons. And, in 1937 the Court, in *United States v. Belmont*, determined that the presidential recognition of a foreign country—in this case the Soviet Union—preempted state laws that did not recognize the Soviet claims to Russian properties. In theory, this ended the ability of the states to recognize pretenders to the Romanov throne as legitimate heirs to govern Russia.

The Burger Court

Judicial biography provides *Goldwater v. Carter* further context. Chapter 3 of this book presents a biography of Judge Oliver Gasch of the US District Court for the District of Columbia. Chapter 4, likewise, presents short biographies of ten judges on the Court of Appeals for the District of Columbia who took part in, or influenced, the decision-making process on appeal. A presentation of a judge's prior judicial rulings and pre-judicial political activities, education, and employment is important for legal history, particularly the legal history of a judicial decision. After all, as the late legal historian Lawrence Friedman once observed, legal history is not merely case decisions and statutes; it involves people and the social, economic, cultural, and political forces of the time. This study is written with Freidman's view of legal history in mind. But, it is important to place the judicial biographies of the nine Supreme Court justices up front here, if for no other reason than the litigants and the judges knew that Goldwater's suit would likely end up with in the Court.

Richard Nixon ran for the presidency in 1968 with a promise to undo much of the "Warren Court's" defendant's rights jurisprudence, if not its civil rights decisions after *Brown v. Board of Education.* When, in 1969, Chief Justice Earl Warren retired from the Court, Nixon selected Warren Burger to replace him. Burger was born in 1907, to working-class parents in Minnesota. He was admitted to Princeton University but could not afford its tuition. Instead, he enrolled in extension courses at the University of Minnesota before attending Saint Paul College and later its law school at night while working as an insurance salesman during the day. This was the type of non–Ivy League background that Nixon championed. Burger's political background included a pre-judicial stint as a Minnesota Republican Party organizer. In 1952, at the Republican

National Convention, he shepherded the state's delegates away from Robert Taft to Dwight Eisenhower, after Minnesota's "favorite son" Governor Harold Stassen did not receive enough votes to remain in contention for the party's nomination. In 1953. Burger became an assistant attorney general in charge of the Department of Justice's Claims Division, where he represented the executive branch in civil suits. In this position, Burger argued to the Court the constitutionality of a national security program after Solicitor General Simon Sobeloff refused to do so. Sobeloff concluded that the program, which did not enable the right of discovering the source of an allegation, violated a professor's constitutional rights, and Burger believed that national security prevailed over the professor's reputation and access to a university.

Three years after Burger joined the Justice Department, Eisenhower nominated him to the US Court of Appeals for the District of Columbia. It took almost a year for the Senate to confirm Burger. Three Justice Department employees accused him of discrimination, but an investigation concluded otherwise. His record on the appellate court evidenced that he was a judicial conservative who sided with the executive branch on national security matters. He also found himself opposite the appellate court's liberals on criminal defendants' rights cases. Burger had opposed the Court's decision in *Miranda v. Arizona* and publicly criticized the decision for hampering law enforcement. When chemistry Nobel Laureate Linus Pauling attempted to sue the Department of Defense over the harm caused by radiation fallout from nuclear testing, Burger called the scientists "crackpots and communists." On the Court he authored decisions upholding the military's authority to prohibit certain political speech on its posts and determined that the army's surveillance program over US citizens was beyond the reach of the federal courts. He also authored the unanimous *United States v. Nixon* decision, arising from the Watergate scandal, which placed significant limits on presidential power to shield the White House from prosecutions and criminal investigations.

William J. Brennan was the longest-serving justice on the Court at the time Goldwater filed his suit against Carter. Appointed to the Court by President Dwight Eisenhower in 1956, Brennan was a World War II veteran and a New Jersey Supreme Court justice. He attended Harvard Law School, graduating in 1931 and was one of the Court's leading liberals during the Warren Court. Although he did not take part in *Brown v. Board of Education*, he voted in favor of other civil rights appeals involving voting rights and equal access to schools and employment opportunities. He also voted in favor of equal pay and benefits for women in a case arising from the US Air Force. Brennan was morally opposed to the United States' involvement in the Vietnam Conflict, but he did not join with Douglas's quest to have the war declared illegal. Unlike most of the other justices—with the exception of Thurgood Marshall—Brennan believed that affirmative action withstood constitutional muster as a means to reverse generations of discrimination, and he also crafted a decision to mandate due process for persons denied governmental welfare benefits. Brennan was not an adherent of executive branch supremacy, and he voted, in a dissent, to curb the ability of the president to have the military surveil US citizens.

In 1958, Eisenhower nominated Potter Stewart to the Court, where he served until 1981. Stewart was born in 1915 to a family embedded in the law. His father was a justice on the Ohio Supreme Court. A graduate of Yale, Cambridge University, and Yale Law School, Stewart also was a naval officer in World War II. Before his military service, Stewart joined a large law firm and represented Proctor and Gamble. In 1948, he was elected to the Cincinnati City Council and then the city's vice mayor's office as a Republican. In 1954, Eisenhower appointed Stewart to the Court of Appeals for the Sixth Circuit and, on learning of Justice Burton's retirement, nominated Stewart to the Court. Eisenhower believed Stewart had "the right political credentials," particularly after being disappointed in Warren and Brennan for their civil rights and individual liberties jurisprudence. Nixon had considered nominating Stewart to replace Warren as chief justice, but Stewart was opposed to the elevation. Stewart tended to side with the press in challenges against government restrictions as well as with litigants claiming civil rights violations. In other matters, including challenges to executive branch authority, Stewart encouraged judicial restraint.

In 1962, President John Fitzgerald Kennedy nominated Byron White to the Court to replace Charles Whittaker. A former National Football League player and World War II veteran, White (who had the nickname "Whizzer" as a result of his football prowess) had shown no fear of southern white supremacists as Robert Kennedy's deputy attorney general and was thought of as a natural choice as a justice. Born in Colorado in 1917 to parents who had not graduated from high school, he was a top scholar and athlete at the University of Colorado, a Rhodes scholar at Oxford, and a Yale Law graduate. In World War II he earned two Bronze Stars and was assigned to the aircraft carrier USS *Bunker Hill*, where he survived a devastating kamikaze attack that killed hundreds of sailors. In 1960, White headed the Citizens for Kennedy organization. When White retired in 1993, the American Bar Association characterized him as a Democratic appointee who more often aligned with conservatives and who did not pursue a consistent jurisprudential doctrine. White supported civil rights legislation, but he also took a "tough on crime" stance in the 1960s and 1970s, and he usually sided with Rehnquist and Burger on decisions impacting national security. During the Vietnam Conflict, he argued against the Court ruling on the constitutionality of the United States' involvement.

President Johnson nominated Thurgood Marshall to the Court to replace Arthur Goldberg in 1966. Unsurprisingly, southern senators, including Strom Thurmond (R-SC), opposed Marshall's nomination. Goldwater was not in the Senate at the time of the vote, but Carl Curtis (R-NE), who later signed on to Goldwater's legal brief, voted to approve Marshall. Marshall was the great-grandson of a slave captured in the Congo region of Africa, and the son of a railroad porter and primary school teacher. Despite his superb undergraduate record at Lincoln University in Pennsylvania (the nation's first historically African American college), the University of Maryland's law school denied him entry because of its segregation policy. He attended Howard University instead, graduating at the top of his class in 1933 and working with the National Association for the Advancement of Colored People three years later.

Marshall had argued before the Court in *Brown v. Board of Education*, as well as in several earlier civil rights victories in state courts. In 1940, in *Chambers v. Florida*, he convinced the Court to overturn the convictions of four indigent African American defendants who had been denied counsel during harsh interrogations. Justice Hugo Black, who wrote the majority opinion, was thoroughly impressed with Marshall's legal acumen. In 1961, Kennedy appointed Marshall to the Court of Appeals for the Second Circuit, and in 1965 Johnson appointed him solicitor general. Once on the Court, Marshall became enmeshed in several decisions related to the Vietnam Conflict. He voted to limit presidential authority in surveillance decisions as well as in selective service cases. However, in 1973 he clashed with Douglas in an appeal arising from the Nixon administration's launching of a new bombing campaign in Cambodia. Marshall believed the war in Vietnam was a travesty and that the attack on Cambodia against the communist Khmer Rouge a grossly immoral act. But, in *Holtzman v. Schlesinger*, he ruled that the judicial branch could not order a halt to the bombing, even though Congress had prohibited the use of appropriations to use military forces outside of Vietnam. Douglas felt otherwise and reinstated a lower court's injunction despite the fact Marshall had earlier refused to do so.

Shortly after Burger's confirmation, and after two failed nominations, Nixon nominated Harry Blackmun, a childhood friend of Burger's. Like Burger, Blackmun had served on a federal appellate court prior to his appointment. He had also been employed as the in-house counsel to the Mayo Clinic and had been affiliated with the Republican Party in Minnesota. Nixon expected that Blackmun would be complementary to Burger, but almost from the start of their judicial tenure on the Court, the two began to diverge. To be sure, they both determined that the Court could not adjudicate questions on the legality of the Vietnam Conflict, and Blackmun sided with Burger on pressing national security cases, including the surveillance of citizens. But Blackmun was more willing to uphold antidiscrimination programs as well as determine that the federal government itself discriminated against minority groups and women. Blackmun has been associated with *Roe v. Wade*. As its author, he has tended to be cast as a nonconservative, but this was not always the case as he voted to uphold the death penalty.

Nixon's third and fourth appointments were as likely to side with claims of national security over individual rights as any justice in the twentieth century. In 1971, Nixon nominated Lewis Powell to replace Black. Born in 1907, Powell served as an intelligence officer in the US Army Air Forces in World War II. His military background included being a distinguished graduate from the Army Air Force's intelligence school, having a role in the intelligence preparations for the Operation Torch landings in North Africa in 1942, and later assisting in deciphering German codes through the Allies' top secret Ultra program at Bletchley Park in the United Kingdom. Powell earned his undergraduate and law degrees from Washington and Lee University in Virginia. After his admission to the Virginia bar in 1930, he pursued a one-year advanced course of study at Harvard's law school, where he studied under Frankfurter. As a leading member of the Virginia bar, in the late 1950s Powell was appointed to oversee denials of exemptions from the national conscription program. In 1981, he voted to uphold a national draft registration that exempted women from having to participate; White, Brennan, and Marshall would dissent from this decision.

In 1969, Nixon nominated Powell to a Blue Ribbon Commission to study the state of the military in expectation of a post–Vietnam Conflict policy. In this role, Powell contributed to the shaping of the all-volunteer military. For much of his career, Powell spoke out against communism as an evil. However, he had his limits in regard to presidential rhetoric. Writing to historian Daniel Boorstin in 1980, Powell complained that the congressional demands for action against the Soviet Union were ill-advised. "All of this talk about war disturbs me more than a little," he penned. "Apart from other reasons, it is little short of madness to talk about fighting the Soviet Union on the Eurasian land-mass eight to ten thousand miles away without adequate bases, means of transport or indeed anything like adequate forces." Included in Powell's objections were the nation's dependence on Middle East oil and a lack of discipline in the armed forces. He concluded his criticism with the observation that he "would have thought any sixth-grade child—after the 1973 embargo—would have known this."

William Hubbs Rehnquist was Nixon's fourth, and most controversial, appointment to the Court. A graduate of Stanford University's law school and a World War II veteran, Rehnquist began his legal career by clerking for Justice Robert Jackson. He also took part in voter suppression activities in Arizona. As a foreshadowing of Rehnquist's national security jurisprudence, in 1953 he conveyed to Robert Jackson his approval of Jackson's stance in the trial of Ethel and Julius Rosenberg. After stating that capital punishment is solely a legislative decision (though he conceded there were sound arguments against its use and that every accused person has a right to a fair trial), he accused the Court of behaving like "a bunch of old women." More important, he was convinced the "Rosenberg case had dragged on too long as it did," and that Jackson had saved the Court's public reputation. In essence, Rehnquist believed in the importance of maximizing penalties to citizens determined to be a threat to national security.

Rehnquist spent the first three years of Nixon's presidency in the Justice Department directly under Attorney General John Mitchell. Like several members of the White House, he worked to roll back the civil rights gains of the prior decade, including making arguments against school busing. He also believed the federal government's power had to be curbed except in matters of national security and foreign policy. Because there was available evidence that Rehnquist had opposed the integration of schools and wanted Justice Jackson to vote to maintain *Plessy v. Ferguson* in *Brown*, as well as evidence of his involvement in voter suppression efforts against Hispanic voters in Arizona, there was considerable opposition to his confirmation in the Senate. Yet, by a close vote, he was confirmed. That he issued a decision in favor of Carter's assertion of power over treaties may have been more of a reflection that he was a firm supporter of presidential authority than an indication of his agreement with Carter's specific policy in question.

When William O. Douglas retired in 1975, President Gerald Ford nominated John Paul Stevens to replace him. Prior to his judicial tenure, Stevens was known for investigating governmental corruption. An Illinois judicial commission had appointed him to investigate payoffs to judges, leading to the prosecution of two Illinois Supreme Court justices in 1969. In 1970, Nixon appointed Stevens to the Court of Appeals for the Seventh Circuit. In the aftermath of Watergate, Ford was more constrained than Nixon in selecting a justice, and Stevens's moderation on the appellate bench made him likely to be confirmed. A native Chicagoan born in 1920, Stevens attended the University of Chicago and then served in the navy in World War II. Following the war, he enrolled in the Northwestern University School of Law, where he earned the highest grade point average in the school's history. After admission to the bar, he clerked for Justice Wiley Rutledge. When Stevens retired, he would be the last justice to have served on active duty in the military. He would also be the last serving justice to have not matriculated at an Ivy League law school until President Trump nominated Amy Coney Barrett to the Court in late 2020. Stevens's early legal interests were not in foreign policy; instead, he concentrated in antitrust law, publishing several treatises and teaching courses in the subject at the University of Chicago. But, over the course of his judicial tenure, Stevens would side with litigants against the United States in appeals arising from the national security policies of Presidents Ford through Barack Obama.

The Political Question Doctrine

The Supreme Court has fashioned constitutional doctrines since its existence as a means for determining when and under what conditions a federal court may adjudicate an issue. Throughout this study, the principle of implied powers and the doctrines of standing, ripeness, mootness, and the political question are analyzed just as the courts would do in *Goldwater v. Carter*. Each of the doctrines was important to the traverse of the lawsuit as well as to its final result. The political question doctrine is important to address not only in the fifth chapter—describing the Supreme Court's decision—but also here in the introduction. This is because the doctrine explains the limits of judicial review inherent in Goldwater's challenge to Carter. There are three independent coequal branches of the federal government. Two of the branches, the executive and the legislative, are deemed "political" because the voters determine who will serve. The judicial branch is another matter. The judiciary is normally reticent to solve clashes between the two elected branches. The judiciary is also reluctant to intervene in certain state political questions. Two prior judicial decisions give the nonjusticiable political question doctrine definition.

In 1840, a large number of Rhode Island's citizens openly rebelled against their state government. The governor and state legislature prevailed when the state militia sided with them and suppressed the rebellion. Rhode Island was the only original state that did not adopt a new constitution after the nation's founding; instead, its government and voting rights were constrained by its colonial charter. When the charter was enacted, the state was largely agrarian, and voting qualifications were predicated on property ownership. By 1840, Rhode Island was a state with an industrial economy and a middle class that did not meet the property qualifications to vote. The US Constitution contains a specific clause guaranteeing to the citizens of each state "a Republican form of government." It is clear that Rhode Island did not have such a form of government. One of the arrested rebels argued this point all the way to the Court, and indeed, his basic premise was correct. Rhode Island was in violation of the Constitution. But, in a decision titled *Luther v. Borden*, the justices determined that the courts could not enforce the clause in question. Rather, Congress, the president, or both could do so. After the Civil War, the Fourteenth Amendment was ratified, enabling the courts to determine that state voting schemes were either constitutional or unconstitutional. Because *Luther v. Borden* was issued as a broad decision limiting judicial review, it would be cited by Carter during the arguments to the Court.

Perhaps the most important opinion in terms of framing the political question doctrine, *Baker v. Carr*, was also central to the Court's action in *Goldwater*, but that opinion arose in a context far different than a foreign policy challenge. *Baker* arose out of a challenge to Tennessee's apportionment of voting districts, which had mirrored the state's demographics from a half century earlier. As noted in greater detail in later chapters, the Court determined that the judiciary had the ability to rule on voting districts where the apportionment of votes resulted in a departure from the representation principles of one vote per person, albeit though not applied to the US Senate. In doing so, the Court recognized there were other categories of issues that constituted political questions outside the judiciary's competency.

In 1969, the Court, in *Powell v. McCormack*, determined that the House of Representatives could not exclude Adam Clayton Powell from his elected seat. The Constitution, in Article I, Section 2, Clause 2, states, "No Person shall be a Representative who shall not have attained to the Age of twenty five Years, and been seven Years a Citizen of the United States, and who shall not, when elected, be an Inhabitant of that State in which he shall be chosen." In other words, as long as Congressman Powell was over the age of twenty-five years and a citizen, and the voters in his district elected him, he was qualified to serve in the House. Powell was, in fact, much older than twenty-five and had served in Congress since 1945, but he was in the midst of a scandal. Not only had an investigation concluded that he misappropriated funds, but the House refused to seat him until the conclusion of its investigation. Powell sued the Speaker of the House, John McCormack, and others to force them to perform their constitutional duty to seat him.

The Court of Appeals for the District of Columbia, in a decision authored by (then) Judge Warren Burger, determined that Powell's suit was nonjusticiable. In other words, Burger determined that Powell's suit was "political" and therefore solely for the House to decide. Thus, to Burger, the federal courts could not grant review of appeals that arose from Congress's internal workings. The Supreme Court, in an opinion authored by Chief Justice Earl Warren, reversed on the basis that the Constitution does not, in its plain text, permit the House to refuse to seat one of its own duly elected members. The House, the Court concluded, may expel a member by a two-thirds vote. Indeed, the plain text of Article I, Section 5, Clause 2 reads, "Each House may determine the Rules of its Proceedings, punish its Members for disorderly Behavior, and, with the Concurrence of two thirds, expel a member." So, while the seating of a member in the House is inherently political, the Constitution did not commit to the House the authority to usurp the will of a district's voters. (Until 1955, Powell was only one of two Black members of the House, and it should not escape notice that the House had voted 307 to 116 to determine his fate in a manner not expressly provided for in the Constitution.) As in the case *of Luther v. Borden*, *Powell v. McCormack* would be cited by the parties for the question of whether the Court had the ability to adjudicate Goldwater's appeal. That is, one of the fundamental issues underlying Goldwater's challenge to Carter was whether, as a result of the Constitution's silence on treaty termination, the federal courts could decide which party was in the constitutional right, or to leave that question to the elected branches of government to decide.

Conclusion

One final comment on the political question doctrine and foreign policy bears mention as it relates to the importance of *Goldwater*, albeit the comment is more important for context than the importance of the opinion. Prior to World War II, judges and justices had participated in significant foreign policy actions at the behest of the executive branch. But the jurists did so in a nonjudicial capacity, albeit one in which the separation of powers seems to have diminished in importance. In the late 1920s, on behalf of President Calvin Coolidge, Justice Willis Van Devanter arbitrated a maritime jurisdictional dispute with Canada. Justice John Jay, at President George Washington's behest, negotiated a significant treaty bearing his name with Great Britain, which lessened tensions with the British Crown and possibly avoided a war in 1795. In 1893, Justice John Marshall Harlan represented the United States in an international arbitration with Great Britain over fishing rights and enforcement in the Bering Sea. He did so after President Benjamin Harrison enlisted him and remained to the satisfaction of Harrison's successor, Grover Cleveland. In 1895, Cleveland appointed Chief Justice Melville Westin Fuller and Justice David Josiah Brewer to represent the United States in the hopes of both asserting US dominance in the Caribbean and diffusing a potential conflict with Great Britain over a border dispute in Venezuela. In an age of "jingoism," both justices succeeded in smoothing tensions with Britain, but they also contributed to the cementing of the Monroe Doctrine into a policy recognized by the European powers. In the late 1940s, President Harry Truman tried to convince Chief Justice Fredrick Vinson to serve as a special emissary to Soviet premier Joseph Stalin in the hopes of reducing tensions.

As noted, the justices involved in these foreign policy actions were not acting in a judicial capacity. But it remains a historic fact that presidents have called on judges to act in nonjudicial roles. One need only view the name of the Warren Commission to understand the recency of extrajudicial activities, however wise or unwise these might be. Whether this facet of history provided to the conservatives challenging Carter a further assumption that the judiciary might be amenable to taking up their cause is difficult to discern. It may have shaped their view of what the federal courts were willing to do in their efforts to stop a treaty revocation with a cherished ally. Since *Goldwater*'s issuance, there have been no publicized extrajudicial activities approximating those of Harlan, Fuller, Brewer, or even Van Devanter. While *Goldwater* likely had nothing directly to do with this, the opinion itself may serve as a reminder against future efforts to enlist the judiciary in the manner of Washington, Harrison, Cleveland, and Truman. Perhaps this is the weakest argument for the opinion being a landmark case among all the others listed, but it remains important as a matter of context in defining legislative and judicial relations.

CHAPTER 1

President Carter, China, and the Coming Clash in the Court

On December 15, 1978, President Carter announced that the United States would formally recognize the People's Republic of China and rescind a long-standing obligation to defend Taiwan. The next morning, Senator Barry Goldwater held a press conference in Phoenix and promised to take Carter to court. "He says he can end it. He is mistaken," Goldwater claimed. "And if he decides to do it on his own, that's why I'm going to take him to court and prove that it's unconstitutional and illegal." From California, former governor Ronald Reagan, a presidential aspirant and Goldwater ally, encouraged a court challenge against Carter. "For the first time in its history, the United States broke a treaty without cause," Reagan insisted. "We callously betrayed a long-time friend and ally who refused to betray us, and we did so with brutal rudeness."

Six days after Carter's announcement, Goldwater held true to his word and filed suit in the US District Court for the District of Columbia. He was soon joined by more than twenty legislators, all of whom were conservatives. This began a yearlong political and legal battle between a president and a former presidential candidate; between a president who took unilateral command of a significant treaty decision and a group of legislators who had previously derided the federal judiciary as being overly "activist"; and between a president who had campaigned on transparency and legislators who were opposed to widening congressional oversight of programs designed to contain and defeat communism. While a significant alteration of foreign policy is fascinating and worthy of a comprehensive study, this book does not center on Carter's presidency or his decision to rescind an important treaty. Rather, as a brief reminder, it focuses on a legislative effort to constrain the presidency in the federal courts and how the Supreme Court, in recognizing an expansive presidential power, enabled the reemergence of an "imperial judiciary."

Coming on the heels of the Camp David Accords in which Carter mediated a historic peace framework between the governments of Israel and Egypt, his China announcement promised nothing short of a reordering of the United States' Cold War policies in Asia. "The United States recognizes the government of the People's Republic of China as the sole legal government of China," Carter informed the nation in a television address. "Within this context, the people of the United States will retain cultural, commercial, and other unofficial relations with the people of Taiwan." If this had been the only statement that a citizen who observed the Cold War from its beginning in 1945 had heard, it still would have been a surprise. Carter's notification signaled a departure from a Cold War dynamic in which many Americans believed that communism was a monolithic entity commanded from Moscow and that China was a key participant in the Soviet Union's expansionist designs. Carter's next statement, however, was a "political bombshell." He announced, "There is one China and Taiwan is part of China." For three decades, the US government had recognized Taiwan as independent of China. Indeed, thrice the US government displayed its willingness to use military force to defend Taiwan.

One reason for the appropriateness of the term "bombshell," beyond the reordering of foreign policy, was that the announcement was made without formal consultation with Congress, and Congressman Clement Zablocki (D-WI), the chairman of the House International Relations Committee, labeled it as such. While campaigning for the presidency in 1976, Carter promised not to abandon Taiwan. This was consistent with the stance of every president since Harry S. Truman, and the protection of Taiwan was hardly controversial. In 1954, when President Dwight Eisenhower presented the Mutual Defense Treaty with Taiwan to the US Senate, it passed with very little opposition. Indeed, only three of the Senate's ninety-six members opposed it. The treaty's supporters recognized that it symbolically stood for more than a two-state alliance. It was important to ensuring that communism did not overtake the United States' strategic allies, and there was a fear of the People's Republic of China. In 1949, the Chinese Communists under Mao Zedong defeated

Chiang Kai-shek's Nationalists, ending a long civil war. Chiang and the remaining Nationalists fled to the island of Formosa, setting up the Republic of China. In the early years of the Cold War, the "fall" of China to communism not only led to a wide-ranging hunt for communists in the United States but also resulted in a belief that communism had to be contained throughout Asia. Containment policies contributed to the United States fighting the attempted spread of communism in South Korea and later in South Vietnam, Laos, and, Cambodia. During the 1954 Taiwan treaty negotiations, Secretary of State John Foster Dulles assured Chiang, "You may be confident that the US will never agree to a submission to the UN on the question of the Chicoms'—the State Department's shorthand statement for Chinese Communists—right to govern Formosa."

Implicit in Dulles's assurances was also the promise that the United States would not diplomatically or militarily abandon Taiwan. Indeed, Dulles stated this much in a confidential communication with Eisenhower. Article V of the Mutual Defense Treaty read: "Each Party recognizes that an armed attack in the West Pacific Area directed against the territories of either of the Parties would be dangerous to its own peace and safety and declares that it would act to meet the common danger in accordance with its constitutional processes." And, when the Senate voted on the treaty, there was a general understanding that unless Taiwan offensively launched a military invasion of the Chinese mainland, the United States would defend Taiwan at all costs.

In the first two decades of the treaty's existence, there was little indication that the United States would not come to Taiwan's defense. For seven months beginning on September 3, 1954, China's military fired artillery at Kinmen and Matsu, two islands occupied by the Taiwanese military and claimed by both Mao and Chiang. On January 29, 1955, after the ratification of the Mutual Defense Treaty, Congress passed the Formosa Resolution authorizing the use of military force to protect Taiwan. American naval forces assisted in the civilian evacuation of the islands, and Dulles publicly expressed the administration's consideration of using nuclear weapons. Three years later, in 1958, Chinese and Taiwanese military forces clashed once more near the disputed islands, and this time a sizable US military force came to Taiwan's defense. Although

Soviet premier Nikita Khrushchev warned that a general war was likely if the United States continued its support, in the end Taiwan maintained an odd and precarious control of the islands, and no major war occurred.

In defense of his foreign policy decision, Carter noted that prior to the communist takeover of China in 1949, the United States and China had a long friendship and that a rapprochement with China promised a return to a prior era, even if the governing ideologies of the two nations were polar opposites. He also reminded Americans that the 1972 Shanghai Communique—an agreement between President Richard Milhous Nixon and Premier Zhou Enlai—stressed that both governments would work toward a normalization of relations. Finally, Carter assured Americans that both China and the United States premised normalization on a guarantee that neither would seek hegemony in Asia and both governments would oppose efforts of other powers to do so. Finally, diplomatic relations with China promised to mitigate the possibility of conflict throughout Asia.

Carter's bombshell announcement was problematic for several reasons. In the words of one historian, the recognition of the People's Republic of China constituted the most dramatic foreign policy development of the 1970s, and this alone would have resulted in several objections in Congress given that throughout the history of the United States it has been rare not to have dissent over foreign alliances. In July 1978, five months prior to Carter's announcement, Senator Robert Dole (R-KS) introduced a resolution to the Senate declaring that Carter would have to consult the upper house on any changes to the Mutual Defense Treaty. Dole and his cosponsors, Senators Jacob Javits (R-NY), Harrison Schmitt (R-NM); S. I. Hayakawa (R-CA), Carl Curtis (R-NE), and Robert Morgan (R-NC), recognized that Carter could establish relations with China, short of a treaty and without Senate consent. But they argued that Carter had to take into account "American and Japanese security interests in the Western Pacific area—which motivated the 1954 defense treaty and which remain important today—before any policy changes are undertaken."

In September 1978, when Carter signed into law the International Security Assistance Act, he agreed with the basic premise of Dole's resolution. Indeed, Dole and Senator Richard Bernard Stone (D-FL) placed into the resolution the following statement: "It is the sense of the Congress that there should be prior consultation between the Congress and the executive branch on any proposed policy changes affecting the continuation in force of the Mutual Defense Treaty of 1954." This amendment, known as the Dole-Stone Amendment, would become important to the district court in its assessment of the merits of Goldwater's suit. Despite Carter's agreement, after signing the bill into law he did not consult with the full Congress before his announcement. Instead, he insisted that he, and not Congress, ultimately decided when and where a treaty would be terminated.

Given the Senate's overwhelming approval of the treaty more than two decades earlier, it was unlikely that the Senate would, if asked, formally renounce the treaty. It is helpful, however, to note that Carter's announcement signified that for the first time since the presidency of Franklin Delano Roosevelt, the United States was going to officially recognize a communist superpower. Yet Roosevelt's recognition of the Soviet Union in 1933 was different than Carter's move to recognize China. When Roosevelt established diplomatic relations with the Soviet Union, Congress did not try to upend his decision in federal courts. And, although displaced former Russian government officers planned to return to power, the US government did not recognize their claims to govern. In contrast, the Taiwanese government, with the United States' full approval, earlier professed to be "China's government" and claimed that the government of the People's Republic of China was merely a conquering power that would be removed once its 900 million people pushed their communist government out.

Despite this book's focus on judicial-legislative relations, it is important to have a basic framework for why Carter acted to recognize China, as well as the motives of his principal congressional opponents. Perhaps the most fundamental reason for Carter's decision was that China possessed one-quarter of the world's population and was a "superpower"; therefore, the United States could no longer ignore this reality. Indeed, the decision to recognize China was hardly a dramatic move if juxtaposed with the foreign policies of the United States' key allies. Great Britain, France, West Germany, Canada, Australia, and Japan had already recognized China, as had most of the governments of the developing world. Canada provided the United States with an example of flexibility from past foreign policy doctrine. On November 17, 1965, the

Canadian government issued a press release explaining that while it "welcomed the opportunity to see Communist China take a seat in the United Nations," this had become impossible because "Peking itself has set a price on participation that is unacceptable." In stating his government's reasons for nonrecognition, Prime Minister Lester Pearson was emphatic that it was unwilling to abandon Taiwan or approve of China's support to a communist insurgency in Indonesia. On October 13, 1970, with Prime Minister Pierre Trudeau as Canada's leader, the Canadian government formally recognized the People's Republic of China, and China had not abandoned any of its demands on Canada derecognizing Taiwan. Nonetheless, Carter's announcement was not only a departure from US foreign policy but also the first time since the nation's founding that the president's congressional opponents challenged a foreign policy decision involving recognition of a foreign country in a lawsuit that traversed to the Supreme Court.

The Setting: An Assertive Congress and the Chaos of the 1970s

Carter became president during a major reevaluation in foreign policy in the sense that both Nixon and Ford had pursued changes in regard to China as well as the future use of military force and economic relationships with unfriendly governments. Shortly after his inauguration, Carter outlined new "cardinal principles" detailing how US foreign policy would be conducted. First and foremost, the United States would incorporate human rights and human freedoms into its foreign policy decisions. Additionally, he intended to stem nuclear weapons proliferation across the world and promised to reduce the nation's strategic nuclear stockpile, and his administration would seek to establish a lasting peace in the Middle East. He did not, however, make normalization of relations with China a centerpiece of his campaign. Nor, in the first six months of his administration, did he publicly mention normalization. Perhaps, because the "far right," led by Governor Ronald Reagan, had almost upended Ford's candidacy in the 1976 Republican National Convention by opposing Ford's overtures to China, Carter muted his intended China policy until the Soviet Union moved large numbers of military advisers into Africa and South and Central America. And, during the first year of Carter's presidency, the Chinese government feted several of his Republican legislative opponents while seemingly ignoring his administration.

For many Americans, prior to 1974, the Cold War appeared to monolithically pit the United States and its allies against the Soviet Union, China, and the various countries ruled by communist regimes. This belief was colorfully manifested in popular entertainment such as the 1962 movie *The Manchurian Candidate.* In reality, the world was not entirely divided between communist and "free." There were, after all, dozens of nonaligned nations, including India, the world's second-most-populated country. (India had gone to war with China in 1962, yet had strong diplomatic relations with the Soviet Union.) And, in reality, while the veneer of a monolithic communism might have provided the American public with a degree of relief at being able to believe there was a right and a wrong, or a "good side" and a "bad side," global politics were far more complex than this veneer. Moreover, the Vietnam Conflict changed perceptions of the United States for many of its own citizens. Presidents Lyndon Johnson and Richard Nixon were hardly transparent on their policies in Vietnam. Daniel Ellsberg's release of the Pentagon Papers confirmed to many Americans that the government had engaged in a costly series of dishonest acts. Evidence of government repression and surveillance over citizens who opposed the war or advanced civil rights, as well as secretive military and intelligence campaigns in Cambodia and Laos, also served to undermine public trust in the government, even before Watergate.

Congress, which had acquiesced to Johnson in 1964 in approving the Gulf of Tonkin Resolution, reasserted its influence over presidential use of the military in foreign operations. In 1970, Senators Frank Church (D-ID) and John Sherman Cooper (R-OH) introduced legislation limiting the ability of a president to send military forces into Cambodia and Laos. Three years later, Church and Senator Clifford Case (R-NJ) introduced additional legislation preventing a president from funding military operations in Vietnam, Laos, and Cambodia without clear congressional approval. And, toward the end of Nixon's presidency, Congress twice passed the War Powers Resolution, theoretically preventing the long-term deployment of military forces unless Congress voted to support the action.

Congress did not merely limit its oversight and fiscal control powers to military operations around the world. After Watergate, special House and Senate committees investigated the government's secretive role in toppling foreign governments and carrying out political assassinations. The evidence produced in these committees included an appalling array of illegal activity inside of the United States such as testing psychotropic drugs on unsuspecting citizens, privacy rights violations, and repeated bungling by the intelligence agencies. Carter was partly elected on the promise to give back to the people of the country a trustworthy government that would, in theory, return the United States to a period prior to the Vietnam Conflict. This promise proved illusory. The war in Vietnam had made it difficult for the public to discern that the global division between communist and "free world" predating 1965 was no longer clear and that military strength was no longer a sole basis to gauge the strength of the nation or the "free world." As a result of dynamic global changes, no president could return the United States to its pre-Vietnam status.

The world economy had become more interdependent in the 1960s so that by the 1970s Western economies were less resilient to inflation and recession. Steel-dumping allegations against the European Economic Community after the 1973 steel crises in which there were devastating steel factory closures in Ohio and Pennsylvania complicated foreign policy. In 1977, Congressman Joel Fisher (D-VA), a liberal Democrat who agreed with Carter's human rights policies, normalization, and the transfer of the Panama Canal, received hundreds of letters complaining that the administration was not supporting domestic steelworkers. Echoing the belief of legislators across the political spectrum, he responded in a form letter to his constituents: "I share your concern that a strong and vigorous steel industry is of vital importance to the United States, not only in terms of its immense contribution to the well-being of the economy, but also because a weak steel industry has profound national security implications for the country." Neither Carter nor Congress, however, could find a means to resurrect the dying steel industry any more than they could solve the energy crisis.

Monetary and tariff disagreements between the United States and its European allies, including Britain, West Germany, France, and Italy, at times appeared more difficult to solve then arms negotiations with the Soviet Union. Indeed, when, in 1969, Nixon tried to establish détente with the Soviet Union through the Strategic Arms Limitation Talks (SALT), he, national security adviser Henry Kissinger, and their Soviet counterparts were able to reach an agreement on capping the numbers of nuclear warheads each country possessed. And, at the 1972 Moscow Summit, Nixon and Soviet Premier Leonid Brezhnev agreed that neither the United States nor the Soviet Union would interfere in the internal affairs of the other. In contrast, at the same time Nixon worked on achieving an accord with the Soviet Union, differences between NATO countries reached a boiling point over the fiscal contributions of each government as well as over Western European economic policies that many in Congress, as well as the Nixon administration, believed to be detrimental to the United States. On top of this, for the first time since 1893, the United States suffered a trade deficit while the Japanese economy surged as imported Japanese cars, computers, televisions, and other manufactured items entered the US domestic market, often at the expense of the American worker. This, in turn, diminished respect that voters had in the nation's political institutions. In the first three postwar decades Americans had adopted the belief that governmental policies shielded them from global economic changes. As a result of economic uncertainties and downturns, another reason for distrust in the government emerged.

Japan presented another problem to the Nixon, Ford, and Carter administrations. In 1976, an executive from the Lockheed aerospace company—one of the United States' largest defense contractors—admitted to Congress that the company had bribed foreign governments, including Japan's prime minister. Lockheed had used "front companies" and underworld criminals, some of whom had committed crimes against humanity in World War II, to accomplish sales of its fighter aircraft and the L-1011, a competitor to the Boeing 747 and Douglas DC-10 passenger aircraft. Whether Nixon and Ford were aware of the scope of Lockheed's malfeasance at the time is unknown, but both administrations had pushed for an enormous financial bailout to the corporation. In the end, Japan's prime minister and other governmental officials were charged with crimes and faced jail time. As a result, the Japanese public had reason to suspect the US government of having taken part in governmental corruption.

Throughout the 1970s, Lockheed was in the news for other reasons of fraud and corruption that affected foreign policy. In the closing days of Lyndon Johnson's presidency, Arthur Ernest Fitzgerald, a high-ranking civil servant in the Department of the Air Force, testified to the Senate that the government's purchase of the Lockheed C-5A Galaxy aircraft—the largest military cargo aircraft of its time—was burdened with cost overruns and the airplane had too many design flaws and maintenance problems to be of use. Fitzgerald insisted that the secretary of the air force, if not the secretary of defense, knew of these problems but pursued the acquisition nonetheless. His testimony implied not only that the government considering bailing Lockheed out of its enormous debt but that the company had contributed vast sums of money to political campaigns and then put Lockheed in a position of power at the expense of the taxpayers.

At a time when the public was discussing the power of the "military-industrial complex," Fitzgerald's testimony was front-page news. Rather than treat him as a dedicated civil servant who had uncovered governmental largesse in a prior administration, the Nixon administration became vindictive and directed Fitzgerald's firing and public humiliation. (For a brief time before he was fired, Fitzgerald was transferred from his high-ranking position to inspecting overseas bowling alleys on military bases.) For the next decade, including after the Civil Service Commission reinstated him to the federal government, Fitzgerald sued Nixon and issued public statements against presidential policies regarding military and foreign affairs. His suit would eventually end up in the Supreme Court. On the 1976 campaign trail, Carter promised to respect civil servants like Fitzgerald—Carter mentioned him by name—but then appointed one of Fitzgerald's tormentors as secretary of defense and backed Nixon's legal defense. Fitzgerald became an anthem for governmental distrust and a warning that the defense industries leveraged an unusual amount of influence in shaping national defense and foreign policies.

There were several reasons Nixon and Kissinger, and then President Gerald Ford, pushed for détente with the Soviet Union, but the foremost among these had to do with a shift of Soviet foreign policy. In 1968, Brezhnev, who served as premier from 1964 to 1982, stated that the Soviet Union had an obligation to protect the governments and peoples of socialist countries against internal threats of capitalism. Brezhnev's doctrine stressed that while national sovereignty was not a basis for sending military aid, threats to international socialism and communism would be a reason to do so. The Brezhnev Doctrine, if embraced by the myriad socialist governments around the world, promised more proxy wars on the level of Vietnam, unless the United States acquiesced to Soviet expansion. Détente, then, was a diplomatic attempt to prevent this from occurring. Of course, not every foreign conflict had its roots in the East-West divide between "free" and communist, but the Soviet Union injected itself into several of the world's conflicts that had roots outside of the East-West ideological divide.

And the world's conflicts were astoundingly costly in human lives. While the United States was mired in Vietnam, a genocide occurred in Nigeria as its minority Ibo population attempted to create an independent nation named Biafra. The Nixon administration did very little to assist either side or work to achieve peace, though nongovernmental organizations and several prominent rock and roll personalities tried to help the Ibo. In spite of congressional concerns, Nixon's response to the Ibo's plight bordered on willful ignorance. When Gilbert Gude (R-MD) argued that in the face of a potential genocide "surely our shared humanity dictates that our responses must not be limited by the jurisdictional boundaries or political differences," Nixon tepidly responded by appointing a retired law school dean to the Nigerian capital of Lagos—far from the people in need—to oversee food shipments. In contrast, the Soviet Union supplied arms to the Nigerian government. The Soviets also backed insurgent movements in Ethiopia during its three-decade-long civil war that resulted in thousands of deaths and the establishment of a pro-communist dictatorship. India and Pakistan went to war as well, and another horrific toll of suffering occurred at the hands of the Pakistani military in East Pakistan before India's military victory and the creation of an independent Bangladesh. Unlike in Biafra, the Nixon administration along with China supported Pakistan, while the Soviet Union supported India. Importantly, while neither the Biafran nor the East Pakistan conflict centered on a question of whether communism or another form of government would prevail, US foreign policy in these conflicts appeared amoral and without direction.

Amoral and directionless foreign policy was not limited to Asia and Africa. While Western Europe was thought to be a grouping of stable allies, in one case it was not. In late 1967 a military junta ousted the elected Greek government. Two years later, fifty-eight members of Congress appealed to Secretary of State William Rogers to limit foreign and military aid to Greece, "the only nation in the Western Alliance in the post–World War II period to fall to a military coup." Congressional interest in Greece was unsurprising. Beyond a sizable ethnic Greek population in the United States, Greece was not merely a democracy; it was where democracy was founded. And, it was a member of NATO. After receiving a tepid response from Rogers, Congressman Don Edwards (D-CA) led the other fifty-seven representatives to appeal to Nixon to cease all military aid to Greece until free and fair elections took place. When this resulted in no satisfactory action, on August 3, 1971, the House took the extraordinary step of voting to discontinue all military aid to Greece over Nixon's threatened veto. The problems with Greece, however, did not abate, in part because of Nixon's intransigence against criticizing that nation, and in part because of the junta's conduct toward Cyprus and the Turkish government's response to the Cyprus situation.

In the first year of Gerald Ford's presidency, the governments of Greece and Turkey threatened each other with war over the control of Cyprus. This raised the specter of two NATO countries going to war. The Turkish military invaded Cyprus after the island's pro-Greek government claimed unification with Greece and abused its Turkish ethnic minority population. Although Ford and Kissinger tried to remain neutral toward both nations, Congress responded by voting to curb all military aid to Turkey. When Ford vetoed the first bill denying Turkey access to US weaponry, Congress passed a second resolution cutting off aid to Turkey unless Ford proved "substantial progress" had been made toward peace in Cyprus. Some conservatives objected even to this resolution. Senators such as Robert Taft Jr. (R-OH)—the son of a former Senate majority leader and grandson of the former Supreme Court chief justice—opposed congressional pressure on the issue of Cyprus and argued that it was critical to have the president remain in charge of foreign policy. But Taft's arguments did not prevail. Congressional foreign policy actions in the Turkish-Greek imbroglio were unusual. Normally Congress accepted a president's foreign policy decisions, even with vocal dissenters decrying the decision. But in this instance, Congress tried to dictate foreign policy to the executive branch.

In March 1975, the North Vietnamese military invaded South Vietnam, in violation of the 1973 Paris Peace Accords. The Paris agreement ending the Vietnam War had been signed between the governments of South Vietnam, North Vietnam, and the United States, and in theory signaled that the United States could return military forces to South Vietnam. Although it was true that shortly after the signatories agreed to cease military operations in 1973, the forces of both sides continually skirmished until the invasion, North Vietnam's invasion violated the peace agreement's clear terms. In 1972, in order to convince the South Vietnamese government to sign the Paris agreement, Nixon promised a resumption of US military involvement if North Vietnam invaded. Ford knew that an overwhelming majority in Congress opposed using any degree of military force, but he also discovered that Congress was unwilling to fund South Vietnam's military. Because he was hemmed in by the 1973 Case-Church Amendment, which prevented the use of funded military assets without congressional approval, Ford could only order the evacuation of US citizens and a few South Vietnamese officials from Saigon as South Vietnam was taken over by the communist North. Shortly after the fall of South Vietnam, Cambodia succumbed to a genocidal Khmer Rouge communist regime. Both Ford and Carter determined not to intervene to stop the over one million deaths that occurred on the "killing fields" of Cambodia, which only ceased in December 1978 with Vietnam's military invasion.

In 1975, Ford appeared to cement a status quo into Soviet-American relations with the Helsinki Accords, though these accords did not prevent the expansion of communism in Africa, South America, and Asia. The Helsinki Accords were a solidification of the détente Nixon had achieved with the Soviet Union during his second term, and they reduced the possibility of war, but they were opposed by conservatives who accused Ford of selling out peoples under communist regimes who desired freedom. In July and August of that year, Ford, along with the leaders of Canada and the major European governments, agreed with Brezhnev that a general framework was essential to reduce East-West tensions and particularly the possibility of war in Europe. Contained within the ten-point agreement was a commitment to human rights, but also a promise of nonintervention in the domestic affairs of the signatory nations. Even Carter, during the 1976 campaign, criticized Ford for permitting the subjugation of Poles, Romanians, and Yugoslavians to Soviet communism. In the presidential debates, Ford stumbled at the question of whether the United States accepted the communist domination of Eastern Europe by claiming that no subjugation had occurred.

Congress also intervened in Ford's foreign policy toward Angola, a former Portuguese colony that gained independence in 1974. American intelligence agencies had conducted clandestine operations in Angola, and as a result of its investigations Congress discovered dozens of operations that otherwise would have been unknown to the public. As in Biafra and Ethiopia, thousands of civilians were killed during the fighting in Angola. Beyond the carnage, Angola presented a complex issue. When it was split into three warring factions, with the Soviet supported-communist faction ascendant, Congress voted to cut off all aid to the other two. In the Senate, John Tunney (D-CA), the charismatic son of famous heavyweight boxing champion Gene Tunney, introduced a measure to prevent Ford from sending military aid and advisers into Angola. Shortly after, Leonard Woodcock, the president of the United Auto Workers, urged the House to back Tunney. (Woodcock, on Carter's nomination and the Senate's approval, would go on to serve as the United States' first ambassador to China.) In early 1976, Congressman Robert Giaimo (D-CT) warned that Ford's use of the Central Intelligence Agency in Angola "conjures up horrifying memories of Vietnam." By the end of January 1976, Ford, to the further anger of congressional conservatives, was legislatively prevented from involving the United States in Angola.

And then there was the oil crisis. Specifically, there were two oil crises in the 1970s. The United States consumed 16.4 million barrels of oil per day in 1970, with Western Europe and Japan using slightly more. Prior to 1970, the United States exported oil, and as a result of large-scale domestic production, gasoline was fairly cheap in comparison to European fuel prices. In 1950, the United States produced roughly half of the world's oil. Yet, by 1970, the United States began to import petroleum. The oil-producing Middle Eastern nations exerted controls over the world economy in a manner not previously experienced. During and after the 1973 Israeli-Arab War, the Organization of Petroleum Exporting Countries (OPEC) began to use oil production as a coercive diplomatic instrument to dissuade Western governments from supporting Israel. Founded in 1960 and mainly centered in the Middle East but also including Venezuela and Ecuador, OPEC possessed leverage in global politics. Within a year, crude oil rose from three dollars per barrel to twelve dollars per barrel. Likewise, in the United States, the cost of a gallon of gasoline rose from an average of thirty-five cents to fifty-five cents, and fuel shortages led to public outrage and inflation. Senator William Fulbright (D-AR), a long-serving foreign policy expert, cautioned that the oil crisis and inflation constituted "a clear and present" danger to the world's democracies. Although some of the Arab nations received Soviet support, the Arab-Israeli conflict was not predicated on the Cold War model, and the OPEC oil embargo proved that emerging nations could drive divisions in the foreign policies of the Western European nations and the United States.

Adding to these complexities, by the time Carter became president, Congress had reasserted itself into foreign policy in another arena. A large number of legislators offered Carter an issue he deemed worthy of pursuing: human rights. To Carter and congressional human rights advocates, détente had achieved an understanding with the Soviet Union that a nuclear war was unwinnable, but that Eastern Europeans and others under communism's control were locked into an existence devoid of political and civil rights. This meant that the United States government had to pressure allies to recognize that they too had to expand basic freedoms or lose financial and military support. They believed that by forcing human rights reforms in the United States' allies, populations under communist rule would likewise demand change. Although human rights, as a foreign policy issue began prior to Carter's presidency, under Carter it became a prominent foreign policy feature.

In 1973, Donald Fraser (D-MN), while chairing a foreign policy subcommittee, accused three past presidential administrations of committing "a consistent pattern of gross violations of internationally recognized human rights." Fraser's investigations into the government's political and economic relations with dictatorships in Africa, South America, and Asia led to restrictions on further trade with dictatorial regimes, including allied governments. In May 1977, at a Notre Dame University commencement speech, Carter claimed that the Soviet Union was no longer a "unifying threat," and the US government had to pursue arms control, end apartheid, and recognize that the peoples of developing countries wanted the same basic rights as were found in the West.

An early instance of a human rights push occurred toward Rhodesia. In 1965, when the United Kingdom demanded that Rhodesia establish a one person, one vote rule and end legal discrimination, Rhodesia's white minority government seceded from the United Kingdom. In turn, the United Nations established an embargo on Rhodesian commerce, and the Johnson administration agreed to put the United States in compliance with the United Nations. Initially, Congress backed Johnson's decision. However, even though a congressional majority favored the embargo, when Senator Harry Byrd (I-VA) introduced an amendment to exempt chrome and other critical defense materials from the embargo, a legislative majority agreed with the exemption. In 1977, Congress, with Carter's encouragement, and despite Goldwater's and the conservatives' resistance, rescinded the amendment.

It was natural for legislators across the political spectrum to distrust the motives of both the Soviet Union and China. After all, one of the principles of communism was that it had to become the global governance system. And so, even when Nixon, a president with conservative credentials, tried to establish a trading partnership with the Soviet Union as a means for boosting the US economy and promoting interdependence, staunch anticommunists such as Senator Henry "Scoop" Jackson (D-WA) and Congressman Charles Vanik (D-OH) inserted into a foreign policy process an amendment placing conditions on the trading partnership. The Jackson-Vanik Amendment required the Soviet Union to annually permit sixty thousand Soviet Jews to immigrate to Israel. The condition of Jews in the Soviet Union had deteriorated in the 1970s to the point where they were being excluded from the government and academia. Although debates on Jackson-Vanik began in 1972, it was not until 1974 that Congress presented a trade act containing its provisions and Ford threatened a veto. The measure came to naught as the Soviet government rejected the trade pact outright in early 1975 and delayed the implementation of SALT II until 1979. Jackson, Vanik, and the Congress as a whole proved, in a manner not seen since Harry S. Truman's presidency, that the legislative branch possessed leverage to upend a president's foreign policies if there was unity to do so. Lacking this unity, there was an open question as to whether Congress could turn to the judiciary for redress.

The Panama Canal's status provided conservatives with the first major opportunity to challenge Carter's foreign and national security policies in the courts. The issue of returning control over the canal was not new in 1977 when Carter announced his intentions to enter into a treaty with the Panamanian government. Indeed, when, in 1965, Johnson announced that he would seek the Senate's approval of a new treaty with Panama, Senator Joseph Montoya's (D-NM) constituents, in an opinion ballot, urged him not to sign any agreement with Panama by a two to one margin. Montoya, a liberal Democrat, listened to them and opposed the canal transfer. But US foreign policy in the decade between 1965 and 1975 had shifted to recognize that foreign governments in South and Central America as well as in Africa and Asia saw US control over their lands as a vestige of imperialism. By 1974, the last of the European empires had come to a practical end, and domestically, liberals and human rights activists believed the Canal Zone symbolized American imperialism. Although Nixon and Ford explored returning the Canal Zone to Panama, the Panamanian government's intransigence and its anti–United States rhetoric as well as domestic opposition from conservatives made it difficult for either president to openly negotiate the return of the canal. As an example, in 1974 Robert Dale Price (R-TX) wrote to his House colleagues that Nixon's negotiation efforts with Panama were nothing more than "a sellout." Price argued that the United States was not a "guest in the Canal Zone; we own the Zone, locks, stock, and water!" One year later Daniel J. Flood (D-PA), who supported Nixon over George McGovern, accused Ford of "surrendering US sovereignty" to Panama. The few conservatives who were willing to negotiate on the return of the canal insisted on a high price for doing so. In 1977, Joseph McDade (R-PA) insisted on massive concessions from Panama for the return of the canal, including a cash buyout.

Even when moderate Republicans like Senate minority leader Howard Baker (R-TN) indicated their openness for negotiations with Panama, conservatives attacked them. When Baker announced he would run for the presidency against Carter in 1980, Republican conservatives assailed his stance on the Panama Canal. As Laura Kalman has pointed out in her comprehensive study on the 1970s, the canal enabled the "new Right" to gain a voice over the older party members, and politicians such as Jesse Helms (R-NC) and Reagan—who proclaimed "we built it, we paid for it, it is ours"—espoused their opposition to handing the canal to

Panama. Perhaps, for this reason, Gilbert Gude, a moderate Republican who had opposed US involvement in the Vietnam Conflict, promised only to consider "what is in the national interest," and the "nation's defense posture," when determining whether to support a shared control over the canal with the Panamanian government.

In 1977, Carter introduced a proposed treaty—in reality two treaties—to the Senate governing the canal's transfer. Ultimately, while the requisite two-thirds of the Senate acquiesced to Carter in approving a treaty to transfer the canal, a majority of Americans opposed the handover. Moderate Republican senator Edwin Brooke (R-MA) found it necessary to defend himself against accusations that he had "allied with Carter and Communists." Frank Church, the chairman of the Senate Foreign Relations Committee, felt compelled to inform his constituents that only when the military leadership of the Department of Defense, the chairman of the Joint Chiefs of Staff, assessed the handover would not threaten national security would he start to examine the treaties. (The term "start" implied to his constituents that he might not vote for the handover.) Brooke would lose his Senate seat in the 1978 general election, partly on the issue of Panama. Church, a long-serving senator, also lost his seat in 1980 partly because of his support for Carter on Panama and China.

Panama was only one of the troubling foreign policy issues Carter inherited. Both Nicaragua and El Salvador appeared to tilt toward communism. In July 1979, a coalition of students and Marxists overthrew Nicaragua's leader, Anastasio Samoza Debayle, ending a quasi-dynastic family's rule that had been in place since 1912. Beginning in 1968, with the help of Cuba, the Sandinista National Liberation Front—or FSLN—waged a civil war against the government, large property farmers, and multinational corporations. In 1977 Carter ceased providing military aid to the Nicaraguan government over its human rights abuses. The Nicaraguan military and police forces had kidnapped, murdered, and tortured thousands of its own citizens, and the FSLN had responded in kind. Conservatives deplored Carter's declination of aid to Nicaragua and blamed him for its subsequent fall to a communist-oriented regime. Conservatives also warned that El Salvador was likely to fall to communism because of Carter's demand for human rights as a basis for US aid.

On October 26, 1979, an assassin murdered South Korea's president,

Park Chung-hee. From the end of World War II, South Korea, like Taiwan, had been a US ally; indeed, from 1950 to 1953, the United States led an international military force in a war against communist North Korea and China, costing the United States more than forty thousand deaths and South Korea, 162,394. After the armistice, US military forces in South Korea consisted of over thirty thousand service members and two major air force bases. Nixon planned to reduce the number of forces both as a show of good faith to China and because the South Korean government under Park had become antidemocratic. Throughout the 1970s Park's government jailed, tortured, and killed its political opposition. In 1974, Congressman Fraser, along with Patsy Mink (D-HI) and Edward Koch (D-NY), authored a petition that was signed by dozens of representatives asking Ford to reduce military aid to South Korea. In a speech to the House, Gilbert Gude insisted that "countries that resort to terror and torture to suppress freedom of expression should certainly not be allowed to do so with our money." During the last year of Ford's presidency, ten congressmen were implicated in a bribery scandal stemming from a South Korea intelligence agent exchanging payments for votes to prevent troop reductions. During the 1976 campaign Carter signaled his intent to continue Nixon's planned military reduction in South Korea, and this, like the Panama Canal handover, led to intense criticism from congressional conservatives. On the basis of human rights, Carter tied troop reductions to government repression. Indeed, he intended for the complete removal of forces to occur within a five-year period, but no reduction took place during his, or Ronald Reagan's presidency.

Conservatives were willing to overlook South Korea's rights record because, in the words of Henry Hyde (R-IL), that nation held an important position in "preventing the number of democracies becoming smaller." Led by Edwin Derwinski (R-IL), Robert Lagomarsino (R-CA), Charles Wilson (D-TX), and John Murphy (D-NY), congressional conservatives voiced their opposition to reducing military forces in South Korea by arguing that North Korea remained a threat and therefore South Korea's repression was necessary. They also pointed out that North Korea, Cambodia, Vietnam, and Uganda had far worse human rights records than South Korea and then complained that although the human rights advocates focused on South Korea, there was little attention placed on these other countries. Criticism against Carter's uneven application of human rights to foreign affairs was not limited to congressional conservatives. Edward Brooke wrote a blistering letter to Carter and Secretary of State Cyrus Vance in response to Carter publicly stating during a formal visit to Romania that Nicolae Ceauşescu acknowledged the importance of human rights. "While it is appropriate that the United States extend the requisite courtesies to other heads of state, it is hardly becoming for the President to intimate that these rulers of communist countries are other than confirmed dictators who have little regard for the sanctity or rights of the individual," Brooke concluded.

Even if Carter had not established full recognition of China, 1979 was a critical year for the foreign policy of the United States, if not also its domestic policy. Although Carter had been elected president partly on the promise of reducing Cold War tensions with the Soviet Union, by the beginning of 1979 the administration had found it necessary to become confrontational with Moscow. Not only had the Soviet Union placed large numbers of its military forces in Afghanistan, but negotiations over nuclear arsenal limitations reached an impasse, and Soviet and Cuban military assistance to African revolutionary groups resulted in a communist-friendly government in Angola. Just four years earlier, congressional conservatives led by Goldwater warned that a lack of support for anticommunist forces would turn Angola into a communist state. Now they claimed that Carter's China policy would result in worse disasters.

Most shockingly, the world witnessed a religious revolution in Iran. The Iranian revolutionaries not only opposed the United States and the West in general but also proclaimed the Soviet Union as their enemy. Iran's deposed leader, Mohammad Reza Pahlavi, had long been an ally of the United States, and his admission to the Mayo Clinic in Minnesota for cancer treatment led to the revolutionaries seizing US embassy personnel and holding them hostage for over four hundred days. With Iranian oil production ground to a halt, the price of fuel doubled for the second time in the 1970s, and the United States once more suffered through gasoline shortages and inflation without commensurate wage or employment growth.

In January 1979, when Carter feted China's leader Chairman Deng Xiaoping, it appeared to Americans that at last stability had been achieved with a former antagonist and the possibility of conflict in Asia lessened. But one month later, Chinese military forces invaded Vietnam in retaliation for Vietnam's invasion of Cambodia. By 1979, Soviet and Chinese relations had frayed once more to the point where the two countries were on a war footing along their immense border.

The United States, Taiwan, and China: 1949–1978

One month after Carter's bombshell announcement, Deputy Secretary of State Warren Christopher announced that in the first two years of Carter's presidency, relations with NATO had been strengthened, "peace between Egypt and Israel that had once been thought of as an impossibility was now quite possible," and nuclear arms negotiations with the Soviet Union were in a promising stage. Not all his claims were immediately evident or accurate. Christopher then turned to China and stated, "After a gap of almost 30 years, the president has taken the historic decision to normalize our relationship with the People's Republic of China." He went on to describe three benefits that normalization would bring to the United States. "Full and normal relations will allow us to work more effectively toward a stable system of independent nations in Asia," he claimed. "It will permit us to encourage an outward-looking China to play a constructive role in the World generally, and it will enable American business to deal on an equal footing with other suppliers as China moves toward modernization."

Henry Kissinger, who served as secretary of state under Nixon and Ford, recalled that when Nixon visited China in 1971, only a small number of Sinologists—scholars engaged in the study of China—viewed the United States' rift with the People's Republic of China as "psychological" rather than as China imperiling the national security. Yet many conservatives and liberals alike believed China harbored expansionist desires and its government was "fanatically ideological and intransigently committed to world revolution." In 1972, Congressman John G. Schmitz (R-CA) warned that any accommodation with China would come at Taiwan's expense, and therefore every true conservative had to oppose Nixon's attempts to create a new relationship with the communist Chinese government. In the article "The Coming Sacrifice of Taiwan," published in a weekly newsletter, Schmitz accused Kissinger of not only "selling out"

Taiwan but also consulting John Stewart Service, a former State Department analyst whom conservatives accused of helping Mao Zedong take control of China. Although Schmitz was voted out of office the following year, to conservatives his warning proved prescient. However, at the time Schmitz spoke, there was also a consensus that regardless of Nixon's "opening of China," the United States' commitment to Taiwan remained in effect and therefore his warning seemed to be foolish. After all, in March 1970, Senator William Fulbright (D-AR), an ardent opponent of the United States' involvement in the Vietnam Conflict, reflected that the then fifteen-year-old Mutual Defense Treaty was "our defense commitment to the Republic of China . . . and . . . absent congressional repeal nothing would affect our commitment to the defense of the treaty area or our ability to meet it."

Following the defeat of the Nationalists and the creation of the Republic of China, for geopolitical reasons the United States was likely bound to defend the island even had a formal treaty not existed. It had practically been a Western article of faith that since Chiang's retreat to Taiwan, the island was an independent nation with lawful status to represent China in the United Nations. In 1950, the Republican Policy Committee, under the leadership of Senator Robert Taft, concluded that as a matter of international law, when the Dutch established a fort on the island in 1624, Manchu China had never effectively ruled the whole of Formosa. And because, at the conclusion of the Sino-Japanese War in 1895, China ceded Formosa to Japan, the People's Republic of China could not claim title to the island. Thus, the United States and Great Britain, which had vanquished Japan in World War II, had absolute authority to recognize Formosa as the Republic of China. Shortly before Taft's publication of the legal status of Taiwan as the Republic of China, he argued to the Senate that the United States had an obligation to protect Taiwan against communist attempts to seize the island if, for no other reason, than to contain communism. "We have given military aid to Turkey and Iran. We have stood firm against the communist advance in Korea . . . in undertaking the airlift in Germany we certainly risked war with Russia," Taft argued before concluding that the United States should permit the people of Formosa to vote on their own future once a peace treaty with Japan had come into effect. Thus, there were two reasons to defend Taiwan: it was an independent nation, and its government opposed communism. It should be noted that Taft opposed most treaties, including NATO. He represented the Republican Party's isolationist wing, but Taiwan was different. His commitment to Taiwan marked the near unanimity across Congress that it was critical to ensure Taiwan's sovereignty.

In 1950, when the communists took control of China, Senator Tom Connally (D-TX) served as chairman of the Senate Foreign Relations Committee. Connally was a staunch anticommunist conservative and loathed any step toward the recognition of a communist regime anywhere in the world. He agreed with Taft on Taiwan's legal status as an independent nation and that the United States had a duty to defend it. While he assured his constituents that there was no indication President Truman sought to recognize the communist Chinese government, he conceded that "so far as actual recognition is concerned, the President has this authority and it is not necessary for him to secure prior approval by the congress." Goldwater, of course, was not bound by Connally's opinion, and the senator had passed away in 1962. Nonetheless, Connally's statement to his constituents evidenced that conservatives were not always in lockstep on the matter of presidential recognition of foreign governments. In spite of a lack of consistency over recognition and treaty revocation, Carter needed Senate allies to oppose Goldwater. Unless a majority of the Senate either favored revocation or remained silent on the constitutional question, the courts might determine—as Justice Lewis Powell later argued in his concurrence—that Carter had acted outside of his constitutional authority.

During the Truman administration, conservative legislators, businessmen, and journalists teamed with the Chinese Nationalists to form a de facto lobby, often referred to as the "China Lobby." Throughout the first decade of the Cold War, Congress conducted investigations to ferret out State Department officials and other government officers who "lost China" to the communists. In hearings often resembling witch hunts, conservative legislators such as Senator Joe McCarthy (R-WI) accused international law scholars, Secretary of State Dean Acheson, and distinguished State Department officers like Owen Lattimore of aiding communism. Hundreds of government workers and university professors lost their jobs and were blacklisted from further government service on specious evidence. In 1957, in *Service v. Dulles*, the Supreme Court—in a decision originating with John Stewart Service's employment termination—appeared to put up a barrier to McCarthy-era excesses in terms of firing diplomatic personnel based on unsubstantiated allegations of communist ties or sympathies, but the decision did not return the reputations of the era's victims. In 1974, when Kissinger sought John Service's advice on China, some conservatives attacked the Nixon and Ford administrations for coddling communist China because they never, despite evidence to the contrary, stopped believing that Service had sympathy for communism.

In 1953, members of the China Lobby formed a political organization, the Committee of One Million, and gained the support of more than a hundred congressmen who promised never to permit the US government to recognize the People's Republic of China. The organization was named after its anticommunist founder, Martin Liebman, collected over one million citizen signatures in opposition to the recognition of "Red China." Early members of the group included Congressmen John Ashbrook (R-OH), Hugh Scott (R-PA), Thomas Dodd (D-CT), and William Proxmire (D-WI). When, in 1964, France recognized the People's Republic of China as a legitimate nation deserving of membership in the United Nations, the Committee of One Million sent out thousands of mailers assuring Americans that there was bipartisan opposition to the United States joining with France. The committee pointed out that both liberals and conservatives in Congress had opposed recognition of China. For instance, in 1961 Senator Clinton Anderson (D-NM), a liberal pro–civil rights legislator assured a concerned Los Alamos Baptist minister he had "made it abundantly clear many, many times: I am opposed to the admission of Red China to the United Nations." Anderson joined the Committee of One Million and, in explaining his reasons for doing so, told his constituents he was "strongly opposed to China's admittance and would do anything he could to prevent their becoming a member of the United Nations."

There are many instances of assurances given to Taiwan prior to Carter's 1978 announcement in which Congress and the Taiwanese would have reasonably believed that the over two-decade-old treaty would remain in effect. Perhaps the most telling occurred a quarter of a century earlier. During the summer of 1951, Justice William O. Douglas had journeyed to Asia, and when he passed through San Francisco on his return, he advocated for the United States to recognize the People's Republic of China. Douglas created a political firestorm for the Truman administration. Senator Everett Dirksen (R-IL) claimed that Douglas's comments proved the administration was soft on communism, and Senator Herman Welker (R-ID) accused Truman of using Douglas to articulate the administration's true position on China, even though Truman had clearly tried to isolate the communists in China. Truman's Democratic allies who normally would have defended Douglas did not do so in this instance. Truman insisted to the public that the government in Taiwan represented all Chinese. And he wrote a private letter to Douglas. "I was somewhat embarrassed by your statement on Communist China," Truman began. "As long as I am President, that cut-throat organization will never be recognized by us as the government of China and I am sorry that a Justice of the Supreme Court has been willing to champion the interest of a bunch of murderers by a public statement." Nixon too attacked Douglas. "There are some who tell us from a practical business standpoint we are foolish in our refusal to recognize Red China and admit its representatives into the United Nations," Nixon claimed, before deriding the justice as a representative of "well-intentioned but misguided people."

In 1975, Averell Harriman, New York's democratic governor and one of the last prominent New Deal men remaining in public service, briefly spoke at General Chiang Kai-shek's memorial service at the National Cathedral in Washington, DC. After eulogizing Taiwan's former leader, the new premier, Chiang Ching-kuo, expressed his thanks to Harriman before adding that Taiwan's people found comfort in the fact the prominent statesman had attended the funeral and professed support for Taiwan. One year later, following the Democratic National Convention, Taiwan's ambassador expressed his alarm to Harriman that neither the Democratic Party nor Carter had spoken about preserving Taiwan's standing or sovereignty. Harriman, for his part, assured the ambassador that the United States was bound by treaty to both recognize and defend Taiwan and the absence of a platform statement should not be worrisome. Four years earlier, Harriman had warned that Nixon's attempts to establish diplomatic relations with China could not endanger Taiwan.

Neither Nixon, Ford, nor Carter wanted to embolden a communist Chinese expansion. There were, to be sure, several practical reasons

Nixon sought for the United States to have a relationship with China. The ongoing war in Vietnam had sapped the domestic economy, and the social divisions within the United States erupted into mass demonstrations against the government. Although Vietnam was not, in 1969, "Nixon's War," it became so by the next year when, without congressional sanction, he ordered an invasion into neighboring neutral Cambodia. That year, mass demonstrations occurred throughout the United States, including those in protest of the National Guard shootings of college students at Kent State University in Ohio and at Jackson State University in South Carolina. Nixon and Kissinger believed that China, as an ally of North Vietnam, and communist movements in Cambodia and Laos could help extricate the United States from the Vietnam Conflict. The two men planned for a post-Vietnam policy in the Pacific in which the United States maintained its alliances but reduced the economic burden of maintaining a large military presence in Asia.

There was also a fraying of relations between China and the Soviet Union that provided Nixon an opportunity to exploit. In March 1969, the military forces of the two nations fought along their border, which resulted in dozens of deaths on both sides. The Sino-Soviet border stretched over forty-five hundred miles, making it the longest in the world, and there were conflicting claims over water rights and river islands. It was startling that the world's two largest communist countries, each embracing an ideology that transcended nationalism and each with a nuclear arsenal, would fight over territory. Yet, the prior year, when the Soviet Union and its Eastern European satellite states invaded communist Czechoslovakia to suppress a pro-democracy uprising, the Chinese government criticized their action as Soviet imperialism. Given that throughout the Cold War, the Soviet Union remained the United States' most pressing threat, the detachment of China and its transition to a Soviet military competitor made it natural for the US government to reassess relations with China. This would take a concerted effort because, across the spectrum, American legislators tended to distrust China, and the few leaders who wanted to move the United States toward recognition saw their efforts fail.

In 1957, Congressman Emmanuel Celler (D-NY), a long-serving House Judiciary Committee chairman, introduced legislation requiring the State Department to issue journalists passports to travel to China. Celler acted after learning that the agency refused to issue a passport to William Worthy, a correspondent for the *Afro-American*, a Baltimore-based news magazine. The following year Celler, with the support of Thomas S. Gordon (D-IL), the House Foreign Affairs chair, introduced H.R. 13652 declaring that freedom of movement "is basic in the scheme of American institutions," and that "the right to travel abroad is part of the liberty which citizens of the United States cannot be deprived without due process of law." It took until 1960 for the House to debate Celler's bill where it met with opposition from conservatives such as Walter Judd (R-MN). Judd, in fact, was one of the leading conservatives on China, and he worked to prevent any step toward recognition, including permitting journalists to travel there. Judd was viewed as a "China expert" among conservatives. After graduating from the University of Nebraska's medical school in 1923, he lived in China as a medical missionary. On his return to the United States, he settled in Minnesota and was elected to Congress in 1942. He was also a founding member of the Committee of One Million. Until the Kennedy administration's second year, the State Department determined not to issue blanket passports to journalists to travel to China. In 1977, Judd wrote to Carter that the recognition of China would be nothing short of an appeasement to the largest violator of human rights.

By the start of Nixon's presidency, there were indications that a growing number of legislators had opened to the possibility of a rapprochement with China. Slowly, in the late 1960s, a small number of legislators evolved from viewing China as an intractable enemy. Their number included Senator Abe Ribicoff (D-CT), who wrote to historian Henry Steele Commager that he renounced his Committee of One Million membership after Commager called US policy on China "the most egregious error in 175 years of diplomatic history." Senator Hiram Fong (D-HI) proved another exception. In 1971, he not only lauded Nixon's visit to China but also tried to create a bipartisan consensus for the United States to have the People's Republic recognized as the sovereign China in the United Nations. But he gained little traction. Henry Reuss (D-WI) was another early exception on the United States recognizing China. On March 23, 1966, Reuss asked the Johnson administration to support China's entry into the United Nations with the understanding that Taiwan would maintain its position there as well. Johnson expressed no interest in doing so.

By the mid-1970s, some of the senators who earlier opposed recognition realized that the United States could benefit from closer economic and diplomatic ties to China if, for no other reason than the Sino-Soviet rift could theoretically be mended and the United States would be in a weakened global position. The most pronounced change in the Senate occurred in 1973 when Henry "Scoop" Jackson stated that full recognition of China was long overdue. He added that derecognition of Taiwan would not harm the United States since the United Nations had already voted Taiwan out of its General Assembly seat. Jackson was generally thought of as a "defense hawk" and had consistently supported Johnson's and Nixon's Vietnam War policies. "It is ridiculous and contrary to our best interests not to have the recognition problem solved at this time," he insisted to the Senate. Robert Taft Jr. informed a Cincinnati reporter that weapons sales in China were important to the United States' foreign policy and influence in the Pacific and Asia. "Without the prospect of effective American support, China's only option is to forestall the Soviet threat by realigning itself with the Soviet Union," Taft argued. "Surely, Moscow would dictate those terms and such a result would be a foreign policy disaster of great magnitude for the United States." This was a change from his father's position on China.

The benefits of cooperation with the People's Republic of China became evident in other areas, including in sub-Saharan Africa. Although Carter had promised to respect Congress, his administration, like that of every president since 1974, cast doubts on the constitutionality of the War Powers Resolution. In 1977, Soviet-backed Katanga forces tried to create an independent state out of Shaba, a province in Zaire. There was evidence of Cuban support to the Katanga forces as well. While the Carter administration had no affinity for Zaire's dictator, Mobutu Sese Seko, Seko was staunchly anti-Soviet. When, in late 1977, the French and Moroccan governments sent military forces to back Seko, Carter informed French premier Giscard d'Estaing he supported the move. Carter also ordered nonmilitary supplies to Seko, and the Chinese government voiced its support for the French, Moroccan, and US actions. In April 1978, when Morocco's forces were in danger of being overrun,

Carter ordered a military airlift to secure their safety. Congressmen Paul Findley (R-IL) and James Leach (R-IA) criticized Carter for failing to comply with notifying Congress of the pending military operation in compliance with the War Powers Act. When the House Foreign Relations Committee investigated the issue, its chairman, Clement Zablocki, announced that Carter was not required to comply with the act over an airlift. However, Congressman Jonathan Bingham (D-NY) disagreed with Zablocki and characterized Carter's perceived lack of compliance with the act a "close call." Seemingly buried within this debate was the fact that the Chinese government publicly supported the United States and, in doing so, evidenced another instance of Chinese-US cooperation against the Soviet Union.

Barry Goldwater: Carter's Challenger in the Federal Courts

In 1964, Goldwater, ran for the presidency against Johnson. Considered a reactionary even by centrist members of his own party, Goldwater lost in a landslide seldom seen in the nation's history. But his loss turned out to be a short-term setback for the Republican Party's conservatives, as four years later Nixon became president. Born in the Arizona Territory in 1909 to a wealthy mercantile family, Goldwater attended a private military school in Virginia and then the University of Arizona before taking over his parents' department store in Phoenix. During World War II, he was commissioned into the US Army Air Forces, where he ferried aircraft to both Britain and China. He was elected to the Senate in 1952 having vowed to reverse the New Deal, and he opposed most federal civil rights programs. As a staunch anticommunist, he voted against censoring Senator McCarthy in 1957, though he later criticized McCarthy's "thirst for power and alcohol." From the start of his Senate tenure, Goldwater tended to align with the Robert Taft wing of the Republican Party, and he had as much disdain for his party's liberals as he did for those in the Democratic Party.

Notably, Goldwater voted against the Civil Rights Act of 1964, insisting that it was unconstitutional for the federal government to police state and local governments and businesses. Although he never signed the

"Southern Manifesto," and, as a reserve general officer, he worked to desegregate the Arizona National Guard, he decried the Supreme Court's alleged activism in cases such as *Brown v. Board of Education* and *Cooper v. Aaron.* He also equated labor unions with organized crime and was the lone Senate vote against a labor bill President Eisenhower introduced to Congress that continued federal recognition of the right of unions to organize. Goldwater also criticized Eisenhower for failing to shrink the size of the federal government. Indeed, he believed that the bureaucracy that grew within the federal government during the New Deal was one of the greatest obstacles to the defeat of communism. He argued that government functionaries had "mightily tried" to defeat Eisenhower's domestic policies. Goldwater would later criticize Nixon for failing to shrink the executive branch bureaucracy, which had grown even beyond New Deal levels during the Kennedy and Johnson presidencies.

Goldwater proved to be far more than an occasional antagonist to Carter. On the day after the 1977 presidential inauguration, Carter issued a proclamation granting an unconditional pardon to citizens who violated the Military Selective Service Act; in response, Goldwater claimed that amnesty for "draft evaders" was "the most disgraceful thing that a President has ever done." He insisted Carter's grant of amnesty would destroy any future attempt to enlarge the military in a national emergency. Although Goldwater's stance, in our present times, might seem horribly reactionary, the weight of public opinion disfavored Carter's amnesty policy. Liberals pointed out that the amnesty order generally favored middle-class whites who fled to Canada or who could afford to live outside of the law, while the poor who actually complied with a draft order and then deserted the military were not granted an amnesty. Conservatives viewed Carter's action as forgiving an unforgiveable treason. Goldwater stood alongside Jake Garn (R-UT) at a press conference and approvingly nodded as Garn claimed that the amnesty "filled him with disgust."

Goldwater's suit against Carter over Taiwan arose not merely as a conservative versus liberal battle, though this was certainly an element in his decision to sue Carter. Goldwater had championed the United States' military involvement in Vietnam, argued that Johnson did not commit enough military forces to assist in the fight against communism there, supported Nixon's use of force in Cambodia and Laos, and believed that Congress had betrayed the people of South Vietnam in 1975 by not permitting military assistance as the forces of the communist North captured Saigon. After the United States failed to save South Vietnam, Goldwater insisted that a US retreat from its possessions or a distancing from Cold War allies would only further empower communism's spread. In this regard, he devalued the aspirations of millions of peoples who had been subjected to oppressive, and often racially bigoted, regimes. He argued that the Rhodesian apartheid government was preferable to majority rule, which he feared would turn to communism if the majoritarian African population were to have full rights. He also backed South Africa's white apartheid government on the basis that it was preferable to a majority-rule government that might be amenable to the Soviet Union.

Goldwater also adamantly opposed the return of the Panama Canal Zone to Panama. When Jesse Helms (R-NC) tried to derail the Panama Canal Treaty by calling for a Senate investigation into a White House–backed committee's fundraising, Goldwater sided with him. He also publicly chastised Arizona's other senator, Dennis DeConini (D-AZ), for "fence-sitting" on the canal issue. He insisted to Senator Paul Laxalt (R-NV), who headed the Senate's investigation into the canal turnover, that giving control of the canal to Panama's president, Omar Torrijos, would pose the gravest national security threat to the United States. In the midst of the Panama Canal debates, Goldwater's attentions turned halfway across the world after Carter announced that he intended to follow through with Nixon's plan to reduce the numbers of US military personnel in South Korea. Goldwater not only asserted that Carter was wrongly abandoning another crucial ally but also feted US army general John Singlaub, who spoke out against Carter on the issue of military reductions in South Korea. After Carter ordered Singlaub transferred out of Korea and the general responded by retiring, Goldwater issued a news release that claimed "the wrong man resigned today" and that Carter "has yet to come up with a military or foreign policy decision that makes sense." Goldwater continued, "Most of them have spelled extreme danger to the United States and the free world."

Goldwater had long opposed recognition of the People's Republic of China for two basic reasons. He believed that Taiwan had been an important ally in containing communism in Asia, and he felt that the act of renouncing the treaty would cause other allies to view the United States as unreliable. In 1969, he met with Nixon to oppose normalizing relations with any communist country, let alone China. Even with the recognition that China's help was essential to ending the Vietnam War and that there was a rift between the Soviet Union and China, Goldwater's opinions barely changed. In 1973, he wrote to a constituent that although "Red China" presented an expansionist threat, he "approved of the President's steps to better our relations with Red China in order to form some type of rational understanding with our major prospective enemies" but "most strongly opposed breaking our ties with one of the most anti-Communist regimes in all of Asia."

In March 1975, when Goldwater learned that Ford intended to journey to Beijing without visiting Taipei, he lobbied the president to change his plans and reinforce to the Taiwanese people that the United States remained committed to their defense. When Ford decided not to do so, Goldwater complained to Taiwan's ambassador, "While it might read favorably on the surface, I think underneath we can see the one China idea and that one China would not be ours." Oddly, perhaps, because Goldwater did not approve of Carter's stated human rights commitment he did not believe that Carter would normalize relations with the People's Republic of China, which, after all, had a lamentable human rights record. This was particularly so when considering that China had backed the Khmer Rouge and insisted that the removal of that government by Vietnam was an act of war.

Once Carter announced his intention to recognize the People's Republic of China, Goldwater explained to Taiwan's ambassador that his lawsuit was "a means to stop a presidential act of dishonesty." On this point Goldwater penned, "Well, after being lied to by President Nixon, President Johnson, President Ford, and Dr. Kissinger, I guess there is not much I can say." As he explained further, "None of us had any idea at all that President Carter was going to take the atrocious step he took." He concluded his letter to the ambassador, "I guess if one had reflected thoughtfully on it, one might have reached the conclusion that the world's largest conglomeration of people could not forever be ignored by the United States, but I never dreamed that, as an American, that any president of mine would lie to me, let alone those I have mentioned plus Carter."

Had Goldwater believed that Carter merely launched the nation into yet another flawed foreign policy decision, it is unlikely he would have sought judicial intervention. But he did sincerely believe that Carter had exceeded his constitutional authority in renouncing the Mutual Defense Treaty. He wrote to one constituent, "My objective is to see that the President cannot get away with breaking the law and to preserve the independence and freedom of 17 million people on Taiwan." In terms of the United States' reliability toward its allies, Goldwater informed another constituent it was necessary to seek redress in the judiciary and obtain a definitive ruling that Carter acted unconstitutionally. "That is why I have gone to the courts to see whether they agree with my position or the President's," Goldwater wrote. "And if they agree with the President's, then there is no treaty we have that is worth the paper it is written on and there will be no countries left in the world that will respect the formal honor of the United States." In addition to exchanging correspondences with Taiwan's ambassador, Goldwater expressed his dismay to several senior Taiwan government officials. When a Taiwanese legislator lamented, "If the pressure from Communist China is strong enough to compel President Carter to violate your own constitution, than the Constitution is at stake," Goldwater wholeheartedly agreed with this assessment.

CHAPTER 2

Goldwater's Congressional Allies and Carter's Tepid Supporters

On December 17, 1978, the editors of the *Arizona Republic* editors accused President Carter of betraying Taiwan. They argued that he used the normalization of relations with China to deflect from his failures elsewhere, claiming that Carter's "Middle East policy was in shambles" and his "Soviet policy floundering." Additionally, the *Republic* hinted that the timing of Carter's announcement was chosen to distract public's attention away from the nation's domestic problems, including rising inflation without commensurate employment and wage growth. The newspaper's editors conceded that China would open up markets to the United States, but like Goldwater, they argued that business interests should not dictate foreign policy, especially with a communist regime. Further, they warned that the abandonment of Taiwan would come with the price of undermining the trust that the peoples of the Philippines, Japan, and Australia placed in the United States. "Carter isn't the first president who has grabbed at an opportunity to pose as a great peacemaker in order to cover up his failures," the editors concluded. "But he is the first to desert a faithful ally, a good friend, and an economically successful country in order to cozy up to a poverty-stricken enemy which still has blood on its hands and will not hesitate to oppose the United States whenever it appears advantageous." It was perhaps foreseeable, that the *Republic* attacked Carter in this manner if for no other reason than its position mirrored that of the state's congressional leaders and, in particular, Goldwater. Indeed, in 1964, the *Republic* endorsed Goldwater over Lyndon Johnson.

Twelve pages after this editorial, the *Republic* reported that Goldwater intended to file a "citizens' suit" in federal court. Goldwater had called Carter a coward, and he posited that eventually the Supreme Court would "have to decide if the president has such powers." He also accurately predicted the Court would rapidly determine his lawsuit against Carter. Yet, however accurate his prediction became, he warned that the Soviet Union's leaders would believe themselves threatened by the possibility of an accord between China and the United States, and then launch an attack in Western Europe. "If Carter's goal had been nothing more than a reasonable attempt to empower China to act against the Soviet Union, then the United States needed only to sell arms to China, rather than abandoning Taiwan," he claimed. Goldwater's prediction regarding the Soviet Union was, of course, wildly wrong, as was his claim that the Japanese and Australian governments opposed Carter's extension of diplomatic recognition of China. To the *Republic*'s credit, it did report, on the same page as Goldwater's comments, that the governments of allied Asian nations viewed Carter's announcement positively. This view, of course, did not include that of the Taiwanese government.

Although the Dole-Stone Amendment might have been thought to be a means for seeking a federal injunction against Carter's unilateral action, at least one other senator believed that more had to be done to create a basis for a court to determine that Carter had exceeded his constitutional authority. On January 15, 1979, Senator Harry Byrd (I-VA) forwarded a "sense of the Senate Resolution." Such a resolution is not binding on the Senate, let alone Congress or the president, but it does explain to the nation that the Senate believes a presidential act is either valid or invalid, or that the action of the government is inconsistent with the best interests of the country. In 1979, the Court of Appeals for the District of Columbia, in deciding a labor union's appeal against wage freezes, determined that such a resolution is not binding on the federal courts. On March 9, the Senate voted against Byrd's resolution, largely because it had not come from the Foreign Relations Committee, but less than three months later the committee reconsidered Byrd's draft resolution, which read "it is the sense of the Senate that treaties or treaty provisions to which the United States is a party should not be terminated or suspended by the President without the concurrence of the Congress," except under limited conditions such as a new treaty taking effect or an act of war against the United States. On June 6, 1979, the very day that the district court issued its ruling, the Senate voted in favor of considering Byrd's resolution over that of competing resolutions, one of which recognized a presidential authority to terminate treaties and another that disclaimed any absolute executive power to do so.

Carter's Conservative Opponents and the Problem of Standing

In the Senate, Strom Thurmond (R-SC), Jesse Helms (R-NC), Orrin Hatch (R-UT), Jake Garn (R-UT), and Paul Laxalt (R-NV) joined in the suit. Carl Curtis (R-NE) also joined, though on January 3, 1979, he retired from the Senate and his replacement, James Exon (D-NE), did not do so. The recently elected Gordon Humphrey (R-NH) joined in the lawsuit before he was formally seated as a senator on January 3 of that year. In the House, seventeen representatives joined Goldwater, including two conservative democrats. Led by long-term conservative John Ashbrook (R-OH), their number included westerners Eldon Rudd (R-AZ), Bob Stump (D-AZ), Don Young (R-AK), Larry George Hansen (R-ID), Steve Symms (R-ID), Robert "Bob" Dornan (R-CA), John H. Rousselot (R-CA), and Clair Burgener (R-CA). From the Midwest, Daniel Quayle (R-IN) and Mickey Edwards (R-OK) signed on to the legal brief. So too from the South did Robert Daniel (R-VA), Larry McDonald (D-GA), Robert Bauman (R-MD), Newt Gingrich (R-GA), and James Collins (R-TX) join in the lawsuit. These men ranked among Congress's most conservative members and while their opponents might have called their legal brief amateurish or ill-advised, the group included a future vice president and House speaker.

Members of Congress cannot automatically sue the federal government in a federal court, and when a member of Congress tries to do so, it is questionable whether they enjoy a status separate from that of ordinary citizens. In order to have a US district court take up a person's or party's cause against the United States, a state, or a governmental agency, the person or party seeking redress must prove that they have standing to sue. A ruling in favor of standing does not necessarily mean that the party claiming standing will prevail on the merits of their claim. Likewise, a party denied standing may have both the facts and the substantive law on their side but cannot establish the means by which the court will hear their cause. Standing may be proved by showing a direct harm or injury. For instance, a person who is lawfully entitled to vote, but is prevented from doing so, has suffered an injury under the law. When a federal or state agency denies a person the ability to make personal decisions regarding the use of their private property, they may possess standing to sue the agency. The same may not be true when a person or party is harmed by the potential actions of a property owner.

As an example, during the Nixon administration, the Department of the Interior was poised to grant the Walt Disney Corporation permission to build a theme park in the Mineral King National Forrest. If Disney had built its intended amusement park, it would have devastated the ecology of the Sierra Nevada range. The Sierra Club, one of the nation's leading conservation organizations, sued on behalf of its concerned members—if not the health of the mountain range and its animal and plant occupants—and insisted that the construction of an amusement park would also harm the public. The Sierra Club further argued that it possessed the specialized scientific and ecological knowledge of the harm Disney's plans would cause. The Court determined, however, in *Sierra Club v. Morton*, that the environmental organization could not "speak" for the population and therefore lacked standing to sue the government.

In 1975, in *Warth v. Seldin*, the Court noted that in determining whether a party has standing to bring a lawsuit against a governmental agency, a federal trial court must determine that the person or party has a direct interest in the outcome of the controversy. In other words, the aggrieved party must have more at stake than a personal dislike of the government's position or must suffer more than an injury common to all of the nation's residents. On the other hand, the Court has recognized that a person or party suing a governmental agency need not be the party most directly harmed by the government's action, and in matters in which Congress has statutorily enabled a "right of action" to sue, another person or party may file suit on behalf of the people most harmed by the government's action.

Not all legal injuries result in standing; indeed, when a legal or personal injury becomes too marginal to the person or party seeking redress, there may be no standing to sue an agency. Thus, if a presidential administration concludes that water regulation should no longer include the prevention of minor amounts of lead or arsenic, a single party will have a difficult time proving that there is standing to sue the agency. This is because Article III of the US Constitution limits the judicial branch to "cases and controversies" in the most direct sense of this term. In 1923, in *Massachusetts v. Mellon*, the Court determined that a taxpayer whose independent suit was consolidated with the state's suit did not possess standing to challenge the constitutionality of a statute because the taxpayer's injury of having a tax increase was common to all taxpayers. In 1968, the Court, in *Flast v. Cohen*, determined that a taxpayer possessed standing to prevent the use of federal tax dollars to pay for religious instruction at a private school. While *Flast* may appear as an instance of overturning *Frothingham*, the arguments raised by Harriet Frothingham and Florence Flast were different. Frothingham claimed that her taxes would increase as a result of the federal government funding state maternity programs to reduce infant mortality and that the federal funding was an unwarranted intrusion into state functions. Flast argued that the use of her taxes to fund religious instruction violated the Constitution's separation of church and state provisions.

In 1974, the Court determined, in *Schlesinger v. Reservists Committee to Stop to the War*, that even though the Constitution's separation of powers doctrine militated against members of Congress serving in the armed forces, concerned citizens did not possess standing to have the courts prevent the secretary of defense from ordering legislators serving in the United States' military reserve forces to active duty. The party challenging the federal government argued, correctly, that when a member of the legislative branch assumes a position in the military hierarchy, the president, as commander in chief, becomes the legislator's senior commander and the legislator is then subject to the president's military orders. This violated, they claimed, the Constitution's incompatibility clause. The remaining part of their argument was that a legislator, while serving in his or her military capacity, weakens the status of Congress, and therefore the legislator's constituent voters are deprived of the full independence of their congressional representative. In turn, they argued, a legislator who serves in the reserve forces makes the legislative branch more subservient to the president than the Constitution permits. Chief Justice Warren Burger authored the majority opinion and determined that citizen standing was too generalized to equate to actual standing. Justices William O. Douglas and Thurgood Marshall dissented from the majority and argued that "the interest of citizens in guarantees written in the Constitution seems obvious."

There is a reasonable question as to why the signatories to Goldwater's suit believed they could prevail in the courts. Traditionally, at least since the New Deal, conservatives, including Goldwater, sought to limit standing as a means for keeping the judicial branch out of political issues. In addition, Goldwater's allies deplored judicial activism, claiming that the Court's decisions on matters such as voting rights and equal access to education and places of business were a matter of judges usurping the will of the legislative branch, and therefore the people. Yet, in *Goldwater*, they sought a judicial remedy in an arena of constitutional silence that could have been addressed through several congressional avenues, including votes to withhold funding from specific programs and ultimately impeachment.

In addition to the lawsuit against Carter over the transfer of the Panama Canal, two of Goldwater's House allies tried to sue Carter in federal court on other matters. In 1978, George Hansen and Larry McDonald filed suit against Carter over granting pardons to draft resisters. (The other plaintiffs in the suit included military veterans, a former prisoner of war, military spouses, and a minor child of a deceased prisoner of war.) Given that the Constitution both grants to the president the power to pardon persons convicted or suspected of federal offenses, and makes the president commander in chief over the armed forces, there should have been little question regarding Carter's constitutional authority to pardon people convicted or suspected of draft evasion. There was, however, a law that required the exclusion of US citizens who traveled to foreign countries for the express purpose of evading military service, and Hansen and McDonald argued that permitting draft evaders a full restoration of their citizen rights unconstitutionally diluted the votes of those citizens who complied with the draft laws. They also claimed that the pardon unfairly favored some classes of people at the expense of others. The Court of Appeals for the District of Columbia ruled against Hansen and McDonald on the basis of standing. That is, the judges on the court expressed that, at best, any injuries suffered by the plaintiffs were too attenuated or common to all citizens to have a basis to argue a claim before the federal courts in the first place.

McDonald and Hansen were not unique in seeking judicial standing against a president. In the 1970s, individual legislators sought various avenues of redress against the executive branch's activities in the federal courts. In 1973, following Nixon's order to bomb Khmer Rouge targets in Cambodia, Congresswoman Elizabeth Holtzman (D-NY), along with several service members, sought to stop this action in the federal courts. Although Justice Douglas believed Holtzman had standing and the Nixon administration violated the law, neither the Court of Appeals for the Second Circuit nor the Supreme Court accepted that Holtzman and her co-appellants had standing to challenge the Nixon administration on the use of the military in a foreign conflict. That same year, the Court of Appeals for the District of Columbia, in *Mitchell v. Laird*, denied standing to several congressmen who sought a judicial determination that because no formal declaration of war had ever been made in regard to the use of forces in Vietnam, Cambodia, and Laos, the use of United States military forces in those countries was unconstitutional. The judges on the appellate court noted, however, that other avenues of redress such as the misappropriation of funds might enable standing. In 1977, that same court denied standing to Congressman Michael Harrington, (D-MA), who had sought a judicial declaration that the Central Intelligence Agency conducted unlawful operations in violation of congressional appropriations limits.

There were notable exceptions to the general nonrecognition of legislative branch standing in the federal courts, but none occurred in the context of foreign policy. In *Kennedy v. Sampson*, the Court of Appeals for the District of Columbia issued a decision that became important to the appellate review of Goldwater's suit. In 1970, Senator Edward Kennedy (D-MA) sued the administrator of the General Services Agency for refusing to publish a law in the *Federal Reporter*. The *Federal Reporter* is the formal means of notifying the public of the nation's laws, and Nixon was statutorily required to publish the law in question. Although both the House and the Senate had overwhelmingly voted in favor of the Family Practice of Medicine Act, Nixon issued a memorandum disapproving this law without formally vetoing it. Nixon's memorandum occurred while Congress was adjourned for its winter recess, although Congress was able to receive Nixon's memorandum during this time.

Kennedy argued to the US district court that by his inaction, Nixon had, in effect, created a "pocket veto" and that the refusal by the General

Services Agency's administrator to publish the law violated the Constitution. Nixon countered that even if Kennedy and his fellow legislators had standing, the congressional recess had made the legislative branch "absent" within the meaning of the Constitution, and therefore the bill had lapsed. The court of appeals determined that as a member of Congress, Kennedy had standing in the court to vindicate his vote for the bill, but on the basis that he represented a majority of the legislative branch and that Kennedy had voted for the law. The appellate court also found that Nixon's argument regarding a congressional recess leaving Congress unable to receive his memorandum to be meritless. While Congress prevailed over Nixon, *Kennedy* appears as a narrow exception to the judiciary's general denial of standing to congressional litigants. This lawsuit, after all, was not premised on Nixon refusing to enforce a law but, rather, on the president being delinquent in not publishing a law based on the White House's specious constitutional interpretation. In 1978, the Court of Appeals for the District of Columbia determined that Congressman Henry Reuss (D-WI) did not possess standing to challenge the administrative authority of the Federal Reserve Bank's board members. Reuss argued that the board members had the ability to affect the nation's economy but had not been appointed according to the Constitution's appointments clause and that, as a result, Congress's authority had been usurped. To the appellate court, this was not enough of an injury to provide standing because nothing in the executive branch's appointment of board members diminished the effectiveness of Reuss's votes in Congress.

In Goldwater's suit, the federal courts could not grant standing merely because of a perception that Carter's recognition of China was inconsistent with his incorporation of human rights as a foreign policy tenet. In addition, the number of signatories on Goldwater's brief might not rise to the level that would cause a court to conclude that there was standing. As an example, Robert Price (R-TX) and Daniel Flood (D-PA) opposed the transfer of the canal to Panama and claimed they possessed standing to challenge Carter in the courts. Their argument centered less on the president's treaty power and more on the constitutional argument that a president could not dispose of federal property without the consent of the full Congress. The Constitution, in Article IV, contains a clause on the disposition of federal property that reads: "The Congress shall have

Power to dispose of and make all needful Rules and Regulations respecting the Territory or other Property belonging to the United States." Implicit in their argument was that the Panama Canal was wholly owned by the United States and Panama could not make a lawful claim on it. This argument, the district court hinted, did not create standing, though the court never took up final argument on the merits of the case. Price and Flood, following their loss in district court, sought an emergency appeal to the Court of Appeals for the District of Columbia. That court, in a decision captioned as *Edwards v. Carter*, sided with the Carter administration in a two-to-one decision. Ultimately, Flood and Price's threatened lawsuit was thwarted because the ceding of the Canal Zone to Panama occurred through a formal treaty process; as a result, the appellate court, in *Edwards*, determined that whatever injury had occurred to Congress, if any, was too speculative and remote to confer standing.

Another difficulty for Goldwater was that Carter never called for the wholesale abandonment of Taiwan, and Congress reacted to his statement by passing legislation guaranteeing Taiwan some degree of sovereign recognition by the United States. On January 22, 1979, Senators Alan Cranston (D-CA) and Edward Kennedy informed Congress that they intended to introduce legislation mandating a continued obligation to defend Taiwan and "assure its peace and prosperity." Cranston had, in fact, assured Carter that he not only supported a "most favored nation" status for China but also backed normalization at the price of rescinding the Mutual Defense Treaty. Cranston, however, believed that if Taiwan were completely abandoned, Goldwater might be able to convince the judiciary that there was a basis for standing.

There were other reasons Cranston acted to protect US-Taiwan relations, albeit in a reduced status than previously. Cranston's staff informed him that mail to his office evidenced a ten-to-one sentiment in favor of maintaining full relations with Taiwan as a recognized country. In response, Cranston promised that he and Kennedy would introduce a separate resolution promising that Taiwan would continue to be militarily defended. He sent out a form letter assuring his constituents that "although many Americans have relatives on the island and others have invested $4 billion in Taiwan's economy," it was in the best interests of the United States to normalize relations with China as long as Taiwan was assured protection. He claimed that his and Kennedy's proposed legislation would give Taiwan assurance that it would not be abandoned, but there was nothing in the proposed act plainly requiring the United States to come to Taiwan's aid. Almost immediately the conservatives objected. "You don't refer to the government and the people of Taiwan which of course, is extremely critical," Goldwater scolded Cranston. "I believe that your legislation should clearly state that the United States will not tolerate aggression in any form by Red China." Goldwater saved his most poignant criticism for the end of his letter: "It further does not answer the question that I have raised in the suit, namely, does the president have the power by law or under the Constitution to unilaterally abrogate treaties of mutual defense," and "if he has the power then I say look out because that is about all that is left in the way of power that is needed for someone to move in and take this country over."

In February 1979, as Goldwater's initial complaint was lodged in the US district court, the House and Senate debated Cranston and Kennedy's measure to "maintain commercial, cultural and other relations with the people on Taiwan on an unofficial basis." This became known as the Taiwan Relations Act, and from April 10, 1979—when Carter signed it into law—the United States has retained diplomatic and economic ties with Taiwan. To date, the act has defined Taiwan-US relations, though none of the senators who joined with Goldwater voted in favor of it. Additionally, conservatives, led by Robert Dole, first tried to place into the act an obligation for the United States to defend Taiwan if China were to try to annex the island; failing this, they tried to place requirements into the act that would make public any future Taiwanese request for arms sales as well as arms sales to China. Dole's efforts in both instances failed. In one sense, the Taiwan Relations Act could have undermined Goldwater's suit because Congress had determined the future course of US relations with that government. On the other hand, the act was not a treaty; it was a statement of domestic law, and there was no language in it which either expressly endorsed or disavowed Carter's actions.

Goldwater's Senate Allies

When Carter made his "bombshell" announcement, Carl Curtis was the longest-serving legislator to declare his opposition to normalization.

Elected to the House in 1938 on an anti–New Deal platform, Curtis sided with anticommunists, opposed unions, and in 1954 vigorously defended Joe McCarthy against Senate censure. Unlike Goldwater and the southern senators, however, he voted in favor of the Civil Rights Acts of 1957 and 1964, though he voted against Title VII affirmative action laws. While Curtis was not always in lockstep with Goldwater, he had a lengthy pro-Taiwan record. On March 26, 1973, he introduced a resolution to express congressional reaffirmation supporting Taiwan. "I believe that time is propitious to introduce a sense of the Congress Resolution which calls on the United States Government to do nothing to compromise the freedom of our friend and ally, the Republic of China and its people," Curtis wrote to his Senate colleagues. "The resolution will reiterate our traditional support for the continued freedom of the Free Chinese." During the 1970s, he was a member of the Senate's Republican Steering Committee, which opposed the Panama Canal treaties, SALT, the Rhodesian embargo, and the Helsinki Accords. While Curtis disagreed with many aspects of Carter's foreign and domestic policies and signed Goldwater's brief, he was soon to depart from the Senate, having decided not to run for reelection in 1978. This became an important aspect of Goldwater's legal brief. Curtis claimed that because he and Strom Thurmond had voted in favor of the 1954 Mutual Defense Treaty, they had an added basis for establishing standing. They reasoned that if Carter unilaterally renounced the treaty, doing so also diluted their voting authority under the Constitution's treaty clause. In a sense, they hoped that *Kennedy v. Sampson* would be expanded to cover their claim.

Strom Thurmond first became a senator in 1954 after serving one term as South Carolina's governor. Born in 1902 in South Carolina, Thurmond attended Clemson University, served in the state government, and was a World War II combat veteran. Like most of his fellow southern legislators, he began his career as a Democrat. In reaction to President Harry S. Truman's support for civil rights, in 1948 Thurmond ran for president as a "Dixiecrat," with the promise to fight against civil rights. Thurmond also opposed Truman's order to desegregate the armed forces. Whereas Goldwater opposed federal civil rights enforcement as a matter of having local communities and states maintain political power, Thurmond simply did not believe in racial equality. He was instrumental in the publication of the Southern Manifesto, which promised southern whites that their elected leaders would undermine *Brown v. Board of Education* and derail federal desegregation policies. Thurmond was highly critical of President Eisenhower's use of the military in 1958 to confront efforts by Orval Faubus, the governor of Arkansas, to keep his state's schools segregated. By this time, Thurmond claimed that the courts could no longer be trusted to protect the "rights" of southern whites, and he called for massive public resistance against integration. Unsurprisingly, he sided with the apartheid regimes of South Africa and Rhodesia and opposed President Johnson's embargo on trade with Rhodesia. Although after the 1948 presidential election Thurmond returned to the Democratic Party, he left that party for good and became a Republican in 1964 in support of Goldwater. Once more, civil rights was the issue that he claimed caused him to do so.

In 1955, Thurmond endorsed the Mutual Defense Treaty. "Letting the communists know that the United States is willing to fight, if necessary, to preserve the peace and to keep our commitments to our allies may well have two benefits," he argued. "It may prevent the Chinese Reds not only from encroachment on Formosa and the Pescadores, it should also knit the Western World more closely against communism because the United States thus assumes a role of real leadership." In 1971, he took exception to Nixon's overtures to China in his weekly news release. "Some people are optimistic that a weakening of U.S. Policy on trade with Communists in Red China will lead to a so-called normalization of relations between these major powers; others feel that Red China offers an untapped market which will earn big profits for American traders," he observed before insisting that "both of these goals are illusions." Thurmond did not stop with his criticism of corporate interests; he also argued that the Chinese government bullied the United States' allies. "Great Britain normalized relations and the British ambassador was unceremoniously kicked out of Peking. France normalized relations and the Maoists helped engineer the riots which led to the downfall of President Charles de Gaulle," he claimed. This was hyperbole as China had little or nothing to do with France's social upheavals in the late 1960s or the aged De Gaulle's departure from office.

Thurmond was at loggerheads with many of Carter's early policies. He referred to Carter's grant of amnesty for draft evaders as a "travesty of justice" and fruitlessly tried to upend it in the courts. Thurmond earlier opposed Gerald Ford's negotiations with the Panamanian president, Omar Torrijos, claiming that any transfer of territory to Panama was "a surrender of rights," and "there is nothing of consequence left to negotiate once we surrender our rights." In 1977, when the Panama Canal Treaty came before the Senate, Thurmond formed alliances to try to defeat any ceding of property to Panama. In a speech to the Young Americans for Freedom—a youth wing of the John Birch Society—he called the canal transfer "the greatest giveaway since God gave man the world for his dominion."

Like Thurmond, Jesse Helms had opposed civil rights and supported Rhodesia and South Africa. He also had close ties to the John Birch Society as well as other anticommunist organizations. Although he was elected to the Senate in 1972 and therefore did not participate in the congressional civil rights debates of the 1960s, as a North Carolina state legislator he had smeared civil rights leaders as being communist dupes, and he opposed the admission of African Americans to the University of North Carolina. In 1976, he supported Ronald Reagan against Ford in the Republican Party primaries and accused Henry Kissinger of weakening the United States. Helms also had ties to Taiwan in the sense that he was a member of the Taipei-headquartered World Anti-Communist League, and at a 1977 conference he warned about China's intended expansion. (Chiang Kai-shek had established the league in 1966). Like Thurmond and Goldwater, Helms had long attacked the federal courts for "judicial activism" not only in civil rights cases but also in cases involving religion in public life. Prior to Carter's presidency, he introduced a bill to strip the federal courts of being able to decide challenges to the constitutionality of prayer in school. Following Carter's China announcement, Helms claimed "no amount of sugar-coated rhetoric by the president can obscure the plain fact that he proposes to sell Taiwan down the river."

Paul Laxalt was born in 1922 in Reno, Nevada, served in the US Army in World War II, and graduated from the University of Denver's law school in 1949. Prior to his election to the Senate in 1974, he served as a district attorney, lieutenant governor, and governor. Some aspects of his political tenure set him apart from Goldwater, Thurmond, and Helms—namely, as Nevada's governor, he purged John Birch Society members from the state Republican Party. Generally, however, he had aligned with Goldwater in decrying judicial activism. Yet, twice in his career he prevailed in the federal courts in highly publicized trials. In between his district attorney tenure and his lieutenant governorship, he successfully represented a casino owner against the federal government over its seizure of the casino's golden rooster statue. He later won a libel suit against the editors of the *Sacramento Bee*, who had accused his family of having ties to organized crime simply because his family owned a casino. (Organized crime members owned some of Nevada's casinos, and in 1970 Ford and Goldwater accused Justice Douglas of consorting with the Mafia over Douglas's chairmanship of a foundation funded by a casino owner.) Laxalt also became one of Reagan's confidants, and in 1976 he advanced Reagan's candidacy at the Republican National Convention, arguing that Ford was too moderate on foreign policy. In the Senate, he led the fight against the Panama Canal Treaty. When, in late January 1979, China's deputy prime minister visited the United States and stated that China's government did not contemplate using military force to take over Taiwan, Laxalt noted that he was not "completely satisfied by the answer."

Utah's two senators hardly differed from Goldwater, Thurmond, and Helms in their foreign policy views and opposition to liberal judicial activism. Like Laxalt, Orrin Hatch and Jake Garn had not been in federal office during the civil rights debates of the 1950s and 1960s. Hatch's first run for public office was the 1976 Senate contest, which he handily won over his Democratic opponent, incumbent senator Frank Moss. Hatch's early focus was to transfer federally controlled open lands to the states for the purpose of economic development. He also spoke against the Equal Rights Amendment, even though Nixon and Ford supported it. Hatch opposed the Panama Canal treaties for the same reasons as Goldwater, calling them "reprehensible." Further, he believed that Carter's termination of the Mutual Defense Treaty was unconstitutional without the Senate's permission. Garn called the treaty abrogation with Taiwan "illegal." In doing so, he criticized Carter's foreign policy and listed the following as its failures: "The breaking of the treaty on the heels of turning back the Panama Canal, withdrawing U.S. troops from Korea, and the administration's unwillingness to link the progress of the SALT talks with acts of aggression by the Soviets and Cubans in Africa." Garn had received significant media exposure in his earlier criticisms of Carter's efforts at nuclear arms reductions with the Soviet Union. Prior to his political tenure, he was a commissioned naval officer and then an Air National Guard pilot. Both Garn and Hatch were proponents of limiting the federal government's size and power and opposed expansive civil rights legislation. Finally, Gordon Humphrey partly campaigned against the Panama Canal Treaty and the recognition of China at the expense of Taiwan, although his main focus in the 1978 New Hampshire Senate election was on curbing federal spending.

Goldwater's Senate allies were small in number, considering that there were dozens of other conservative legislators. Although several conservative and Republican senators believed that Carter had thwarted the law, they were reticent to sign on to Goldwater's brief. For instance, Jacob Javits (R-NY) argued that while Carter had the authority to create an understanding with China, doing so without consulting the Senate violated the 1978 International Security Assistance Act. Yet he explained his reluctance to sign with Goldwater as not wanting the judiciary to intrude into congressional business. Richard Stone, as well, did not want to sign on to the brief. Although Stone believed that Carter had acted against the intent of Congress, he was not convinced Carter had acted unconstitutionally. Three staunch conservatives, Alan Simpson (R-WY), Richard Lugar (R-IN), and John Danforth (R-MO), did not join with Goldwater after concluding that the courts were unable to intervene and it was unwise to ask them to do so. As a general theme, while the conservatives expressed doubts that the courts possessed jurisdiction to rule on the issue, they also fretted that if the courts determined that there was jurisdiction, future conservative administrations would have to confront an active judiciary if Goldwater succeeded.

Goldwater's House Allies: Arizona Conservatives and Anti–Civil Rights

In 1972, Nixon faced challenges from within his party not only from liberal Paul McCloskey (R-CA) but also from legislators on the so-called far right. The far right, as represented by the American Conservative Union, believed Nixon had intentionally reneged on his promise to shrink the size of the federal government and return power to states and municipalities. (Goldwater, in contrast, believed Nixon's attentions had been chiefly focused on foreign policy and, as a result, had failed to defang the federal bureaucracy that had grown under Franklin Roosevelt and Lyndon Johnson, but he did not seek to challenge Nixon for the party's nomination.) The American Conservative Union and the Liberty Lobby, another anticommunist organization, selected John Ashbrook to challenge Nixon. Ashbrook had been a founding member of the Young Americans for Freedom, an organization dedicated to right-wing causes. The organization also lobbied the government to prevent corporations from conducting trade with the Soviet bloc. Ashbrook was not merely consistently anticommunist and conservative; he opposed détente or, for that matter, any other accommodation with the Soviet Union. He denounced corporate and political leaders who tried to open Eastern Europe and other communist areas to trade. In 1979, he demanded that the United States ally with Ian Smith's apartheid government in Rhodesia and abandon the embargo. That same year, he signed on to Goldwater's brief against Carter.

Although the House does not have a formal role in treaty approval, Ashbrook is worthy of detailed description here because he not only personified the conservative opposition to Carter but also had long encouraged the public to distrust the judicial branch. Ashbrook had opposed Abe Fortas's nomination to the Court in 1965 and planned to impeach the justice in 1969. One year later he joined with Ford and demanded Justice Douglas be impeached. Ashbrook had long railed against judicial activism and was convinced that the Warren Court, if not the judicial branch as a whole, fostered communism. This belief was not unique to him. Right-wing organizations such as the John Birch Society, along with anti–civil rights legislators, had characterized the judiciary as a communist bastion. Even though by 1979 the Warren Court was almost a decade removed from the nation, and Douglas, Fortas, Warren, and Hugo Black were no longer deciding appeals (Warren and Black died in 1974 and 1971, respectively; Fortas resigned in 1969; Douglas retired in 1975), Ashbrook worried over the precedent that he believed their judicial activism enabled. The very year that Ashbrook allied with Goldwater to seek redress in the courts against Carter, he introduced a resolution to have Judge Frank J. Battisti of the US district court impeached in the House. Battisti's alleged offense, according to Ashbrook, was a judicial order to desegregate Ohio's public schools. In contrast, when, in 1974, Battisti dismissed charges against eight Ohio National Guardsmen accused of unlawful killing in the Kent State University shooting in 1970, Ashbrook vocally lauded the decision.

A native of Youngstown, Ohio, Ashbrook was born in 1928 and attended Harvard University and the Ohio State University School of Law. He inherited his father's newspaper, the *Youngstown Independent*, in 1954 and was elected to Congress in 1960. He also came from a political family; in fact, he was elected to the congressional district once held by his father. As early as 1961, he encouraged Goldwater to challenge Kennedy's seemingly inevitable reelection campaign. Ashbrook voted against both the 1964 Civil Rights Act of 1964 and the 1965 Voting Rights Act of 1965, and he opposed federal efforts at school integration. On June 28, 1966, he accused the Johnson administration of being an unwitting part of the "Red China lobby." In reality, no "Red China lobby" existed, and this was a smear against the administration. Ashbrook conceded this point, but he accused the officials who promoted university exchanges and greater openness with the People's Republic of China of empowering communism to spread "according to Mao Zedong's alleged designs." These "designs" included the defeat of South Vietnam and pushing the United States out of Asia.

In 1972, Ashbrook challenged Nixon in the Republican primaries, mainly because of his disagreements with Nixon's domestic record but also because of the continuation of détente and Nixon's efforts at developing relations with China. "The plain and simple truth is that President Nixon seems to have forgotten the very people who elected him," Ashbrook claimed, before informing conservatives that he had William F. Buckley's support as well as that of the American Conservative Union and the Young Americans for Freedom. "We have seen him lead the triumphant charge of the Red Chinese into the United Nations," Ashbrook lamented. "We have seen our ally of thirty years standing, Nationalist China[,] cynically expelled from the United Nations while we stood by and did nothing."

In 1978, Ashbrook penned an article in the conservative *Washington Report* as a retort to the *New York Times*, which had published an editorial by Senator Howard Metzenbaum (D-OH) titled "China: A 20th Century Miracle." Metzenbaum had advocated establishing diplomatic relations with China and complimented Chinese technological advances as a boon to the world. "No admirer of Hitler or even the most abject apologist for Stalin ever made a more brazen, sweeping defense of the masters of the Gulag or Buchenwald than the *New York Times* [and Metzenbaum] did this very year for its pet totalitarians in Peking," Ashbrook countered. "In the same liberal organ which demands human rights over property rights when dealing with South Africa . . . it includes this snide and effete question: should we make Peking's handling of what Americans call human rights of the Chinese people an obstacle for normalizing diplomatic relations . . . ?" Given Ashbrook's past support for Goldwater and his stridency that any compromise with a communist government spelled the end of democracy, it was hardly surprising that he would sign on to the brief, let alone become the House leader for Goldwater's cause.

Joining Ashbrook, Robert Bauman called Carter's announcement "the greatest act of appeasement since Neville Chamberlain went to Munich in 1939." Elected to the House from Maryland's Eastern Shore in 1972, Bauman was also staunchly conservative in foreign policy. Indeed, he specifically campaigned against recognizing China and pledged support to Taiwan. He was also a part of the "New Right," which extended its aversion to civil rights to opposing busing, a woman's right to have an abortion as encapsulated in *Roe v. Wade*, the teaching of evolution in public schools, and the Equal Rights Amendment. He also advocated for a "right" to have Christian prayers in public schools. Ironically, in the immediate aftermath of the Court's decision on presidential authority to terminate treaties, Bauman was arrested for soliciting a male child. In 1972, Virginia's Fourth District's voters sent Robert Daniel Jr., a descendant of Supreme Court justice Peter V. Daniel, to Congress as its first Republican representative since Reconstruction. The prior year, prosegregation Democrat Watkins Abbott had announced his retirement, and the contest for his seat pitted the conservative Daniel against a centrist Democrat and three independent candidates. Born in Spring Grove, Virginia, in 1936, Daniel served in the US Army and the Central Intelligence Agency before becoming a financial analyst and YMCA director. He also earned a bachelor's degree from the University of Virginia and a master's degree in business administration from Columbia University. He claimed that recognizing China would lead to the United States being unable to stop the spread of communism across Asia.

Idahoan Steve Symms, like Bauman, was elected to the House in 1972 as a conservative Republican. He had served in the Marine Corps from 1960 to 1963 and was a newspaper owner and apple farmer prior to his congressional service. He would go on to defeat Frank Church in 1980, and in 1988 he falsely accused Kitty Dukakis, the spouse of Democratic presidential candidate Michael Dukakis, of burning an American flag. During the 1980 Senate campaign, Symms claimed that Frank Church was "chummy" with Fidel Castro and had voted against a strong national defense. As a part of the "New Right," Symms opposed abortion to the degree that as a senator he voted against Sandra Day O'Connor's confirmation to the Court. In 1978, he accused the Carter administration of endangering the national security by "giving the Panama Canal to Torrijos."

George Hansen, the second Idahoan to join with Goldwater, served in the House from 1965 through 1969, and again from 1975 to 1985. His political career ended in a federal conviction for various frauds and a four-year prison sentence. (It was his second conviction, but Idaho's Second District voters overlooked Hansen's first criminal conviction and returned him to office.) Aside from the federal convictions, Hansen was known for his anticommunist stridency, support for Nixon's Vietnam policies, opposition to giving Panama any measure of control over the canal, and frequently accusing the Internal Revenue Service of abusing the public. During the Iran hostage crisis, Hansen traveled to Tehran to try to broker a release. Like Bauman and Symms, he opposed both abortion and busing.

Two of Georgia's congressmen, Newt Gingrich and Larry McDonald, joined with Goldwater for reasons akin to the others. Carter's actions, they argued, were a betrayal of an ally and an assertion of unprecedented presidential authority. Elected to the House in 1978 while employed as a history professor, Gingrich had headed the group Georgians against the Proposed Panama Canal Treaties, evidencing his opposition to Carter's foreign policies. McDonald was one of two Democrats to join with Goldwater against Carter. In 1983, while traveling with 268 other passengers and crew on a Korean Airlines 747 shot down by the Soviet air force, McDonald was the only congressman killed by the Soviet Union during the Cold War. Born in 1935, he earned a medical degree from Emory University and then was commissioned into the US

Navy as a flight surgeon. He was also a cousin of General George S. Patton, and according to some of his congressional contemporaries, he possessed the general's intensity. While stationed in Iceland from 1959 to 1961, he developed a hatred of communism and joined the John Birch Society. McDonald opposed school busing and other federal civil rights programs, and he ran for Congress in 1974 as a states' rights Democrat. In 1978, his district's leaders voted to censure him "for the dishonorable and despicable act of calling himself a Democrat." There were reasons for the vote beyond his affiliation with the John Birch Society. He had not supported Carter in the presidential race against Ford, and he opposed the idea that the Constitution contained implied powers. He also voted against the creation of Martin Luther King Day, claiming that King had been a communist. In spite of the censure, his ideology was popular with his constituents to the point that he won reelection even though it was publicly known that he had been arrested for failing to pay court-ordered alimony.

The other Democrat to side with Goldwater, Bob Stump, not only was a native Arizonan but also became a Republican in 1981 after supporting Reagan over Carter. Stump was not known as a vigorous member of the House. According to one opponent, he was intentionally ineffective so that no negative news stories were written about him. Stump's reasons for joining with Goldwater may have matched those of his House peers. Yet it also appears that he wanted to run for the Senate when Goldwater retired. Joining Stump from Arizona was Eldon Rudd, who was first elected to Congress in 1976. Rudd had served in the Marine Corps during World War II, graduated from the University of Arizona Law School in 1947, and then became an FBI agent. His FBI duties included investigating Lee Harvey Oswald's activities in Mexico prior to the Kennedy assassination. A staunch anticommunist, Rudd opposed congressional efforts to curtail clandestine intelligence and military activities to topple the Nicaraguan government in the 1980s. He reacted to Carter's announcement with the argument that in abandoning Taiwan, "the United States would set a bad example for the rest of the world."

From California's congressional delegation, Clair Burgener was elected to the House in 1972 and served for five terms. Originally from Utah, he moved to San Diego after military service in World War II, became an actor and realtor, and then rose through a succession of local and state political offices before coming to Congress. He campaigned on stopping immigration from Mexico. In 1975, he introduced a bill to prohibit the United States from ceding any measure of control over the Panama Canal. Another Californian, Robert "Bob" Dornan, was one of the more boisterous members of Congress. He served in the US Air Force as a fighter pilot, and after his active service ended, he took part in combat missions as a journalist in the Vietnam Conflict. In the 1960s he participated in the civil rights movement by registering African American voters in the southern states. After an unsuccessful campaign to become mayor of Los Angeles in 1972, he ran for Congress in 1976. In an apparent reversal of his earlier commitment to civil rights, he proposed a law to permit private schools to be segregated without a loss of tax-exempt status. He also campaigned against a woman's right to abortion. Dornan later became known for assaulting a Democratic congressman, and he used epithets to describe gays and lesbians. He vigorously criticized Carter's foreign policies on Panama and sided with the white Rhodesian government.

Frank Church and the Counterweight to Goldwater

Frank Church, the chairman of the Senate Foreign Relations Committee, was Carter's ally on most foreign policy matters. (Carter believed that Church unduly favored Israel over Palestinian claims of sovereignty, which led to tensions between the two men.) Church was also an instrumental senator in shaping the nation's foreign and military policies in the 1960s and 1970s. He believed that diplomacy was a better means to contain communism than military force. In 1975, Church argued that the United States had "to come to her senses about the limits of her power and the confines of her real national interests." He insisted that the use of diplomacy rather than the threat of military force would not turn the country into an isolationist state much as it had been in the 1920s. Rather, he argued that because the world had become "complicated and interdependent," a reemphasis on diplomacy was necessary to stop "adventuring in Asia and pouring out billions of foreign aid, where the only return has been animosity and unwanted entanglements." Like Carter, Church sought military force reductions in South Korea, claiming the United

States had undertaken "the extra-expense of stationing troops in Korea 20 years after the threat to that country has passed." He also opposed sending military equipment or financial aid to Turkey after its forces invaded Cyprus. Church is perhaps best remembered today for having led an investigation into the government's covert intelligence activities in 1975, resulting in the Foreign Intelligence Surveillance Act of 1979. He considered running for president in 1976 and formed an exploratory committee and also entered the Massachusetts primary. *Washington Post* reporter George Lardner observed that Church's candidacy was a long shot and a gamble, but he was more of a "choir-boy than a riverboat gambler." The gamble did not pay off as he failed to win any delegates. Carter gave serious consideration to having Church as his running mate before selecting Senator Walter Mondale (D-MN).

Born in Boise, Idaho, in 1924, Church served as an army intelligence officer in World War II. After the war, he earned a bachelor's degree from Stanford University and a law degree from Harvard. In 1956, Idaho's voters elected him to the Senate, where he supported civil rights and in 1964 voted for the Gulf of Tonkin Resolution. Shortly after the 1964 vote, however, he warned against the buildup of military forces in Vietnam and by 1966 became a staunch opponent of the military escalation of the Vietnam Conflict. Church suspected that both Johnson and Nixon deceived the public on foreign and military policy, and he believed that the 1970 invasion of Cambodia violated international law. Along with John Sherman Cooper (R-OH), he introduced an amendment to cut off all funding for military operations in Laos and Cambodia. Although the bill succeeded in the Senate, but failed in the House, it represented one of the first instances of large numbers of legislators attempting to stop a president from sending the military into a foreign conflict. Three years later, Church and Clifford Case (R-NJ) convinced Congress to cut off all funding for military operations in Cambodia past August 15, 1973. Goldwater, Thurmond, and Curtis voted against both of these measures.

Church did, in fact, take strong human rights positions prior to Carter's presidency. Between 1964 and 1976, he worked to have Rhodesia's apartheid government economically starved from US commerce so that the country's majority African population could finally obtain a representative government. In 1973, he voted against exempting chrome from a United Nations embargo against Rhodesia, explaining to his constituents that Rhodesia's government was in violation of international law. Harry Byrd and an alliance of congressional conservatives, including Goldwater and Thurmond, convinced a majority of the House and Senate to permit chrome importation despite the embargo. In 1976, Church reaffirmed his opposition to enabling any trade with Rhodesia, based on its apartheid structure. He also targeted South Africa for economic sanctions, arguing that political and economic support to the apartheid government there was detrimental to spreading democracy, and he voted to prevent covert intelligence operations in Angola and Central America.

Church backed Ford's and Carter's efforts to negotiate with Panama for the return of the canal. His purpose for doing so was to delegitimize imperialism. In 1973, he argued that the canal's transfer was long past due. "One must recognize, that Panama has felt the smallest and most helpless in this hemisphere, that she has been badly mistreated in the way that we have operated the canal and by what we have paid for our loose hold there," he conveyed to his constituents. "The resentment, which you can surely understand, in a small country dealing with a country as big as ours, has flared up in violence and in bloodshed in the years past." Church went on to argue that the United States' continued possession of the canal was a boon to communism rather than a strengthening of national security. In November 1977, with the success of the treaties in the Senate in doubt, Church redoubled his efforts to convince the public that Carter was in the right. "Every Latin American country sides with Panama in the view that our occupation of the Canal Zone represents the last vestige of colonialism in the Western Hemisphere," he insisted. "They resent it much as we resented French control of the Mississippi River in the early years of the last century."

Church's view on China evolved during the Cold War. In 1964, he professed a strong commitment to prevent China's recognition in the United Nations. "As you know, the Truman, Eisenhower, Kennedy, and Johnson Administrations have all refused to recognize Red China and have opposed its mission to the United Nations," he informed constituents who voiced opposition to France's recognition of China. "I have consistently supported Senate Resolutions opposing the admission of Red China to the U.N. and recognition of that country by the United States." However, less than fifteen years later, Church argued that China and Russia were no longer monolithic and had conflicting goals as well as disparate foreign policies. "From the very practical perspective of foreign trade, China can be an extremely important new market for trade, he claimed. "Whether we must sever relations with Taiwan or whether we can recognize both China simultaneously, I think is the question and ideally we should try to maintain relations with both." Thus, when Carter determined to rescind recognition of Taiwan, Church was not—at least as a matter of public record—fully in lockstep with the president.

When Carter announced recognition of China, Church expressed his support. "There is no reason for us to become involved in an armed struggle between the two giants of the Communist world. We haven't formed an alliance with China," he argued. "All we have done is to recognize the government which for the last quarter of a century has governed the Chinese people." Church's endorsement of Carter's treaty abrogation plans was to prove important to the Court of Appeals for the District of Columbia in the late summer and early fall. As chairman of the Senate Foreign Relations Committee, he had the ability, unless overridden by a Senate majority, which would require Democratic defections, to control the tenor and timing of the committee's debates over the treaty revocation issue. He also obtained the support of key Democratic senators to serve as a counterweight to Goldwater's claims of standing.

On national defense matters it would be hard to find a more hawkish senator than Henry Jackson (D-WA), who unhesitatingly sided with Carter on normalization. In the early 1970s, Jackson began to have doubts about allying the United States with Chiang and Taiwan. "The greatest mistake in American diplomacy and intelligence during this century was our failure to understand mainland China; the fact that while they were communists, they were not Russian," Jackson stated in 1980. However, he did not concern himself with the question of whether Carter had the unilateral authority to withdraw from the treaty. Although he did, in fact, believe Carter possessed this authority, he also was adamant that the containment of the Soviet Union was the paramount foreign and national security policy concern facing the United States and China simply did not constitute a threat.

Along with Church and Jackson, Robert Byrd (D-WV), a former ally of Goldwater and Thurmond, proved to be another formidable foreign policy ally for Carter. When the Ninety-Sixth Congress convened on January 3, 1979, the Democratic majority retained Byrd as Senate majority leader, a position he had held since 1977. Unlike many other Democratic legislators, Byrd enjoyed a good personal relationship with Carter, and Byrd had traveled to Europe as Carter's emissary to calm German and French fears on the United States' response to the energy crisis. In early 1977, Byrd endorsed the Panama Canal treaties. He provided a caveat regarding his support for Carter by insisting that the United States had the right to militarily defend the canal in perpetuity. He also noted that after traveling to Panama he and his fellow senators had gained President Torrijos's promise "to better human rights and civil liberties in Panama by abrogating oppressive laws."

Byrd's ascension to majority leader not only included running against Kennedy for the position but also was a remarkable achievement in the sense that in the 1950s and early 1960s he had aligned with southern segregationists. Although he did not sign the Southern Manifesto in 1956, he had been a Ku Klux Klan member and helped filibuster the 1964 Civil Rights Act. He also voted against the 1965 Voting Rights Act, and in the early 1970s he opposed school busing. Yet, beginning in the late 1960s, he transited from segregation politics to supporting civil rights as a result, he later claimed, of his growing Baptist faith. He also, by 1968, opposed the United States' involvement in the Vietnam Conflict. By the time Carter assumed office, Byrd had begun to draw plaudits from civil rights groups for reversing himself on the federal government's authority to enforce equal treatment under the law. Carter relied on Byrd's advice on matters beyond Panama, including whether to fire Thomas "Bert" Lance as director of the Office of Management and Budget and formulating the nation's energy policies. Byrd also encouraged Carter to increase the size of the armed forces in response to the Soviet Union's expanding influence in Africa and eventual invasion of Afghanistan. Carter eventually did so.

Like Church, Byrd had not always supported recognition of China, and he certainly did not entertain doing so at Taiwan's expense. In 1971, Byrd welcomed the United Nations' seating of China in the General Assembly but cautioned, "only if Nationalist China retains its seat, both in the General Assembly and in the Security Council." Byrd also expressed worries over the dual recognition of China and Taiwan over the long term. "Announcing the two-China policy is one thing—making it work is quite another," he argued before insisting that the US government should never abandon Taiwan. Two months after welcoming China's admission to the United Nations, he scolded both the Nixon administration and the international body for expelling Taiwan. "This reprehensible slap at a country which has consistently supported the U.N. since its inception can have no other effect than the further weakening of the U.N. itself," he insisted.

In 1975, when Byrd traveled to China, he reported to his constituents that while the country remained under communist control—he stressed that there were no privately owned vehicles—China had made tremendous progress in caring for its people. "Everywhere there is cleanliness and there is order," he stressed. "Prostitution has been eliminated, unemployment and inflation are non-existent, although there is underemployment, and the streets are safe." He indicated that among the Chinese government's major concerns were Soviet attempts at hegemony and the establishment of Soviet military bases in Vietnam. In addition, he pointed out that the Chinese government was very interested in how Congress influenced the United States' foreign policies toward Cyprus and Angola, and with the Helsinki Accords. While Byrd insisted he remained convinced of the superiority of American democracy, he believed that greater efforts toward normalization were imperative. When, in late 1978, Carter announced a change in relations with Taiwan and China, Byrd agreed that it was the right time to do so, as long as Taiwan's security was assured. Indeed, Carter had quietly sought out Byrd's agreement to the termination of the defense treaty prior to announcing normalization.

Carter, of course, also had Alan Cranston on his side. Elected to the Senate in 1968, Cranston had served in the military in a journalist capacity in World War II. He also argued that the United States should actively participate in establishing a world government, a position that placed him at odds with traditional beliefs on US sovereignty. A vocal opponent of the Vietnam War, Cranston had endorsed normalization as early as 1972, and even placed some of the blame for US-China tensions on the US government. "For more than 20 years there was deep hostility between Communist China—officially known as the People's Republic of China—and the United States," Cranston argued. "Our own country's attitude was typified by ostracism rather than diplomacy, by antagonism rather than reconciliation. In the past few years, however, both countries have decided to improve relations, in the hopes of reducing the danger of war and securing the stability necessary for peace." Prior to Carter's announcement, Cranston traveled to China and met with Deng, who made it clear that while the Chinese wanted normalization, full diplomatic relations could only come about after the Mutual Defense Treaty was formally abrogated.

On March 2, 1979, Cranston claimed that while he supported normalization, China had to withdraw from Vietnam in order to contain the spread of conflict in Southeast Asia. Cranston feared that the Soviet Union would send military forces to Vietnam and a larger war would occur in the region. In order to show his commitment to the preservation of democracy, he reminded his listeners that his and Kennedy's proposed legislation would make it clear that any attack on Taiwan would represent a threat to the United States. "U.S. recognition of China does not mean the abandonment of Taiwan," Cranston argued. "It is just plain common sense to face up to the reality that the real government of 900 million people in China is in Peking and Taipei." Within three weeks of Cranston's comment on Chinese withdrawal from Vietnam, the Chinese military had, in fact, returned to Chinese territory. Thus, Cranston was able inform his constituents that he could fully support normalization without endangering Taiwan.

Cranston, Byrd, Jackson, Kennedy, and Church were Senate leaders, but they were also only five senators out of the total hundred. Harry Byrd, an independent from Virginia (as opposed to Carter's ally Robert Byrd from West Virginia) did not join in the lawsuit against Carter either, which may have undermined Goldwater's suit in the long term. Although the Virginian Byrd had been an independent after leaving the Democratic Party over civil rights, he continued to caucus with the Democratic Party, yet often voted with the Republicans. The eldest son of his father who also served as a senator, Byrd was appointed to the upper house in 1965 to replace his father, after a long career as a state legislator, newspaper editor, and naval officer. He led Virginia's state legislators in a "massive resistance" campaign against *Brown v. Board of Education.* In 1966, he was elected as a Democrat in a special election to serve out the duration of his father's term. But in 1970 he left the party and became an independent. Six years later, when he defeated retired admiral Elmo Zumwalt to retain his seat, he insisted that Taiwan was an ally of the greatest importance to the United States. Byrd was a "defense hawk" and had supported the Vietnam War as well as the containment of China, but he did not believe the issue could be resolved in the courts.

Other prominent Democrats gave Carter verbal support, including, unsurprisingly, Abe Ribicoff. But so too did Sam Nunn (D-GA), who by 1979 was considered a "defense hawk" in the same manner as Jackson. Both of Hawaii's senators, Daniel K. Inouye (D-HI) and Spark Matsunaga (D-HI), came out in favor of Carter. Both men had served in World War II and were decorated veterans. John Glenn (D-OH), Birch Bayh (D-IN), Quentin Burdick (D-ND), and Edwin Muskie (D-ME) gave Carter their endorsement on normalization as well. Indeed, not one of the fifty-eight Democrats defected from Carter and joined with Goldwater. Perhaps most surprising in their absence from the debates over normalization was the southern bloc of senators who had opposed federal civil rights programs and aligned more with Nixon than with liberal Democrats. Yet Howard Heflin (D-AL), Russell Long (D-LA), John Stennis (D-MS), and Ernest Hollings (D-SC) sided with Carter. As a result, a majority of the Senate either aligned with or acquiesced to Carter.

Goldwater's lawsuit against Carter occurred during a transitional time for the Republican Party in the Senate. By the late 1970s, young Republican conservatives from the South and West had established themselves as the virtual leaders of the Republican opposition to Republican moderates in the Senate. This dynamic explains Laxalt, Hatch, Garn, and Helms joining with Goldwater and Thurmond. It also partly explains why more Republican senators did not sign on to Goldwater's suit, though the absence of Robert Dole, William Roth (R-RI), Alan Simpson (R-WY), John Danforth (R-MO), Richard Lugar (R-IN), and John Tower (R-TX) presented Goldwater to the federal courts as speaking from a truly minority position. Even so, the absence of these men did not indicate their approval of Carter's action. Rather, they appeared to see the issue as one that could only be resolved at the polls in 1980, and many of them agreed that the Soviet Union was the paramount threat to the world. Milton Young (R-ND) is a case in point. Having served in the Senate since 1945, he was a staunch anticommunist who had backed Robert Taft over Eisenhower at the 1952 Republican National Convention. He had also voted against censuring Joseph McCarthy in 1954. To be sure, Young did not trust China, and he was appalled by Carter's efforts at normalization, but he determined that if weakening the Soviet

Union came at the cost of relations with China, doing so was a more palatable evil.

Finally, a small number of liberal Senate Republicans openly sided with Carter over Goldwater. Charles McCurdy Mathias (R-MD) had, at one time, praised Nixon for establishing relations with China and noted that he was willing to accept Taiwan's reduced status. Likewise, Clifford Case backed normalization and the treaty abrogation. Carter also had support from Robert Packwood (R-OR) and Mark Hatfield (R-OR). Case, Mathias, Packwood, and Hatfield had endorsed the Panama Canal treaties and tended to view the United States' international role much as Carter did. They also had a history of opposing their conservative Republican peers in other foreign policy areas. When, in 1977, Robert Dole tried to pass an amendment prohibiting the United States from approving World Bank loans to Vietnam, Laos, and Cambodia, Carter obtained the support of Packwood, Hatfield, Mathias, Javits, and Case to defeat the amendment. None of these Republican senators agreed to sign on with Goldwater, though they expressed doubts as to whether Carter possessed the unilateral authority to ignore the prior year's legislation, indicating a requirement that the president actually consult with the Senate. In the end, their absence from Goldwater's suit—just like the absence of southern democrats—weakened Goldwater's position to argue for standing.

CHAPTER 3

In the Court of Oliver Gasch

Shortly after Goldwater filed his lawsuit, he published his legal arguments as to why an injunction against Carter was necessary in the *American Bar Association Journal.* In an article titled "Treaty Termination Is a Shared Power," he provided a number of historic examples of the Senate taking a direct role in the termination of treaties. Goldwater warned that if Carter's actions were left unchallenged in the courts, nothing would prevent a future president from rescinding any defense treaty, including the North Atlantic Treaty Organization (NATO). He recognized that while the Constitution itself was silent on treaty revocation, there were several examples given by the nation's founders that they intended Congress, and in particular the Senate, to have a shared power with the executive branch in treaty termination. For instance, he cited John Marshall's statement that the Constitution intended to enforce the national obedience to treaty agreements. In quoting James Wilson, one of the Constitution's signatories, that "a country which violates the sacred faith of treaties, violates not only the voluntary, but the necessary law of nations," Goldwater insisted this proved that a president needed congressional sanction to rescind a treaty. None of these statements, however, constituted a judicial determination. To this end, Goldwater relied on Justice James Iredell's seriatim opinion in *Ware v. Hylton* that Congress alone possessed the authority to declare a treaty terminated.

Seriatim opinions occur when the justices issue separate opinions. This type of judicial opinion writing no longer exists in the United States; indeed, the United States appears to be the first of the legal systems that originated in British law to abandon the practice of seriatim. Seriatim makes it more difficult to ascertain the extent of a ruling. Nonetheless, Iredell, who served on the Court from 1790 to 1799. left an important imprint on modes of constitutional interpretation. *Ware v. Hylton* arose from Virginia's state government renouncing a debt that one of its citizens owed to a British entity. The debt had accrued prior to the Constitution. But the peace treaty with Britain specifically provided for the recoupment of lawful debts in both countries, and a federal district court had recognized the debt as valid. In his seriatim, Iredell intimated twice that Congress alone "has authority under our government" to declare a treaty terminated.

Goldwater may have selectively used Iredell's quote out of context, and the seriatim reads more like a dissent than an agreement, but the justice's words gave strength to Goldwater's position. Iredell's full wrote read: "If Congress, therefore (which, I conceive, alone has such authority under our government) shall make such a declaration in any case like the present, I shall deem it my duty to regard the treaty as void and then to forbear any share in executing it as a judge." Thus, Iredell articulated his belief that until Congress renounced a treaty, a justice had to side with the party seeking its enforcement. (Unlike the other justices, Iredell did not believe the debt in question was enforceable due to its coming into existence prior to the treaty.) And while the fundamental issue in *Ware* was whether a state government could shun a treaty in contravention of the Constitution's supremacy clause and not whether a president could renounce a treaty, the Court, in *Ware*, upheld the principle that a treaty, once approved by the Senate, becomes the law of the nation. In 1920, the Court reaffirmed this principle in *Missouri v. Holland*, in which the state of Missouri challenged the federal regulation of migratory game birds in compliance with a treaty and the Court dismissed the state's challenge.

The Court of Oliver Gasch

In 1965, President Lyndon Johnson appointed Oliver Gasch to the US District Court for the District of Columbia. The Senate confirmed Gasch without any votes in opposition. Senators James O. Eastland (D-MS) and Roman Hruska (R-NE), who were to soon upend Johnson's attempts at having Justice Abe Fortas confirmed as chief justice and Judge Homer Thornberry confirmed to the Court, lauded Gasch. So, too, did liberal senators such as Philip Hart (D-MI) and Walter Mondale (D-MN). When, in 1983, a portrait of Gasch was scheduled to be unveiled at the federal district courthouse in the capital, Justice William Rehnquist asked for Judge George MacKinnon, a judge on the Court of Appeals for the District of Columbia, to provide the keynote speech. "Being a fair judge connotes much more than impartiality," MacKinnon began. "In the person of Judge Gasch, it includes legal intelligence of the highest order, high ethical principles, humanitarian compassion for his fellow man, a deep sense of majesty for the law, and the courage and wisdom to stand against temporary pressures and expedience." Perhaps this statement of admiration for Gasch partly contextualizes the fact that MacKinnon was the only appellate judge to argue that Gasch's final ruling on Goldwater's appeal had to be upheld. But it is important to point out that while MacKinnon was a staunch conservative and Gasch did not politically align with him, many liberal jurists shared MacKinnon's esteem toward Gasch.

In the history of the federal judiciary, most of the nation's district court and appellate judges have labored under relative obscurity. Only a few, like John J. Sirica, who presided over the Watergate break-in trials, became well known and have remained so. Judges such as David Pine, who ruled against President Harry S. Truman in the steel seizure case in 1952; Luther Youngdahl, who resisted the worst excesses of "red-baiting" during the trial of Owen Lattimore, a prominent Sinologist accused of communism; and Gerhard Gesell, who presided over a significant "Iran-Contra" trial, are barely known today, even though the nation's newspapers and television and radio news reported on their rulings. Yet Pine, Youngdahl, and Gesell shaped the law in a manner seldom achieved by federal trial judges. Gasch falls into the same category as these three men in terms of shaping the law, and like them, the publicity that accompanied the trials he presided over did not translate into a broader historic memory of him.

Born in 1906 and educated at Princeton University, in the 1928 presidential election Gasch campaigned for Democratic governor Al Smith against Republican secretary of commerce Herbert Hoover. In 1932, Gasch earned a law degree from George Washington University while working as a Washington Railway and Electric Company clerk. After Gasch's law school graduation, Senator Carter Glass (D-VA), obtained a position for him with the District of Columbia's general counsel. In World War II he served in the US Army as a judge advocate and by war's end had been promoted to the rank of lieutenant colonel. In this capacity, he advised General Douglas MacArthur on courts-martial and the treatment of Japanese prisoners of war, including a captured general, Tomoyuki Yamashita. Indeed, Gasch had a role in drafting war crimes charges against Yamashita for mass atrocities committed in the Philippines. After the war, Gasch briefly assisted Alexander Holtzoff, a US district court judge in Washington, DC, in investigating the fairness of wartime courts-martial, which led to the creation of the modern Uniform Code of Military Justice. Unlike Holtzoff, however, Gasch publicly advocated that courts-martial were fair and not in need of further reform. After being appointed to the bench, Gasch opined that a president possessed almost unfettered control over the military.

In 1956, President Dwight Eisenhower appointed Gasch as US attorney for the District of Columbia. When Johnson first sought judicial nominees for the district court, Thomas Corcoran, a New Deal adviser to Roosevelt, recommended Gasch. For most of his life prior to becoming a judge, Gasch identified as a Democrat but had not registered as being a member of any party. Gasch later recalled that Corcoran advised him that because Johnson wanted to nominate a Republican to the bench, he should affiliate with the Republican Party. This sleight of hand, if true, was easy for Gasch to accomplish because of his work in the Eisenhower administration. In his first action as a judge, he dismissed a criminal indictment against three defendants charged with securities fraud after concluding the US attorney had delayed the trials to the detriment of the defendants' ability to mount a full defense as required by the Constitution's Sixth Amendment.

Gasch not only served as the trial judge in *Goldwater* but also presided over three significant political corruption trials, those of Johnson's confidant Robert "Bobby" Baker and two congressmen. Baker, a former Senate page and secretary to Johnson, was implicated in a fraud scheme involving vending machine contracts in defense industries as well as kickbacks to politicians. The trial could have upended Johnson's presidency. Senator John J. Williams (R-DE) had led an investigation into Baker shortly before President Kennedy's assassination, but by the time Baker went to trial, Johnson was already president. In the end, Baker was convicted and imprisoned, but no discernible harm came to the Johnson administration. Also, in Gasch's court, Congressman Charles Diggs (D-MI) was convicted of violating the federal mail fraud statute after it was discovered that he accepted or demanded kickbacks from his staff. Daniel Flood, who has already been mentioned for opposing the Panama Canal treaties, was indicted for perjury for lying about payoffs he received in exchange for steering federal defense contracts to corporations. Flood's prosecution ended in a mistrial, and doctors diagnosed him as unfit to participate in a second criminal trial. Gasch entered a ruling dismissing the indictment.

Aside from his ruling in *Goldwater* and judicial service in political corruption trials, Gasch was influential in shaping the law in several other decisions, many of which were reported in the nation's major newspapers such as the *New York Times* and *Washington Post*. In his first year on the bench, he dismissed a "home-rule" case for Washington, DC, and referred to the legal theory of home rule as "insubstantial." In 1973, he ordered the Nixon administration to comply with the intent underlying congressional funding of the Environmental Protection Agency. Gasch's ruling in this instance particularly gave Goldwater hope that his suit against Carter would be favorably resolved in the district court. Two years later, Gasch determined that the Consumer Products Safety Commission had the authority to prevent the sale of high-tar cigarettes, even though in 1960—prior to the creation of the commission—Congress had specifically exempted tobacco from the Federal Hazardous Substances Act. In 1976, Gasch ruled in favor of a Georgetown University student against the university in a case that might have been overturned by the Supreme Court in *Bakke v. Board of Regents* had Gasch not denied a postponement to the university for hearing the case. Gasch determined that the university unlawfully denied a white student a scholarship in favor of minority students and ordered the university to repay the student the tuition costs he had incurred. Georgetown did not appeal the order.

In 1974, Gasch ruled that dozens of arrests of Quakers who peacefully protested the United States' involvement in the Vietnam Conflict were illegal, and he ordered a full expungement of their arrest records as well as attorney fees awards against the government. He also imposed a fine on the Greyhound Bus Corporation for making illegal contributions to President Richard Nixon's reelection campaign. In 1976, he decided that the executive branch could, in the absence of express congressional opposition, close a military installation regardless of the economic impact on civilian employees and the local community. He also dismissed a corporation's lawsuit against Nigeria after concluding that the federal courts did not possess jurisdiction over sovereign foreign governments. Almost contemporaneous with Goldwater's appeal, Gasch determined that the United States could not be sued by veterans who were injured by the use of Agent Orange in Vietnam. Although the government's use of the Agent Orange defoliant and its deleterious health effects on both service members and Vietnamese citizens, were and remain controversial, it is noteworthy that the court of appeals upheld Gasch's ruling.

By the time Goldwater filed suit, Gasch had a two-decade-long friendship with Chief Justice Warren Burger. During the period Gasch served as a US attorney, he reported directly to Burger, who headed the Department of Justice's civil division. In 1955, Burger appointed Gasch to represent the executive branch in a politically contentious appeal involving a service member transferred to the control of Japanese prosecutors. In what became captioned *Wilson v. Girard*, Gasch argued, and the Court agreed, that status of forces agreements—that is, agreements between a foreign government and the United States that the United States would maintain court-martial jurisdiction over service members—did not vest service members with the right to be prosecuted in a military court-martial instead of a foreign trial. The decision to extradite, Gasch argued, was based on presidential prerogative in foreign affairs. Gasch's decision to ultimately side with Goldwater was not necessarily a departure from this jurisprudence on presidential authority, but in ruling against Carter, he imposed a significant restraint on presidential control over alliances.

January 1 to June 6, 1979: The Disintegration of World Order

In the six months between the time Goldwater announced his intention to file suit against Carter and the district court first taking up the issue, both US foreign policy and the domestic economy were thrown into disarray. When, on January 1, 1979, the leaders of China and the United States determined that normalization would occur within the year, this newfound relationship promised a geographic zone of stability on an increasingly fragmented globe. In mid-January, Shah Mohammad Reza

Pahlavi, Iran's monarch, fled from Tehran to Egypt as the Iranian government crumbled under a burgeoning rebellion. Iran's revolution began as a seemingly liberal fight for greater freedoms, but it was co-opted by Shia Islamists. Two weeks after the Shah fled, Ayatollah Ruhollah Khomeini returned to Tehran from his Paris exile and rapidly assumed control over the government. Also in early 1979, a civil war erupted in the Central African nation of Chad. While Chad was not necessarily a key interest to the United States, it was clear that Libya's dictator, Muammar Gaddafi, a sponsor of terrorism against the United States, was seeking to expand into that nation. Twice in 1977, Carter had personally warned Gaddafi to refrain from assassinating US ambassadors, and he certainly wanted to stop the Libyan dictator from expanding his power over other peoples. Thus, at the end of the first month of the year, when Deng Xiaoping traveled to the United States and met with Carter, it appeared that two of the world's three adversarial superpowers were at least lessening the prospect of international conflict in one region of the world. But, even this promise had a rough start because of simmering issues between China, Vietnam, Cambodia, and the Soviet Union.

As the US military exited South Vietnam and Cambodia in 1973, communist insurgencies in each country grew in strength, and did so with Chinese, Soviet, and North Vietnamese support. Yet, behind the facade of a unified communist front in Southeast Asia, the Chinese and Soviet governments competed for regional influence. Prior to the 1975 unification of Vietnam, the North Vietnamese government feared Chinese expansion because, historically, China had alternated between dominating and controlling Vietnam. Even during older periods in which Chinese overlords were removed from outright power in Vietnam, Vietnam's rulers had, at times, been vassals of the Song and Ming dynasties. When North Vietnam and South Vietnam gained independence from France in 1954, the North Vietnamese communist government under Ho Chi Minh aligned with China more as a matter of unity against the West than out of a shared kinship or trust. In 1975, the unified Vietnamese government under Le Duan looked to the Soviet Union as its protector and viewed China as a likely enemy. Given the Sino-Soviet split, this may have been the most practical course for Le Duan's government to take, though it further enabled the United States to reach out to China.

By 1975, Cambodia had fallen under the control of the genocidal communist Khmer Rouge. Between 1975 and 1980, over 1.5 million Cambodians lost their lives in a communist-led genocide. Led by Pol Pot, the Khmer Rouge developed close ties to China and gained recognition in the United Nations. Goldwater and his allies, along with members of Congress from both parties, were troubled by Carter's acquiescence to China on this issue. If US foreign policy was to be governed by human rights, they queried, how was it possible not to demand China cease supporting the Khmer Rouge as a condition of normalization? The issue with Cambodia, however, was far more complex than Carter's critics presented to the public. Beginning in 1973, the Khmer Rouge murdered a large swath of Cambodia's Vietnamese ethnic minority, and although the Vietnamese communists and Cambodia's Khmer Rouge aligned to defeat the United States as well as the pro–United States Cambodian government under Lon Nol, China and the Khmer Rouge were, at best, temporary allies, and only so because of a common enemy.

After the 1972 Paris Peace Accords, the Khmer Rouge began to attack North Vietnamese border villages. Independent of the Khmer Rouge, ethnic minorities in Vietnam resumed guerrilla-level warfare against the Vietnamese government. In an odd alliance, the United States and China armed Vietnam's ethnic minorities to fight against Le Duan's government. Known as the United Front for the Liberation of Oppressed Races—or FULRO—ethnic Montagnards and Hmong fought an insurgency against the Vietnamese government for more than twenty years. At times, the Khmer Rouge supplied arms for the FULRO and even participated in small strikes on the Vietnam-Cambodia border. In response, on December 25, 1978, Vietnam invaded Cambodia.

On January 29, 1979, when Deng Xiaoping and Carter signed accords establishing formal diplomatic relations between China and the United States, Deng informed Carter of the possibility of a Chinese invasion of Vietnam. According to national security adviser Zbigniew Brzezinski, Carter did not demand the Chinese refrain from launching a military attack, though he expressed a desire for China not to do so. China's purpose for invading, however, was limited to proving to the Soviet Union that its support of Vietnam (or other Asian countries) would not serve as a deterrent to China's foreign policy, and to undermine Vietnam's ability to remain in Cambodia. In other words, the Chinese government did not intend to occupy Vietnam and be drawn into a never-ending war.

Cambodia and Vietnam presented a "thorny issue" for the US government, in terms of normalizing relations with China, because conservatives feared that the Chinese government sought territorial expansion. Public opinion would have made an attempted rapprochement with Vietnam into a political liability. As of 1979, neither Cambodia nor Vietnam had formal diplomatic relations with the United States. It was unlikely that diplomatic ties could be established with the Khmer Rouge any more than diplomacy could be achieved with Khomeini in Iran. In 1975, Cambodian military forces seized the USS *Mayaguez* and captured American sailors. President Ford's attempts to negotiate the release of the sailors proved unsuccessful, and as a sign of further difficulty, Thailand's prime minister insisted that the United States could not use military bases in his country against Cambodia. The Chinese government, moreover, rebuffed a request to assist in the release. A military rescue effort occurred, though it resulted in high casualties, in what perhaps became a prelude to a failed hostage rescue attempt in Iran in April 1980. Additionally, American naval aircraft sunk Cambodian gunboats and bombed targets in Cambodia. In the end, the Cambodian government released the sailors but claimed the *Mayaguez* was on a Central Intelligence Agency mission, and was not a legitimate merchant ship. The fact that China's government kept silent, without assisting the United States, angered congressional conservatives, and this remained in the public memory at the time of normalization.

Yet both Ford and Carter were willing to look past China's declination of assistance regarding Cambodia, and Carter, along with Ford and Nixon, did not openly condemn China's invasion of Vietnam on February 27, 1979. Their relative silence—in particular Carter's—is explainable. Vietnam had violated the 1972 Paris Peace Accords and also imprisoned, tortured, and killed hundreds of South Vietnamese who had supported the United States. More important, it would have been untenable for Carter to condemn China's move into Vietnam and continue with normalization. As an added benefit to strengthening US foreign policy, the Soviet Union appeared powerless to support its Vietnamese ally, checking its ability to expand into Southeast Asia. On the other hand, China appeared to be conducting the very type of aggression that Carter and Deng insisted neither country intended to conduct. Even though China removed its forces from Vietnam by the end of March 1979, the invasion was recent enough to be referenced in the June hearings in Gasch's courtroom.

Aside from the Chinese invasion into Vietnam, the symbolism and promise of normalization might not have been readily apparent to either its critics or the American public in light of events between Deng's visit and the time Gasch issued his first of two decisions. Simply, the world appeared to erupt into regional conflicts. In April 1978, a pro-Soviet faction murdered Afghanistan's president and took over control of the government. On February 14, 1979, Adolph Dubs, the US ambassador to Afghanistan, was killed after being taken hostage by antigovernment soldiers in Kabul. While it remains unclear why an anti-Soviet group would kidnap Dubs, the Soviet military and Afghan police bungled a rescue attempt that resulted in Dubs's murder. Although neither Carter nor Deng seemed to accurately predict Soviet conduct at the time, in a short period a rural Afghan religious insurgency took form and challenged the ability of the secular, pro-communist government to rule Afghanistan. Ultimately, the Soviet Union would send large numbers of forces and commit crimes against humanity while trying to enforce the Brezhnev Doctrine in Afghanistan. Deng, in turn, would permit the United States to conduct electronic surveillance operations into the Soviet Union from China. When Goldwater appeared before Gasch for the first time, the parties to the suit, as well as Gasch, understood that Afghanistan had become increasingly unstable and the Kremlin considered Afghanistan in its sphere of influence. The specter of a new Russian conquest for warm-water ports was a frequent theme for conservatives to expound. This presented another global flash point that aligned China and the United States against the Soviet Union. Indeed, both Carter and Deng condemned the Soviet actions. This aspect of Chinese policy was not referenced in Gasch's court.

Equally troubling to US foreign policy was a deteriorating situation in Iran. Unlike Afghanistan, Iran was a key United States ally. Iran's Shah, Mohammad Reza Pahlavi, had been in power since World War II, but he also was a draconian ruler. And he had maintained power in the 1950s as a result of US and British clandestine operations to overthrow Mohammad Mosaddegh, a progressive prime minister who had sought to nationalize Iran's oil production and other industries to the detriment of American and British corporations. In 1953, in what became known as Operation Ajax, the CIA convinced the Shah to depose and prosecute Mosaddegh for treason in a military court. While Mosaddegh was convicted and sentenced to three years in prison, other cabinet officials were sentenced to death and ultimately executed. Although, by the late 1970s many Americans did not know about or had forgotten this episode, it left a lingering distrust toward the United States among the Iranian people and was used as an example by the Shia Islamic revolutionaries as evidence of US malfeasance.

During the 1976 presidential campaign, Carter accused the CIA of being "a national shame" and tried to reform it by appointing Admiral Stansfield Turner, a career naval officer who did not possess an intelligence background, to become its director. In 1977, Turner testified to Congress that the agency had conducted psychological experiments on people without their knowledge. Carter took cognizance of the Church and Pike committees and imposed limits on the CIA through executive orders as well as by disapproving several planned overseas operations. Following Carter's directions, under Turner, the agency reduced the number of agents working on covert operations from twelve hundred to slightly more than four hundred. Partly as a result, a small number of intelligence agency employees began to "leak" secrets from past operations in violation of their employment contracts with the agency, and while Turner supported Carter's attempts to corral the agency, he also wanted to prosecute leaks in the criminal and civil courts. Attempts to silence former agency personnel turned critics did not initially go according to plan and had deleterious effects on the agency's effectiveness, which became known to the public.

When, in early 1978, the CIA issued its first assessment of Pahlavi's ability to confront dissidents, it advised Carter that the Shah's position in power remained sound. The agency also did not consider the potential power of Shia extremists and instead characterized the Shah's dissenters as "fragmented and not wedded to a singular goal." While it was true that socialists, liberals, and college students opposed the Shah, there was a growing opposition to him among the Shia clerics, and the agency did not warn of the possibility that the Ayatollah Khomeini might return from his Parisian exile to take control of the country. Yet this is precisely what occurred.

On January 16, 1979, the Shah left Iran to go into exile, and less than one month later Khomeini returned to Tehran. He quickly removed the temporary government and assumed control over the country, in the process establishing a theocratic state. The same day that Afghan militants kidnapped Dubs, Iranian revolutionaries attacked the US embassy in Tehran and took hostages. Khomeini's government defused the temporary—or first—hostage crisis, but it was clear that Iran was neither an ally nor a stable country for the foreseeable future. Indeed, Iran rapidly became an antagonist to the United States and Europe. In addition, its oil production and transportation were stifled as a result of internal chaos, leading to a second oil crisis in the decade and another devastating shock to the US economy. Goldwater, Thurmond, and other conservatives argued that if Carter's administration had "bungled" in regard to Iran, owing to an overall foreign and national security incompetence, then naturalization with China would likely prove to be another disaster, albeit one of much greater proportions.

Even Carter's energy policies lurched into a public relations disaster. There were, in theory, viable alternatives to foreign oil dependency, and earlier Carter had championed nuclear power, but domestic events would make an expansion of nuclear energy politically and socially untenable. The United States led in the field of nuclear power, a technology that harnessed the energy emitted from the atom as opposed to mining ancient deposits of decayed organisms that could be burned as fossil fuel. Nuclear power appeared to offer the United States a means to achieve energy independence from the Middle East and to do so without the rampant pollution caused by fossil fuels. Prior to 1979, the public largely accepted the promise of nuclear power as a means for producing vast amounts of electricity. Of course, the mining and milling of uranium into usable fuel rods did have an environmental impact, but nuclear power plants did not belch carbon monoxide and sulfur into the atmosphere, and clean air coupled with electricity was a welcome change from the prior century of gas, coal, and oil burning. Nuclear energy even promised a solution to the recent discovery of "acid rain," a product of fossil fuel burning and other industrial pollution that led to deforestation and fish depletion. In short, nuclear power seemingly offered environmentalists a better choice over coal and oil, and there was a consensus in the United States regarding the desire to remove foreign influence in energy supply and pricing.

On March 16, 1979, the movie *The China Syndrome* portrayed a potential nuclear meltdown caused by corporate malfeasance and operator negligence. Two weeks after the film's release, a significant accident occurred in Pennsylvania at the Three Mile Island Nuclear station. The Three Mile nuclear plant suffered a partial meltdown that threatened to spread lethal doses of radiation across central Pennsylvania. In the end, the partial meltdown was contained and there were no cases of radiation poisoning such as later occurred at the Soviet nuclear plant at Chernobyl in 1986 where forty-two people died. However, antinuclear activists and a public increasingly disenchanted with the government almost ended new nuclear plant construction, and the United States remained subject to OPEC's whims for the foreseeable future. That Carter had a degree in nuclear engineering from the US Naval Academy and previously campaigned on the promise of safe and efficient nuclear energy production did not help bolster his presidency. California's democratic governor, Jerry Brown, and Senators Alan Cranston (D-CA) and S. I. Hayakawa (R-CA) called for closing all nuclear plants in that state. Others followed suit. Once more, Carter's view of the United States' place in the world, this time on the possibility of freedom from oil gouging, looked like a leadership failure.

The week of June 6, 1979, in which Gasch took up arguments and issued a ruling, was no less chaotic than the prior six months. Moreover, Gasch was not immune to the news of the world during this week, though his ruling did not indicate that the United States' position in the world swayed him. On May 29, a bomb exploded outside of the Cuban embassy building in Washington, DC. Although no one was injured, a group self-titled as Omega 7 took responsibility and demanded Cuban military forces leave Angola. That same day, Carter announced that oil shortages were likely to last into the foreseeable future unless the nation embraced conservation measures. He also conceded that although the Senate had approved the Panama Canal treaties, Congress had not acted to implement the treaties, and in a short time the canal would be left undefended. He expressed doubts that, even that in the face of rising oil prices, he could convince Congress to vote in favor of a windfall profits tax. He also acknowledged that Senator Edward Kennedy might present difficulties to his reelection campaign not only through a primary challenge but by fostering disunity in the party.

In addition to China's invasion of Vietnam and the mass refugee issues created by the Vietnamese invasion of Cambodia, the world's stability was in question in other areas. Soviet aggression was reported around the world. Even though three days before Gasch issued his ruling, the *Times* reported that Carter believed there were "modest gains" with the Soviets in resecuring détente, there were troubling actions by the Soviets. One day before Gasch issued his ruling, the Department of Defense announced that the Soviet Union had surpassed the United States' conventional nonnuclear military capabilities on land and in the air. The morning that Gasch issued his ruling, the Japanese government warned that the Soviet Union had built a significant military presence in the contested Kuril Islands, and this undermined the prospects of peace in the Pacific. Japan had long claimed the islands as part of its historic lands, but at the end of World War II, the Soviet Union occupied the island chain. At the same time, the Soviet government protested the election of three representatives from West Berlin to the European Parliament and threatened some type of retaliation. In the midst of an endangered détente, Brezhnev formally asked for talks with the People's Republic of China to enter into a new alliance. Deng rebuffed him.

Foreign policy disputes with allies also were causing headaches for the United States. In an attempt to alleviate the rising price of oil, Carter granted a five-dollar subsidy to families for each barrel of imported home heating oil. Without Carter's intervention, Americans living in cold-weather states would face prohibitive costs to keep their homes and small businesses livable in the winter months. In response to the subsidy, the European Common Market, the predecessor to the European Union, protested and threatened economic retaliation. Western Europe's concerns with the subsidy were based on an international shortage of oil caused by the upheaval in Iran, leading to fears of a deep recession in Europe. At the same time, NATO leaders objected to Carter's attempts to reopen the Strategic Arms Limitations Talks with the Soviet Union without significant European involvement.

Outside of Europe there was disarray with other allies. On May 10, the *New York Times* reported that the South Korea government, in an act that Carter would hardly approve of, jailed seven journalists for violating a law that made it a crime to print articles critical of the government. Also, Carter threatened to remove the United States from the World

Health Organization after the Arab nations sought to block Israel's access to that agency. Although Carter supported Israel being a member of the World Health Organization, he roundly criticized Prime Minister Menachem Begin for enabling the buildup of settlements on the West Bank and imperiling chances of peace with the Palestinians. Added to concerns over the West Bank, Israeli military forces along with Christian militia in Lebanon exchanged artillery fire with Muslim forces, while Lebanon itself descended into a civil war. Further, the Turkish government, which had asked for extensive loans from both Europe and the United States to alleviate economic misery and currency devaluation, disagreed with conditions attached to the loans.

Much of the media's reporting centered on Iran. On May 24, Khomeini declared that secularists were an enemy as much as the Shah had been. Attacking Iran's nationalist opposition, who had initially supported the Shah's removal, Khomeini argued, "Our problem is not oil, our problem is not the nationalization of oil. Our aim is Islam." Two days later, Khomeini accused the United States of trying to assassinate one of his lieutenants, Ayatollah Hashemi Rafsanjani. This was one of the many factors that contributed to a complete collapse of relations with the new Iranian government. Khomeini's conduct also personally affected at least one member of Congress. After Senator Jacob Javits introduced a Senate resolution condemning the widespread extrajudicial killings in Iran, Iran's Shia leaders denounced Javits on the basis of his Jewish faith and threatened him with murder. Yet, news media also reported that a public affairs firm employing his wife, Marion Javits, received over a half million dollars from the Shah in the preceding five years. On June 1, Iran formally rejected William Cutler as the US ambassador and demanded the United States send another person.

Standing in the District Court of Judge Oliver Gasch

On December 22, 1978, Goldwater filed his complaint against Carter seeking "declaratory and injunctive relief." In the lawsuit's prefatory heading, Goldwater gave notice that he sought to have the court "declare unconstitutional and illegal, and enjoin, set aside, annul, suspend, or otherwise declare invalid and of no effect, the purported notice by defendant President Carter to the Republic of China to terminate the 1954 Mutual Defense Treaty . . . without the advice and consent of both Houses of Congress." The twin basis Goldwater advanced to prove standing was that Carter's action denied his "right to vote" in the Senate and was necessary to protect "his sworn duty to preserve, protect, and to defend the Constitutional allocation of powers to the Executive and Legislative branches of the federal government." Thurmond and Curtis added an important element to their arguments for standing: the fact that they had voted for the 1954 treaty. As for the representatives, they claimed standing on the same basis as Goldwater.

Led by Attorney General Griffin Bell, the Justice Department argued that Goldwater lacked standing to challenge the treaty termination, and even if standing were recognized, the appeal constituted a nonjusticiable political question. As noted in chapter 2, standing is the first hurdle that a party in a lawsuit must prove in order to get a claim heard in federal court. Members of Congress were not customarily permitted to sidestep this hurdle, though the level of proof for standing may have occasionally flexed in their favor. Even if a member of Congress could convince a court on the issue of standing, some claims would be deemed as inherently political, and if the judiciary were to take up the issue, courts feared that the authority of the legislative and executive branches would be damaged. Known as the political question doctrine, and therefore not justiciable at the courts, the doctrine was first recognized by the Court in 1803 in *Marbury v Madison.* At times the doctrine of standing and the political question doctrine were intertwined so that it became difficult for the public to know why a court dismissed a case. In 1967, the Court of Appeals for the District of Columbia determined, in *Luftig v. McNamara,* that the federal courts were not competent to adjudge questions of foreign and military policy as these questions were political in nature. Four years later the US District Court for the District of Columbia dismissed the claim by Senator Mike Gravel (D-AK) and twenty members of the House of Representatives against Secretary of Defense Melvin Laird that the war in Vietnam was being waged in an illegal manner. Judge William Blakely Jones, a contemporary of Oliver Gasch, determined that Gravel's claim presented a nonjusticiable political question that could only be resolved by the two elected branches of government.

When, in 1977, Congressman Michael Harrington (D-MA) filed suit to have a court declare that several CIA operations were unconstitutional, the US District Court for the District of Columbia dismissed the suit on the basis of a lack of standing. Harrington also lost his appeal in the US Court of Appeals for the District of Columbia. That court, however, articulated a four-part test to determine congressional standing in suits against the government. First, the party would have to prove that he or she had suffered an injury. Second, a statute or the Constitution itself would have to protect the party against the injury. Third, the party would have to be able to link the injury as being caused by the action of the government. Finally, there would have to be some proof that the court would be capable of curing the injury. Harrington had argued that as a member of Congress he voted to allocate funds for specified uses, and the CIA had exceeded the intent of Congress. Moreover, he alleged that because the CIA had violated other laws with the use of these funds, Congress had been injured in conducting its legislative duties as mandated under the Constitution. The appellate court recognized that Harrington had interests in his status as a member of Congress in the areas of impeachment, appropriations, and general lawmaking, but this did not empower the courts to make a judgment on the CIA's activities. Importantly, the court cautioned that if Harrington had specialized standing to challenge the CIA—an executive branch agency—then other members of Congress could turn the courts into "roving commissions" to examine any executive branch action. Instead, Congress itself would have to act to upend an executive action, rather than the courts.

After arguing he possessed standing, Goldwater next turned to the substantive constitutional question as to whether the Constitution required Senate or full congressional action in treaty terminations. Goldwater insisted that because, under Article VI of the Constitution, a treaty was considered the "supreme law of the land," and only Congress could terminate a law, the termination of a treaty was no different. He conceded that although the 1954 treaty had an exit clause within its tenth article, nothing in the treaty itself envisioned that a president could unilaterally act to invoke its clause. To the contrary, he argued, both the Constitution itself by the language of Article VI and the language of international law as captured in the Vienna Convention on the Law of Treaties defined the term "party" as "a state which has consented to be bound by the treaty and for which the treaty is in force." Finally, Goldwater insisted, the 1978 Dole-Stone Amendment to the International Security Assistance Act bound Carter to put treaty revocation to a vote. He reminded the court that Carter had signed the amendment. Goldwater's complaint next turned to the past practice of treaty termination, noting that of the forty-eight treaties that had been terminated since the nation's founding, forty-four had been terminated by the actions of Congress. The four other treaties were "allegedly terminated by a president, but under circumstances where it became impossible to perform the obligations specified." Goldwater concluded with a prescient admonition that "if left unchallenged, the unilateral action by defendant Carter will set a dangerous precedent which enables him to abrogate or terminate any defense treaty at will, such as the North Atlantic Treaty Alliance."

On June 6, 1979, Gasch issued his initial ruling in which he explained that Goldwater lacked standing to challenge Carter's decision to terminate the Mutual Defense Treaty. He prefaced his ruling by observing that Carter's decision to recognize the People's Republic of China "represented a significant change in the relationship between the two countries." He also expressed his belief that the power to terminate treaties was shared between Congress and the president. After providing a brief history of the Mutual Defense Treaty along with Carter's actions, Gasch turned to the nature of the treaty itself. He acknowledged that the treaty possessed a clause permitting termination, but he also noted that this clause was silent on how the treaty could be terminated. However, he cautioned, while the Senate did not remove its authority to oversee the treaty, including its termination, the issue before the court could only be addressed if Goldwater possessed standing. In contextualizing standing, Gasch provided an overview of the Dole-Stone Amendment and observed that while Goldwater claimed the requirement of presidential consultation with Congress prior to revoking the treaty had never been complied with, Carter countered that he had consulted with individual members of Congress. Carter's position, moreover, was that by announcing his intent to remove the United States from the treaty, full compliance had been achieved. Gasch disappointed both sides in pointing out that while there was a clear argument between the parties as to whether compliance with a statute had occurred, he could not provide an answer. This was the essence of the political question doctrine.

Yet, throughout his ruling, Gasch hinted that Goldwater was in the right and Carter wrong. For instance, Gasch provided an overview of presidential treaty termination history, finding that since the beginning of the nation, over fifty treaties had been terminated through various means. "Some have been terminated by legislative action; some have been terminated by the President with the concurrence of both houses of Congress; some have been terminated with senatorial consent; and some have been terminated by the President acting alone," he observed. However, as to this last category—unilateral action—Gasch also indicated that "presidential terminations have been in situations in which it might be inferred that the Congress had no reason to question presidential action." Gasch minimized this category's importance by citing an instance in which President Calvin Coolidge terminated an anti-smuggling treaty with Mexico, on the basis that the Mexican government proved unable to effectively enforce it. Gasch's reliance on this episode was not wholly accurate. Coolidge referred to the treaty termination as "a small treaty we had with Mexico covering the question of smuggling." Two senators objected to Coolidge's action, but both of them were frequent critics of Coolidge's policies. Senator George Norris (R-NE) warned that the end of the treaty would enable US citizens to import arms into Mexico to foster further political upheaval at the behest of the Doheny and Sinclair oil interests, and these interests had been at the center of the Teapot Dome scandal. In the early 1920s, President Warren G. Harding quietly transferred authority over the naval petroleum fields in Wyoming and California from the naval department to the Department of the Interior. Secretary of the Interior Albert Fall entered the government into private leasing arrangements with the Doheny and Sinclair oil companies, and he received kickbacks in return. The Teapot Dome scandal grew to include the attorney general's brother and other government officials, and it tarnished Harding's legacy as well as undermined trust in the government. In addition to Norris, Senator William Borah (R-ID) openly argued that the Senate had to at least give an opinion on the treaty revocation. In response to Borah, the Senate Foreign Relations Committee determined that it would not discuss the treaty revocation until the next Congress.

Gasch observed that Goldwater's suit was not unusual in the sense that since the height of the Vietnam Conflict, members of Congress had asserted special standing as a means for redressing grievances with the executive branch. These included a senator's opposition to the presidential appointment of members to the National Petroleum Council, several representatives seeking an injunction against granting inventors at government research laboratories exclusive patent rights, and another challenge from sixty members of the House of Representatives seeking a declaratory judgment that the Panama Canal treaties were unconstitutional. Gasch insisted that before it was possible to review the substantive claim against Carter, he first had to address standing, and that there were no special standing measures for assessing congressional claims.

Much of the district court's focus was on the more recent decision, *Kennedy v. Sampson*, in which the Court of Appeals for the District of Columbia recognized a narrow avenue for standing in congressional suits. As a reminder, *Sampson* arose from Nixon's exercise of a "pocket veto" when he claimed that Congress had gone into a recess. But the appellate court determined that Nixon's actions had impaired a power of Congress and in that instance, Congress was, in fact, in "session," in the sense that it was able to receive executive communications. However, Gasch found *Sampson* inapplicable to Goldwater's suit, even when applied to Thurmond's and Curtis's separate claims. This was because, in *Harrington v. Schlesinger*, a suit arising from a congressman's challenge to defense spending, the Court of Appeals for the Fourth Circuit determined that once a bill became law, Congress's interests in seeing the law enforced were indistinguishable from those of the citizenry at large. That is, the enforcement of laws in a general sense was too tangential to confer standing to citizens' groups.

Gasch next observed that because there were "no specific standards" he could find for assessing a question of congressional standing, he believed he had no choice but to review Goldwater's appeal under an "injury in fact" test and then assess it for justiciability under *Baker v. Carr. Baker*, however, was not a question of foreign policy and arose as a voting apportionment issue. In 1962, the Court took up an appeal that arose out of a challenge to Tennessee's state legislative districts. These districts favored rural counties over the state's cities as a result of Tennessee not having drawn a new district map since 1901. On appeal, conservatives argued that the drawing of state legislative election districts was a matter of legislative prerogative and presented a political question that the federal courts could not solve. The Court, in an arduously long decision and to conservatives' ire, formulated a six-part test and determined that the federal courts could oversee legislative redistricting if the voting districts imperiled the "one person, one vote" standard. Gasch did not spend much space, however, in referencing *Baker* other than to point out that if he were to take up a new suit against Carter, he would have to apply the *Baker* "injury in fact" test.

Gasch concluded his ruling with the admonition that until Congress acted against Carter, he could do nothing in the matter. Likewise, if Congress approved of Carter's treaty termination action on Taiwan, then Goldwater's suit was moot. Importantly, however, Gasch did not convey that Congress had to fully oppose Carter, to achieve standing. He also did not require the Senate to formally renounce Carter's actions. Instead, he expressed, "If the Senate or the Congress takes action, the result of which falls short of approving the President's termination effort, then the controversy will be right for a judicial declaration respecting the President's authority to act unilaterally." When Gasch dismissed the lawsuit, he did so by advising that Goldwater's suit could be renewed if Congress as a whole, or the Senate alone, expressed its disapproval of Carter's unilateral action. Gasch's ruling was more than a hint for the Senate to act and for Goldwater to renew the suit against Carter. Thus, it was unsurprising that the *Washington Post* placed on its front page a headline that read, "Senate, Court Suggest Carter Overreached on Taiwan Treaty," and the *Chicago Tribune* reported that Carter had lost in Gasch's court.

The Further Descent into Chaos

On July 15, 1978, Carter informed the nation in a televised address that the country had descended into a "malaise," and there was a crisis of confidence in its leadership. Carter spoke of the lack of trust in government since the Vietnam Conflict and the seeming inability to curb inflation and restart employment. He promised to wean the United States from foreign oil imports. One week later, Carter purged half of his cabinet in a move that had no recent precedent. To be sure, Nixon sought the resignations of his first secretary of state, William Rogers, and Secretary of Defense Melvin Laird before he began his second term. But Carter was barely through the first half of his term when the country saw the resignations of the secretaries of the Treasury, the Department of Transportation, the Department of Energy, and the Department of Health, Education, and Welfare. In addition, Attorney General Griffin Bell resigned from the Justice Department. The press, moreover, reported that the White House had issued "evaluation forms" for its staff to declare their loyalty, a move that was widely ridiculed in Congress and the press as sophomoric.

On July 22, 1979, Benjamin Wattenberg, a Democratic Party adviser, lamented to the *New York Times* that the United States had retreated from it superpower role against the Soviet Union. While Wattenberg acknowledged that Carter's administration had, in 1978, increased defense spending, he countered that this was enough because, from Egypt to Vietnam, there was "an arc of crisis." He argued that not enough had been done to assure the United States' allies that they would be shielded from chaos and communist infiltration by American diplomatic, economic, and military might. Wattenberg observed that in Africa, South Korea, and even with the United States' nuclear deterrent, Carter had been weak in the face of communist aggression. He claimed that Carter's focus on human rights, which was supposed to have forced the Soviets to leave parts of the world alone, had only undermined American allies. While the editorial contained no mention of China, from a conservative anticommunist perspective, the recognition of China at the expense of Taiwan fit nicely into a narrative of American weakness. This narrative would also be present in Gasch's court when it determined whether Goldwater actually had standing, and, if so, whether the court could issue an injunction against terminating the Mutual Defense Treaty.

Between June 6 and the beginning of September, the world continued to spiral into uncertainty, although improved relations with China offered some respite. Moreover, Carter had become increasingly willing to confront the Soviet Union. On September 30, he warned the Soviet and Vietnamese governments that any threats to Thailand's territorial integrity would be viewed as an act of war resulting in intervention in concert with a 1954 agreement made with Thailand. (Ironically the agreement with Thailand was similar to the Mutual Defense Treaty.) In spite of China's military operations in Vietnam, Vietnamese military forces continued to drive Khmer Rouge forces east into Thailand, escalating tensions between Vietnam and Thailand. Carter's warning to the Soviet Union was welcomed in China. Carter, in turn, applauded the Vatican's announcement that it would seek closer diplomatic ties to China.

It was also possible that the United States and China could work to reduce civil war and nation-state conflicts in Africa. The possibility of greater cooperation in Africa was already seen, with the United States, France, Morocco, and China working to prevent Soviet-supported rebels from taking over Zaire in 1978. In April 1979, Tanzanian military forces and Ugandan rebels overthrew Idi Amin's dictatorship. Amin had established relations with China, and in 1975 he praised China for working to end apartheid in Africa. The Chinese government had retained its diplomatic ties in Uganda, and these could be used to prevent the country from falling into a Soviet sphere of influence after Amin's ouster. On August 5, a military coup in Equatorial Guinea overthrew Nguema Masi's brutal dictatorship, which had overseen the massacre of thousands of its citizens. Equatorial Guinea was a former Spanish West African colony located between Gabon and Cameroon, and its government had diplomatic relations with China and France. By the end of the month, the coup captured Masi and his cabinet, conducted a military trial, and sentenced several of the captured men to death. The new government welcomed the continuation of China's diplomatic presence but remained closed to most other nations. On September 21, a military coup overthrew Emperor Bokassa I of the Central African Empire—today the Central African Republic—and replaced him with a former prime minister. Bokassa had massacred over one hundred school children, in addition to thousands of perceived political enemies, before being deposed. As in the case of China's relations with Equatorial Guinea, China was one of the few governments to have full diplomatic relations with the Central African Empire. Because preventing the expansion of Soviet influence was, at the time, considered to be a key US foreign policy tenet, China's diplomatic ties could prove useful.

On September 22, Panama's government asserted its right to occupy the Canal Zone regardless of whether Congress enacted implementing legislation. By the end of the month, however, Carter was able to secure the necessary votes in the House to pass legislation on the transfer of the canal. This occurred in the face of conservative lobbyists threatening to spend millions of dollars in primary contests against Republicans and conservative Democrats who sided with Carter. Three months earlier, Carter openly acknowledged that his noninterference doctrine in Central America was in shambles in Nicaragua and the position of that country's anticommunist dictator, Anastasio Samoza, had become untenable. Backed by Cuban and Soviet military advisers, a communist insurgency overthrew Samoza in mid-July. Samoza unsuccessfully tried to seek refuge in the United States. When Carter refused him permission to remain, the exiled dictator warned that other South and Central American countries would fall to Soviet-backed communist factions. Senator Orrin Hatch, one of the signatories to Goldwater's suit, excoriated Carter for permitting communism to become the governing force in Panama, Nicaragua, and Paraguay.

In early September, the CIA announced that a fully equipped Soviet army brigade was stationed in Cuba. Retired general John Singlaub—whom Carter had removed from command in South Korea one year earlier—claimed to the *New York Times* that the Soviet military had placed nuclear-capable units in Cuba. If true, this would mark the first time since the Cuban Missile Crisis in 1962, which had brought the United States and Soviet Union to the brink of war, that a nuclear-capable force was on the island. The *New York Times* and other major newspapers reported that both Gerald Ford and Henry Kissinger asserted that during Ford's presidency, there was no evidence of a Soviet buildup in Cuba, leaving the impression that Carter had, as in the case of Iran, been caught flat-footed. The previous year, Carter promised Senator Stone that the administration would resist the establishment of any Soviet military bases in Central America before voting on the Panama Canal Treaty. As late as August 1, 1979, Carter assured Senator Church and the Foreign Relations Committee that there were no Soviet combat forces on the island, beyond military advisers. But on October 1, the State Department announced that there was, in fact, a Soviet brigade, and Carter demanded the Soviets remove it. In the end, the Soviets refused to do so, claiming that the military forces had been in Cuba since the end of the missile crisis. This, along with Soviet aggression elsewhere, led to the collapse of the second Strategic Arms Limitations Talks and the possibility of a renewed nuclear arms race.

Although the Soviet Union's military forces invaded Afghanistan on December 24, well after Gasch's second ruling, Soviet involvement in

Afghanistan was a headline news matter. Between June and September, Soviet Army helicopters dropped napalm on rural villages, and Islamist rebels killed Soviet military advisers as well as some of their family members. Over the summer, rebel forces besieged an Afghan military base. In a series of events eerily reminiscent of post-Diem South Vietnam, Afghanistan became a growing quagmire for the Soviets. By early August, Afghanistan army units had mutinied against their government, and Brezhnev sent forty-five hundred military and civilian defense advisers into the country. The *Washington Post* reported that Soviet military advisers aided the forces loyal to Afghanistan's president, Noor Taraki, defeat a rebelling force. In spite of Soviet help, in mid-September, one of the rebelling military units attacked the capitol palace and deposed Taraki. One week earlier, Brezhnev promised full support to Taraki, and the possibility of Soviet military intervention grew even though Taraki's successor, Hafizullah Amin, was a fervent communist. The Kremlin next backed Amin, though Soviet agents assassinated him in late December.

And then there was Iran. In early July, Khomeini expelled American journalists. On July 29, the *New York Times*, *Washington Post*, and other major newspapers, as well as the CBS evening news informed the public that the CIA had failed to warn of the Iranian revolt against the Shah. The *Times* noted that Khomeini had published a book years earlier on his goal to turn Iran into a theocracy, yet the intelligence agencies only learned of the book after he assumed power. It was as though the West had only learned about communism during the Cold War even though Karl Marx had published *Das Kapital* and *The Communist Manifesto* considerably earlier. The previous day, the newspaper headlined that tens of thousands of Iranians demonstrated in Tehran, shouting, "Death to the leftists, Carter, Sadat, and Begin." By August 1, Khomeini's government seized local newspapers that had reported unfavorably in the eyes of his government, and twenty-two journalists were sentenced to death. Besides expelling American journalists, the Iranian government started to remove European journalists as well.

It appeared that no force within Iran could counter the strength of the Shia Islamists. Even ethnic minorities who had held out against prior attempts to destroy their leadership had little success in holding on to their lands. Kurdish insurgents fighting against Khomeini's regime were crushed by Iranian military forces. So, too, were the small numbers of ethnic Turkmen and Baluchis subjugated. Other ethnic and religious groups faced persecution as well. Religious leaders in Iran's historic Jewish population as well its Baha'i faith were arrested, tortured, and killed. After three Lebanese Shia men hijacked an Alitalia DC-8 and demanded that the Lebanese government release their leader, Khomeini welcomed the hijackers in Tehran. And, Khomeini expressed solidarity with the Palestinian Liberation Organization. It became increasingly clear that a new wave of terrorism was likely to occur as a result of Khomeini's support for Iran's perceived enemies.

The Senate Acts and Gasch Issues Goldwater a Favorable Ruling

On June 7, the *New York Times* ran a headline that read, "Senate Rebukes Carter over Ending of Taiwan Pact." In taking Gasch's "hint," the Senate indeed worked quickly to establish the requisite standing that Gasch had noted was needed before his court could take up the substantive issues in Goldwater's suit. In the July 1979 issue of its journal, the American Bar Association observed that while Goldwater's suit had been "snagged" on the question of standing, Gash left open the possibility for reconsideration. To the bar association, Gasch had purposefully telegraphed the means for Goldwater to continue on in the suit. In the House of Representatives, George Hansen, Robert Stump, Robert Bauman, and John Ashbrook introduced resolutions similar to the original sense of the Senate Resolution that had foundered prior to Gasch's ruling dismissing Goldwater's (and their) lawsuit. The House, however, did vote on any of these resolutions. The Senate was more proactive.

After Gasch's dismissal of Goldwater's suit, the Senate voted in favor of adopting a proposed resolution by Senator Harry Byrd's (I-VA) that read, "It is the sense of the Senate that approval of the United States Senate is required to terminate any mutual defense treaty between the United States and another nation." Byrd's resolution was hardly a departure from the Dole-Stone Amendment of the prior year. On the one hand, the Senate voted in favor of Byrd's original amendment prior to the Frank Church–led Foreign Relations Committee's attempts at rewording it. On the other, Byrd's resolution did not note whether the

Senate's view was prospective or retrospective. Had the resolution been prospective, it would not have applied at all to Carter's actions. The resolution was simply a statement by the majority of the Senate that believed Carter was at least required to submit the termination of the treaty to the Senate for a vote. It was not binding law. Yet Goldwater's position was strengthened by the Senate in other ways during the debates on Byrd's resolution. Notably, two more senators who were not a part of the lawsuit insisted that Carter had acted illegally. Senators John Warner (R-VA) and Walter Huddleston (D-KY), in pressing for the resolution, argued that it was essential to preserve Taiwan's democracy as well as the Constitution's role for the Senate.

The Senate also received competing resolutions from Senators Church and Goldwater. Goldwater's resolution claimed that Carter had violated the Constitution. Church, who served as chair of the Senate Foreign Relations Committee, proposed a resolution that did not condemn Carter's actions or call for a full Senate vote on any substantive matter. Instead, Church's resolution warned, "A court action could set back Washington's China policy, which . . . most of the country supported." Church explained to his constituents, "We have stopped viewing China and Russia as a monolith and now perceive them as separate countries, often with conflicting goals and foreign policies." He also urged people to consider that normalization would erode Brezhnev's expansionist policies, and concluded, "The Soviet Union, for instance, is very concerned with any friendly approaches we make that improve our relations with China. And, from the very practical perspective of foreign trade, the PRC can be an extremely important new market for trade."

The majority of the Senate, by a vote of fifty-nine to thirty-five, voted to later consider Byrd's resolution and did not take up either Goldwater's or Church's proposed resolutions. Byrd's amendment at least condemned the principle of unilateral presidential action in treaty termination, and Goldwater believed this was enough to petition Gasch to reconsider the issue of standing. On October 2, Goldwater filed a motion to Gasch to reverse his prior ruling. The Federal Rules of Civil Procedure apply to most noncriminal trials in US district courts and are designed to ensure uniformity and efficiency in the court system. Rather than appeal directly to the Court of Appeals for the District of Columbia—the linear step in an appeal—Goldwater wisely determined that it was best for the district court to review its earlier rulings based on the Senate's action with the Byrd Resolution. Goldwater's decision, moreover, comported with Rule 59(e) of the Federal Rules of Civil Procedure.

There was nothing unsavory about Goldwater's actions. In 1962, the Court determined, in *Foman v. Davis*, that it was preferable to have an aggrieved party file a motion to a district court for reconsideration of a ruling than advance a cause to an appellate court. *Foman* was not, to be sure, an appeal arising out of a challenge to presidential authority. Rather, that appeal came to the Court from a daughter's challenge to her mother's will. Rule 59(e) does not require that new evidence be introduced, though in the case of Goldwater's appeal, Congress had taken action in response to Gasch's June 6 ruling, and Gasch treated the resolution as evidence. In considering whether to grant Goldwater a rehearing, Gasch concluded that while the vote in favor of Byrd's amendment was not a complete renunciation of Carter's actions, the Senate had implicitly rejected Church's resolution and therefore the majority expressed a disapproval of Carter.

Carter, through Attorney General Benjamin Civiletti, continued to argue that Goldwater lacked standing to challenge the treaty termination, and even if standing were granted, Goldwater's suit was a nonjusticiable political question. Carter further argued that because presidents possessed an authority to recognize foreign governments, and the Court, during Franklin Roosevelt's presidency, acknowledged this authority in regard to a unilateral diplomatic recognition of the Soviet Union, then the derecognition of a government was a corollary authority vested solely in the presidency. Added to this argument was a further claim that because the normalization process was already taking effect, if the district court were to rule against the administration, presidential authority over foreign policy would be weakened in all foreign policy matters. Implicit in this warning was that if the court were to rule in Goldwater's favor, Carter would be unable to quickly respond to the Soviet Union over Afghanistan's or Iran's provocations against the United States and its allies. His administration specifically insisted that the "unusual need for unquestioning adherence to a political decision already made," and the "potentiality of embarrassment from multifarious pronouncements by various departments on one issue," required the federal courts to abstain from ruling on Goldwater's suit. In other words, Carter urged the court to consider that even if the administration were in the constitutional wrong, the court should take into consideration the potential damage to presidential authority in foreign policy if it were to rule on a wrongful act by overturning it. Such an argument was the very essence of an imperial presidency that the administration had campaigned against in 1976, and that scholars had warned the nation about.

Gasch would disagree with almost the entirety of Carter's position. On October 17, 1979, he issued his second decision and determined that Goldwater met the requirements of the appellate court's four-part standing test, and that the suit against Carter did not run afoul of *Baker* on the political question test. As an inconsequential victory for Carter, Gasch continued to reject the proposition that Thurmond or Curtis enjoyed special standing simply because they voted in favor of the Mutual Defense Treaty in 1954. This decision, in effect, maintained the Fourth Circuit's holding in *Harrington v. Schlesinger.* And he did not restate the facts leading up to the lawsuit, other than to accept that Byrd's resolution had been an affirmative statement of the Senate and therefore the issue became justiciable. While Gasch conceded that Byrd's resolution merely expressed "a sense of the Senate" and could hardly be considered decisive, when coupled with the fact that the Senate did not disapprove of individual legislative suits, this was enough of a basis to permit consideration of the suit on the merits.

In terms of the political question doctrine, Gasch concluded that because there was a difference between the president's and Congress' foreign policy authorities, the judiciary possessed the ability to resolve a constitutional question when the two political branches clashed. He conceded that this was not true in all instances, such as a presidential determination as to when a foreign group is a legitimate representative of another nation. But he also reasoned that although there was a potential legislative remedy such as impeachment, this did not prevent judicial branch intervention. The basis for Gasch's conclusion was that he believed treaty termination was a shared power between the political branches. "Unlike its careful allocation of the power to enter into treaties, the Constitution contains no specific reference to the manner in which treaties are to be terminated," Gasch began. "Nor is there any definitive evidence of the intentions of the Framers." Added to this constitutional silence, Gasch believed that because there was a lack of consensus among constitutional law scholars over Congress's role in treaty termination, it was critical for the court to settle the dispute between Goldwater and Carter.

Gasch found Carter's other claims of executive branch authority unpersuasive. Carter had argued that the removal of the United States from a treaty was akin to the removal of cabinet officers. Perhaps wondering whether Carter was seeking a judicial referendum of his recent decision to force the resignation of half of the cabinet secretaries, Gasch responded that the presidential power to remove cabinet officers from their position had, at best, a minimal impact on the nation. In contrast, he countered that the termination of a treaty "impacts upon the substantial role of Congress in foreign affairs especially in the context of a mutual defense pact involving the potential exercise of congressional war powers and is a contradiction rather than a corollary of the Executive's enforcement obligation." In response to Carter's claim that a president is the sole spokesman for the nation's foreign policy, Gasch replied that being the sole communicator of foreign policy and sole organ of it were two vastly different matters. Gasch found Carter's claim that because a president had the constitutional authority to recognize the legitimacy of a foreign government, a president could withdraw recognition also irrelevant. While Gasch recognized that in 1942 the Court had upheld the president's authority to recognize a foreign government as "a modest implied power," he determined that the ability to terminate treaties, even when done in conjunction with the recognition of a foreign government, was hardly a modest act.

As a signal warning not only to Carter but also to future presidents who would assert unilateral authority over foreign policy, Gasch adopted Justice Frankfurter's cautionary words from *Youngstown Sheet and Tube v. Sawyer* that "the accretion of dangerous power does not come in a day. It does come, however slowly, from the generative force of unchecked disregard of the restrictions that fence in even the most disinterested assertion of authority." Because of the Constitution's silence in treaty termination, Gasch determined, the framework of the Constitution had to be assessed as a whole. Gasch did not simply rely on his own legal acumen; he also sought scholarly guidance.

International law has been shaped by many scholars, but in the traverse of Goldwater's appeal in the district and lower appellate courts, one scholar appears to have had a pronounced influence. By the time Goldwater's suit came before Gasch, Columbia University law professor Louis Henkin was one of the leading international law scholars, so it is unsurprising that Gasch referenced his work. Born in Russia, Henkin immigrated to New York City as a young child and graduated from Harvard Law School in 1940. Between clerking for Judge Learned Hand on the Second Circuit and Justice Felix Frankfurter on the Court, Henkin fought in the European theater during World War II, earning the Silver Star for bravery in combat. He later served in the State Department and then taught at Columbia University. As of 1978 he had authored influential treatises on war powers, presidential and congressional authority in international law, and human rights. For this reason, Judge Earl O'Connor referenced Henkin's work in determining that Carter did not need the Senate's consent to return the contested medieval regalia in US custody to Hungary. And Congress had used Henkin's expertise on the issue of treaty termination. That Gasch relied on Henkin is evident not only in the decision but also in his judicial notes, which now reside at Georgetown University's law school.

Henkin did not, to be sure, recognize a presidential authority such as Carter had exerted in regard to either the regalia or a sole presidential authority for treaty termination. He recognized that the existence of this authority remained an open question not only because of the Constitution's silence but also because the Court's treatment of history in regard to treaties was both limited and fractured. But he recognized that certain powers conferred to Congress such as the authority to declare war and enable commerce and the legislative role in the national defense might support an argument for greater congressional oversight in treaty enforcement or the lack thereof. In the first decision in which he ruled against Goldwater in June 1976, Gasch cited Henkin on the issue of the political question doctrine. In the later decision in which he ruled in favor of Goldwater, Gasch cited Henkin four times for the purpose of highlighting the possibility that there was a Senate role in treaty termination and that where a treaty was not wholly self-executing—meaning it had required additional legislation for implementation—there was a greater argument for the Senate. To Gasch, the Mutual Defense Treaty fell into this category as Henkin had described it. Perhaps highlighting the influence of one of the the nation's leading international law scholars might appear as a distraction, but Henkin's influence continued into the phase of Goldwater's suit before the US Court of Appeals for the District of Columbia.

In assessing the Constitution's framework in light of the allocation of powers for a treaty termination, Gasch saved his opinion of Carter's actions for the end of his decision. "At least under the circumstances of this case involving a significant mutual defense treaty with a faithful ally, who has not violated the terms of the agreement," Gasch penned, "any decision of the United States to terminate that treaty must be made with the advice and consent of the Senate or the approval of both houses of Congress. That decision cannot be made by the President alone." Thus, Gasch had conferred on Taiwan the title of a "faithful ally" and determined Goldwater's arguments to be constitutionally sound and Carter's actions to be unconstitutional. In this first phase of the litigation, Goldwater and the conservatives achieved a victory over Carter and his allies. Yet, in conformance with Congress's historic legislative mandate, previous Congresses had created avenues to appeal, and other courts would hear the challenge.

CHAPTER 4

The Court of Appeals, the Merits of the Case, and Conflict with Iran

Judge Oliver Gasch's ruling in favor of Goldwater dominated the news for just one day. On October 18, 1979, the *New York Times* front page read, "Judge Rules Carter Cannot Bypass Congress in Ending Taiwan Treaty." The *Washington Post* headlined, "President Carter Violated the Constitution by Unilaterally Terminating the United States' Mutual Defense Treaty with Taiwan." The CBS evening news broadcast as its top television story that Carter lost in court and the treaty with Taiwan was safe for the present. The *Chicago Tribune* reported that Goldwater lauded Judge Oliver Gasch. "I am elated at the court's ruling," Goldwater ebulliently declared. "It is the first time in this nation's almost two-hundred years of constitutional history that a judge has ruled on the power of treaty termination." One day later, Carter informed the nation that he would appeal Gasch's ruling to the Court of Appeals for the District of Columbia.

Gasch's ruling received mixed reviews in the Senate. Majority leader Robert Byrd (D-WV) expressed doubts that the appellate court would uphold the ruling. So, too, did Carter's ally at the helm of the Senate Foreign Relations Committee, Frank Church. Minority leader Howard Baker (R-TN) asked that the Senate hold a nonbinding vote specific to the issue of the Mutual Defense Treaty's termination, but he too believed that Gasch had gone too far in his ruling because the Senate had not yet held a formal vote on termination.

On November 13, 1979, Assistant Attorney General John Harmon argued to an eight-judge, en banc panel of the Court of Appeals for the District of Columbia to overturn Gasch's decision. Harmon had clerked for Justice Lewis Powell after graduating from Duke University's law school and had a sense that the Court—if it reviewed the decision—would determine it exceeded the bounds of judicial review based on standing. Five other Justice Department attorneys joined Harmon on the appeal, including Robert E. Kopp. One year earlier, Kopp had represented Carter against the congressmen who tried to prevent transfer of the canal to Panama. Goldwater was represented by attorneys who possessed impressive credentials, including Eugene Rostow, a former undersecretary of state in President Lyndon Johnson's administration and a vigorous opponent of détente. While Rostow served as "of counsel" to the legal team, J. Terry Emerson (a former Senate counsel), Daniel J. Popeo (the founder of the influential conservative-leaning Washington Legal Foundation), and Paul Kamenar represented Goldwater in the appellate court as well as before the Supreme Court. Popeo and Kamenar, like Kopp, took part in the Panama Canal litigation in the Court of Appeals for the District of Columbia, albeit in opposition to Carter. One attorney Goldwater had wanted decided not to join in the lawsuit. Goldwater had earlier personally lobbied for Stanford Law professor Gerald Gunther to head his legal team, but Gunther demurred, having already communicated with Judge Carl McGowan on the court of appeals over the issue of presidential treaty termination. By the time of the lawsuit, Gunther, a former law clerk for both Judge Learned Hand and Chief Justice Earl Warren, was one of the more prominent constitutional law scholars in the nation. Because he articulated to McGowan that although he believed Goldwater possessed standing in a general sense, Carter was in the right on the matter of presidential power, he decided to remain apart from the litigation and not risk McGowan's recusal.

At the core of Carter's claims of presidential authority to terminate treaties was an argument that in twenty-six instances of treaty termination, a president had acted without Congress's permission thirteen times. Although it is unclear as to why Carter's legal team arrived at the number twenty-six, this undersold their position as almost double that number of treaties had been terminated. Emerson countered that a total of fifty-two treaties or treaty provisions had, in US history, been terminated and that four of the times Carter cited had, in fact, been accomplished after Congress specifically approved termination. As for the other instances of treaty termination, Emerson argued that varying degrees of legislative approval preceded the presidential action.

Senator Baker opted to file an amicus brief with the court of appeals.

That Baker did so bears on the role of the Senate in the court process. The previous December he had announced that he would run for the presidency, and when queried on his position regarding Goldwater's suit, he responded that he did not oppose normalization of relations with China, only that Carter had not sought the Senate's approval to do so. The term "amicus" means "friend of the court." Amicus briefs allow a person or organization who is not a part of an appeal to file a legal argument in an effort to educate the court on an important matter. While persons or organizations may have a financial interest in the outcome of an appeal, the primary constraint on amicus practice is a prohibition that the named parties to a lawsuit not work in concert with the amici. In this instance, Baker was to argue to the appellate court that Goldwater was in the wrong in claiming that a judicial remedy was possible on the basis of a constitutional question, while Carter was also in error for his claims of unilateral treaty termination power.

Baker was not alone in filing the amicus brief, but he appears to have led in the effort by first seeking advice from the Senate's legal counsel on how best to protect the Senate's interests. On November 7, 1979, the Senate's legal counsel advised Baker that a bipartisan effort to urge the court of appeals not to define the Senate's treaty termination authority as a matter of constitutional law was critical to preserving the Senate's power. Baker and Robert Byrd also agreed that it was important to argue to the appellate court that its judges issue a "sweeping statement to the effect that all questions touching foreign relations are political questions." In other words, they worried that if the appellate court were pushed to define a constitutional constraint in treaty termination, it would weaken Congress in the long term because it would enable a president to exit treaties without congressional consent, and the only avenue left for Congress would be for the House to initiate impeachment proceedings. And if the court determined that a political question prevented review over all foreign policy matters, impeachment would become more commonplace.

There was a bipartisan consensus in the Senate for the appellate court not to issue a broad decision that would shut the door to judicial review in future congressional appeals as well. Part of this had to do with a fear that the court would narrow the doctrine of congressional standing into a nullity. Again, if the federal court were to be closed to Congress, the legislative branch would be corralled into facing the choice of an impeachment or acquiescing to a presidential action viewed as unlawful. For this reason, the Senate amicus brief asked the judges to confine their analysis to the Mutual Defense Treaty's provisions and whether the positive vote on Senator Harry Byrd's resolution conferred standing. Baker, Byrd, Warren Magnuson (D-WA), Claiborne Pell (D-RI), and Mark O. Hatfield (R-OR) signed the brief. These were some of the more senior senators; in particular, Magnusson was president pro tempore, the second-highest-ranking official of that body.

The amicus brief was to prove influential in the appellate court's decision. Importantly, no judge voted to reverse on the basis of a nonjusticiable political question doctrine. But not all the senators who signed onto the Byrd Resolution agreed to sign the amicus. Secretary of State Cyrus Vance assured a number of senators that the United States would continue to be locked into several agreements with Taiwan, ensuring the island's freedom from China. "Since all other countries which had previously normalized relations with the PRC had without exception taken the position that all their bilateral agreements with Taiwan became null and void simultaneously with the severance of their diplomatic relations with Taiwan, we believed it was essential we made clear that there would be no hiatus in relationship and that the agreements with Taiwan continued to have legal validity despite the withdrawal of recognition," Vance informed Senator Jacob Javits (R-NY). Javits, who had supported Carter's foreign policies, fretted about Taiwan's status to the point that he commissioned a study of the various obligations the United States might still have with the island. What ultimately stopped him from signing the amicus brief to the court was Vance's assurance that even if the court of appeals sided with the Carter administration, the Taiwan Relations Act legally enabled the United States to militarily defend Taiwan if China attacked.

The Court of Appeals for the District of Columbia

The Court of Appeals for the District of Columbia has been called the nation's second most important federal court, ranking only behind the US Supreme Court. Christopher P. Banks, in his *Judicial Politics in the D.C.*

Circuit, noted that at the time of *Goldwater*, the appellate court "consisted of several judicial all-stars," with a "core of unusually gifted judges." The judges participating in the en banc panel did not include those judges on senior status but did include J. Skelly Wright, Harold Leventhal, Edward Tamm, Carl McGowan, Spottswood Robinson, George MacKinnon, Malcom Wilkey, and Patricia Wald. Although these judges represented a cross section of the nation's jurisprudential spectrum, there was, with the exception of MacKinnon, a noticeable lack of affiliation, for or against Carter, based on presidential appointment or prior political service. And the court would depart from the normal panel and determine the issue as a whole, or en banc.

An en banc panel is not the norm in the federal courts of appeal, but it is also not unheard of. The term "en banc" is from the French, rather than Latin—in itself not the norm in American law—and it means "all of the judges." Usually, the nation's federal appellate courts convene three-judge panels as a method of deciding cases. Because the nation's appellate courts may have more than ten judges appointed to them, not counting judges on senior status, an en banc panel can be quite large. Senior status is a form of retirement, and judges on senior status may decide cases if the court is overloaded with work; although they cannot not sit en banc, nothing prevents the senior judges from trying to exert their influence on the serving judges. Two of the judges, David Bazelon and Charles Fahy, had opined on Goldwater's argument, but Fahy died months before the appellate court heard argument and Bazelon seems not to have played a role. When a federal appellate court meets en banc, it usually does so on a party's motion to reconsider a previous ruling from a three-judge panel. In rarer circumstances, an en banc panel might convene without first having a three-judge panel issue a decision so as to expedite the full array of an appeal to the Supreme Court. In *Goldwater*, the en banc occurred too rapidly have the decision advanced to the Supreme Court in the likelihood that the losing party would appeal. Equally important, the need for a ruling was urgent as a result of the oncoming treaty termination date. Two of the judges, Abner Mikva and Roger Robb, recused themselves from the decision, leaving eight judges to decide the issue. Judges will recuse themselves from voting on a case for a variety of reasons, but one of the most common is that the judge has a personal interest in the outcome or a relationship with one of the parties that would create an appearance of a judiciary that was neither fair nor impartial.

Wright, Leventhal, McGowan, Tamm, Robinson, Wilkey, and MacKinnon were already veterans of two significant en banc decisions centering on the executive branch. In 1971, in a lawsuit against the *Washington Post* (and in a separate lawsuit against the *New York Times* in the Court of Appeals for the Second Circuit), President Richard Nixon attempted to stop the publication of a vast historical study on the US government's role in the escalation of the Vietnam Conflict. In what was known colloquially as the Pentagon Papers case, the Court of Appeals for the District of Columbia upheld the *Washington Post*'s First Amendment right to publish government documents. In that instance, Wilkey and MacKinnon dissented, while the others, including Bazelon, crafted a decision favoring freedom of the press. The Supreme Court upheld the majority and overturned the Second Circuit, which had reached the opposite result. Two years later, in other Watergate-related cases, the District of Columbia appellate court issued en banc decisions requiring the Nixon administration to provide evidence to the House Judiciary Committee as well as enabling the transfer of grand jury transcripts to the committee.

The appellate court had also already decided on one challenge to Carter's foreign policy actions. In *Edwards v. Carter*, Fahy and McGowan ruled that the sixty members of the House of Representatives lacked standing to bring suit to stop the transfer of the canal to Panama. MacKinnon dissented from their decision. The district court that first heard the lawsuit determined, in February 1978, that the representatives' argument that Carter and the Senate, in attempting to agree to a treaty that disposed of United States property, had violated the Constitution because Article IV gives to both houses the authority to determine whether the disposal of federal property may occur. On April 16, 1978, the appellate court upheld the lower court's ruling but on different grounds. Fahy and McGowan determined that the purpose for the clause in Article IV on property disposal had to do with protecting the property of the states and not the treaty-based renunciation of title to overseas properties. Moreover, Fahy and McGowan concluded that while the representatives might be able to articulate an actual injury, the injury itself was too ambiguous and the property disposal provision too remote from the treaty clause to confer standing. However, the language Fahy and McGowan used in *Edwards* has relevance to the appellate court's *Goldwater* decision seventeen months later. "The transfer of property contemplated in the current instance is part of a broader effort in the conduct of our foreign affairs to strengthen relations with another country, and indeed with the whole of Latin America," Fahy and McGowan concluded. "The Framers in their wisdom have made the treaty power available to the President, the chief executant of foreign relations under our constitutional scheme, by and with the advice and consent of two-thirds of the members of the Senate present, as a means of accomplishing these public purposes." Thus, McGowan acknowledged the existence—and he deemed it important—of an unhindered presidential foreign policy power in matters where the Constitution was silent.

Within a day of Carter's appeal against Gasch's decision, Chief Judge Wright urged the appellate court to vote for an en banc decision rather than a normal three-judge panel. Had the appellate judges not unanimously voted for an en banc review, Wright and Judges Abner Mikva and Edward Tamm would have been assigned to the case. However, because Mikva had recused himself, it was unclear who might have substituted in for him. The decision to advance to an en banc panel was not unanimous as Tamm and Wilkey voted against doing so. Nonetheless, the requisite number of votes were obtained for en banc review. Wright then issued an order for the district court to produce a complete transcript of the arguments made before it. He also established a deadline of November 5 for the receipt of legal briefs from both Carter and Goldwater and set November 8 as a deadline for response briefs from both sides. On November 8, the Department of Justice asked for a short extension of time. Emblematic of the crisis with Iran, the White House memorandum to Wright stated that the counsel who drafted the government's briefs needed the permission of the assistant attorney general to file, but that officer was unavailable and "at the White House because of the Iranian crisis."

Shortly after issuing the scheduling order, the International Law Institute at Georgetown University forwarded an amicus brief arguing that the issue before the court was inherently political and therefore constituted a nonjusticiable issue. This amicus brief aligned with the White House's position. On November 8, Wright, with the support of his fellow judges, denied amicus counsel the ability to provide an oral argument to the court. He also advised the judges that there was likely to be an audience beyond the appellate court's normal capacity. Three days later, the parties argued their positions to the en banc appellate court.

On November 15, while the appellate court deliberated, the Senate tried to take up the issue as to whether the Byrd Resolution was retrospective or prospective. If the Senate determined that Byrd's resolution was retrospective, there would be a clear statement to the appellate court that the Senate believed Carter had acted unconstitutionally. If the resolution were to be considered prospective, all the Senate would have accomplished was to give a warning to Carter, as well as future presidents, not to unilaterally revoke treaties. Thus, in addition to the Senate's amicus brief encouraging the court to rule on the specific language of the Mutual Defense Treaty and avoid sweeping doctrinal statements, the Senate's inaction on Byrd's resolution left the judges wondering whether the majority of the Senate believed there was a constitutional crisis created by Carter's actions. The court took the unusual step of seeking clarification from the Senate's parliamentarian, who responded that "no final action has been taken on Senate Resolution 15, and the Senate may reconsider in the future." Thus, the appellate court went on to decide the appeal without the benefit of a Senate statement on an important matter

The appellate court issued its decision on November 30. Judge Harold Leventhal participated in the discussions and voted with the en banc majority, but he died unexpectedly before the decision's publication. One day after oral arguments, Carter ordered a freeze on the government of Iran's funds held by US banks. Between November 4 and the end of the month, Congress almost unanimously backed Carter's efforts to confront Iran, as it became clear that he might need the full constitutional commander in chief authorities exercised in past presidencies during times of international conflict. Simply, Iran had become an explosive issue, and its government was clearly on a "war footing."

On August 8, 1988, the *New York Times* characterized the life of Judge J. Skelly Wright in an obituary headline that read: "A Liberal in Most Eyes, but Southerners Called Him a Traitor." Four months before issuing his concurrence in *Goldwater*, Wright had authored a decision for a three-judge panel that concluded that Nixon, along with national security adviser Henry Kissinger, H. R. Haldeman, and former attorney general

John Mitchell could be sued for the illegal wiretap of Mortin Halperin, a subordinate of Kissinger's on the White House national security staff. The case went to the heart of the intersection of foreign policy and national security on the one side and liability for governmental malfeasance on the other. Its origins are important to the question of presidential power to act in secrecy. After the *New York Times* reported on a secretive bombing campaign in Cambodia, Kissinger asked the Federal Bureau of Investigation to clandestinely record Halperin's conversations as well as those of his wife. A district court judge sided with Halperin against Nixon, Haldeman, and Mitchell, but not Kissinger. The three-judge panel, in *Halperin v. Kissinger*, upheld the lower court, except on the question of Kissinger's immunity from liability. Although the appellate court did not conclude that Nixon or Kissinger was guilty of wrongdoing, the decision, if left intact, enabled a jury or a judge serving as a fact finder to do so. In essence, Wright did not believe in a presidency immune from civil liability because this would place a presidency above the law

Wright was a pro–civil rights judge. He grew up in New Orleans, graduated from Loyola of New Orleans Law School, served as an assistant US attorney as well as in the Coast Guard in World War II, and in 1947, President Truman appointed him as US attorney for Louisiana. As a federal prosecutor, Wright oversaw the prosecutions of members of Huey Long's political machine. Although Long was assassinated in 1935, his political machine dominated Louisiana's politics into the early 1950s. In 1950, Truman appointed Wright to a district court judgeship in the Eastern District of Louisiana, and in 1962 President John F. Kennedy appointed him to the Court of Appeals for the District of Columbia. As a result of his pro–civil rights decisions, he was given the nickname "Judas Wright" in the South, and the Ku Klux Klan burned crosses on his front yard. Kennedy had considered appointing Wright to the Court of Appeals for the Fifth Circuit, but segregationist senators led by James O. Eastland (R-MS) informed Attorney General Robert Kennedy they would block a vote. The southern senators, however, chose not to derail Wright's appointment to the DC court. In 1967, Wright issued a desegregation order to the District of Columbia's public school system, which became a model order known as the Wright Decree.

Outside of civil rights enforcement and in addition to his treatment of Nixon and Kissinger, Wright was not an advocate of executive branch supremacy. In 1971, he dissented from a three-judge panel's decision to issue a temporary restraining order to the *Washington Post* over the Pentagon Papers case. Wright penned, "To allow a government to suppress free speech simply through a system of bureaucratic classification would sell our heritage, far, far too cheaply." An en banc panel, in reversing the decision, sided with him. Two years later he voted to uphold Judge John J. Sirica's order to the Nixon administration to turn over the contested White House recordings related to the Watergate scandal. Wright was also a prolific legal scholar who wrote on subjects such as judicial rulemaking, the relationship between the First Amendment and campaign financing, and civil rights and school desegregation. During the time the appellate court deliberated on Goldwater's appeal, Wright authored a defense of affirmative action programs in the *University of Chicago Law Review*, but he also sided with Carter's decision to force Iranian students to report their status to the Justice Department.

Carl McGowan was a graduate of Columbia University's law school, a World War II veteran, and a Northwestern University Law School professor; he had worked on Illinois governor Adlai Stevenson's 1952 presidential campaign and served as an assistant to him. From 1936 until 1939, he was in private practice in New York and then joined the Northwestern University law faculty. After the Japanese attack on Pearl Harbor, McGowan was commissioned as a naval officer. Following a stint as general counsel for the Office of War Mobilization, at war's end he returned to Northwestern. In 1962, Kennedy nominated McGowan to the appellate court, but Congress did not act on the nomination before it recessed, and Kennedy resubmitted the nomination the next year, this time successfully. McGowan, like Wright, was not an unbridled advocate for executive branch supremacy. In 1977, he authored a Freedom of Information Act decision against Henry Kissinger that further enabled citizens to obtain government information against the government's objections.

President Lyndon Johnson nominated Harold Leventhal to the appellate court in 1965. Leventhal and McGowan were classmates at Columbia University's law school. Leventhal began his legal career by clerking for Chief Justice Harlan Stone and then worked as a government lawyer. In World War II he served as a Coast Guard officer and became a Nuremberg war crimes prosecutor under Justice Robert Jackson. In 1952, the national Democratic Party hired him as its general counsel, and he remained in that position until Johnson appointed him to the appellate court in 1964. When the Senate Judiciary Committee voted unanimously to forward Leventhal to the Senate for a vote, there was no dissension against the nomination in the Senate. Like Wright and McGowan, Leventhal voted to uphold significant federal civil rights enforcement programs. He also authored several scholarly articles on a wide range of legal subjects and became known as "the principal author of the modern law of administrative government." One year into his judicial tenure, he wrote a majority opinion overturning three contempt convictions for members of a women's peace group subpoenaed to testify before the House Un-American Activities Committee. Leventhal generally sided with presidential authority over the military, particularly in regard to upholding policies that discriminated against gays and lesbians. The last issue that he took part in prior to his death arose from the Carter administration's attempt to curb demonstrations against the Shah. Although Leventhal took part in the deliberations on Goldwater's challenge to Carter and cast his vote with the majority, he did not live to see the actual decision published to the public.

Johnson also appointed Spottswood William Robinson III to the District Court for the District of Columbia in 1964 and the appellate court in 1966. Robinson was confirmed by a vote of seventy-three to seventeen. Thurmond and Goldwater, along with the pro-segregationist bloc, voted against his confirmation. After graduating first in the Howard University Law School class of 1939, Robinson had a distinguished career as a civil rights advocate arguing cases alongside Thurgood Marshall, including *Brown v. Board of Education*. Between 1961 and 1963, he served on President Kennedy's Civil Rights Commission, at the same time he was dean at Howard University's law school. On the bench Robinson authored a decision enabling private citizens to sue for libel against journalists who mixed in disputable "facts" with opinion in a defamatory manner. He sided with Wright, McGowan, and Leventhal on school desegregation cases, but he dissented from a decision in which the Department of the Navy was permitted to administratively discharge sailors suspected of homosexual conduct without substantial proof that the conduct occurred or undermined the navy's ability to function. By the time of Goldwater's appeal, Robinson had a reputation as an ally of indigent persons, including crafting a decision that waived court fees for poor citizens filing for divorce.

Carter appointed Patricia Wald to the Court in 1979. A 1959 Yale Law graduate, Wald clerked for Judge Jerome Frank at the time of Ethel and Julius Rosenberg's appeals after their espionage convictions. While a judge's decision is her or her own, it is worth noting that in working on the Rosenberg appeals, Wald was exposed to judicial decision-making in one of the most contentious and controversial death penalty trials and appeals in US history. Following her clerkship with Judge Frank, she worked at the influential Washington, DC, law firm Arnold and Porter, and then in the Johnson administration. During the early years of Carter's presidency, she was an assistant attorney general. Wald was confirmed to the court of appeals four months before hearing Carter's challenge to Gasch's ruling. Her confirmation was not welcomed by conservatives. Senators Paul Laxalt (R-NV), Strom Thurmond, and Alan K. Simpson (R-WY) opposed her for allegedly being "too liberal." Joining them was Gordon Humphrey (R-NH), who accused her of "wild and wacky" ideas regarding children's rights. In 1986, when Wald became the chief circuit court judge, the *Washington Post* noted that she was well known as a judicial liberal and her advocacy of children's rights was unparalleled by that of any other judge. After her judicial service, she went on to adjudicate cases on the International Criminal Tribunal for the former Yugoslavia and became a leading scholar in both intelligence law and mental disability law.

The appellate court's moderate to conservative judges included Edward A. Tamm, who graduated from Georgetown University's law school in 1930 and served as an assistant to FBI director J. Edgar Hoover from 1940 to 1948. President Truman appointed Tamm to the district court in 1948, and Johnson elevated him to the appellate court in 1965. Although Hoover backed Tamm's appointment, the Republican-led Senate initially refused to act on it. Truman used a recess to secure Tamm's judgeship, knowing that the Republicans would have voted in favor of him under other circumstances, which is, in fact, what occurred. As a district court judge, Tamm ordered the National Labor Relations Board to objectively resolve disputes between rival unions after he found that the board unfairly favored one union over another. He also refused to rule in favor of actors and playwrights who had been targeted by means of an anticommunist blacklist. While Tamm did not provide relief to persons accused of communist leanings, he dismissed contempt indictments of suspected Chicago Mafia leaders called as witnesses before a Senate committee after he determined that the committee had exceeded its authority. In 1955, Tamm ruled that the military did not possess court-martial jurisdiction over civilian spouses who accompanied their husbands overseas. The Court would later adopt Tamm's rationale in *Reid v. Covert*, a decision that significantly narrowed executive branch control over US citizens residing on overseas military bases. Tamm also determined that the Federal Communications Commission's ban on seven words considered to be pornographic constituted an unsupportable censorship and therefore the ban was a violation of the First Amendment's right to free speech. Although Tamm was viewed as collegial by his fellow judges, at times he was outspoken against the court's liberal wing.

Appointed by Nixon in 1969, George MacKinnon was perhaps the court's most conservative judge at the time of Carter's appeal from Gasch's decision. It appears that some of his reputation has been negatively shaped by Judge Laurence H. Silberman, a senior judge on the appellate court who died in late 2022. In an oral history of his judicial experience, Silberman recalled an instance in which he observed MacKinnon, while serving as a judge, discussing legislation with Nixon. If true, this would have been inappropriate, but Silberman portrayed MacKinnon as a "political hack," even though those were not his precise words. MacKinnon was not a "hack," but his views were occasionally at odds with the majority of his peers on the appellate court.

MacKinnon later recalled that when he went to the court "Bazelon and Wright were masticating the criminal law," and he saw it as his duty to put an end to it. He was a national security hawk who insisted, in his dissent in *Agee v. Muskie* (which later became titled *Haig v. Agee*), that the executive branch could revoke a citizen's passport, if the president or secretary of state deemed the citizen dangerous to the nation's security. On top of this, after the 1970 Kent State University debacle in which members of the Ohio National Guard fired on students, killing four and injuring nine, MacKinnon insisted that the soldiers had acted in self-defense, and he intended to argue this point to Nixon. He also believed that the 1970 invasion into Cambodia—the event that precipitated massive domestic unrest—was a lawful act of national defense.

Although he was a national security hawk, he possessed an intolerance for the government's maltreatment of certain individuals. In regard to Ernest Fitzgerald, he tried to find a means to award interest on back pay after the Civil Service Commission ordered Fitzgerald's reinstatement to the Department of the Air Force. In the end, because Congress had not statutorily authorized back pay, the best MacKinnon could accomplish was to emplace into a three-judge decision that the court "had sympathy" for Fitzgerald's position. Fitzgerald was not the only person MacKinnon believed had been wronged. Shortly before Carter announced normalization with China as a policy, MacKinnon wrote to him asking that he exercise clemency for Patricia Hearst. The granddaughter of newspaper magnate William Randolph Hearst, Patricia Hearst had been kidnapped by members of a domestic terrorist organization but then joined with them in their criminal activity. "I previously wrote to President Ford about this matter but I want to repeat my observation that the handling of Patricia Hearst's case by her lawyer and family was not in her best interests," MacKinnon argued to Carter. "She committed the offenses while she was still subject to the Youth Corrections Act and if the case had been properly handled she would have obtained a Youth Corrections Act sentence that would have certainly not led to the long confinement that she has suffered."

A 1929 graduate of the University of Minnesota School of Law, MacKinnon began his law career as a counsel to an investment firm and at the same time was employed as the University of Minnesota's assistant football coach. From 1934 to 1942, MacKinnon served in the Minnesota legislature and aligned with Republican governor and presidential aspirant Harold Stassen. MacKinnon served in the navy in World War II and in 1946 was elected to the House of Representatives, where he assisted in writing laws restricting the political activities of labor unions, such as the Taft-Hartley Act. MacKinnon also teamed with Nixon during the House Un-American Activities Committee investigation into Alger Hiss and later, in 1952, served as research director for the Nixon for Vice President Campaign. In 1953, President Dwight Eisenhower appointed MacKinnon as US attorney for Minnesota. In that position, he led a significant prosecution against Teamsters Union president James Hoffa.

When MacKinnon died, the *New York Times* noted that he had the unusual distinction of the Supreme Court adopting his dissents as the law of the land more than any other judge during his lifetime. MacKinnon's record on executive branch authority was mixed. In the 1980s, he led the court to avoid accepting a collateral appeal on the Iran-Contra investigation that could have delayed the investigation. And he generally supported the constitutionality of a court-appointed independent counsel to investigate executive branch malfeasance even though this construct raised a significant separation of powers question, yet he also did not believe it was unconstitutional for the army to conduct surveillance operations on US citizens. In May 1979, Chief Justice Burger, on Attorney General Griffin Bell's advice, named MacKinnon to the Foreign Intelligence Surveillance (FISA) Court. In this position, he issued wiretap and surveillance warrants to the National Security Agency and the FBI. Yet, MacKinnon also voted to uphold Judge Sirica's order to the Nixon administration on turning over recordings to Congress. In 1971, he dissented in the Pentagon Papers case, arguing that the *Washington Post* could be restrained from publishing information the administration deemed hazardous to national security.

MacKinnon was in the minority in *Edwards v. Carter* and was noted for issuing lengthy dissents. When Congressman Edwards sought an injunction based on MacKinnon's dissent, the newest justice, John Paul Stevens, denied Edwards after determining that the sixty members of the House did not have standing and were unlikely to prevail. MacKinnon, in his *Edwards* dissent, highlighted his view that the Cold War necessitated the maintenance of strategic bulwarks against communism. Justice Department attorney Robert Kopp recalled that in oral arguments, MacKinnon "sometimes liked to ask questions that were a bit off topic." The Panama Canal issue presented MacKinnon with such an occasion. During the arguments in *Edwards*, MacKinnon quizzed Kopp about the Battle of San Juan Hill—a battle that had been fought in Cuba during the Spanish-American War and had little to do with the issue before the court. When Kopp, in MacKinnon's estimation, did not express sufficient historical knowledge of the canal, MacKinnon "delivered a lecture from the bench."

Malcolm Wilkey was another judge appointed by Nixon. He replaced Warren Burger after Burger was confirmed as the Supreme Court's chief justice. A World War II veteran and graduate of Harvard Law School, Wilkey had served in the Justice Department during Eisenhower's presidency, rising to become the US attorney for the Southern District of California, and later was employed as the general counsel to a major international mining corporation. When, in early February 1970, Nixon nominated Wilkey to the appellate court, the Senate confirmed him with no opposition. Wilkey was hardly a judge in the Warren Court mold. He opposed the Fourth Amendment's exclusionary rule, which enabled defendants to have courts suppress evidence obtained in violation of the amendment, and argued that it had hampered law enforcement. He was staunchly anticommunist to the point where, in 1981, he controversially accepted an "investigatory trip" at the behest of the South African government to occupied Namibia. The South African military had occupied a part of Namibia, and Wilkey apparently accepted apartheid as a legitimate form of government. He claimed that South Africa was an important ally in the fight against communism, notwithstanding its entrenched racism that relegated its majority African population to social, economic, and political positions of servitude. In 1981, when President Ronald Reagan tried to appoint Wilkey to the Iran Claims Tribunal, some of Wilkey's fellow judges advised Reagan not to do so as several cases involving Iran were before the appellate court. Wilkey concluded his judicial career by leaving the judiciary in 1985 and being appointed ambassador to Uruguay.

It is unlikely that the two judges who recused themselves from Carter's appeal from Gasch's ruling would have changed the outcome, had they decided to remain on the case. At most, the two recused judges would have been on opposite sides, though MacKinnon intimated that Roger Robb would have dismissed the suit on the basis of standing. Robb graduated from Yale University's law school in 1931 and later served as a special counsel to the Atomic Energy Commission. In this capacity, he oversaw the security clearance revocation of J. Robert Oppenheimer. Yet Robb was, in at least one respect, a model lawyer who would not turn down the representation of a defendant regardless of the unpopularity of the defendant's status. Earlier in his career, he was appointed to represent Earl Browder, the leader of the Communist Party of the United States, in a contempt trial. Although Robb was a staunch anticommunist, Browder lauded his vigorous lawyering. Robb did not face opposition to his judicial nomination; indeed, Goldwater was an advocate for Robb's appointment. As a private attorney Robb represented Fulton Lewis and other anticommunist and religious radio and news personalities. He also represented Goldwater in the senator's libel suit against a magazine that printed a defamatory article. The suit against the magazine owner traversed to the Second Circuit, which found for Goldwater. The Supreme Court denied certiorari, though Justices Hugo Black and William O. Douglas would have overturned the award against Goldwater on free speech grounds.

Abner Mikva would have likely sided with Carter, and although he did not openly state his reasons for recusing himself, his biography evidences that he embraced a broad reading of judicial ethics rules in his decision to recuse. Mikva graduated from the University of Chicago School of Law, clerked for Supreme Court Justice Sherman Minton, served in both the Illinois legislature and Congress as a liberal Democrat, and in 1978 was nominated to the appellate court by Carter. The Senate confirmed Mikva by a closer margin than that for his contemporaries: fifty-eight to thirty-one. Conservatives, including Thurmond and Goldwater, opposed Mikva. So too did the National Rifle Association, which spent more than $1 million in advertising against his judicial nomination. The primary rationale employed by the National Rifle Association against Mikva was that as a member of the House of Representatives, he voted in favor of a judicial pay raise and then sought a life-tenured judicial position. The reality underlying this action was that the association was looking for a means to prevent someone they believed would support firearms regulations from becoming a judge. Goldwater had a different objection to Mikva and informed his constituents, "In general I think the judicial nominees of Presidents whatever party are entitled to great consideration but not when there is a significant question relative to their ability or legal background or when there is past evidence of wrongdoing of any kind." Although Goldwater did not directly accuse Mikva of wrongdoing, he noted to several constituents that he doubted Mikva was capable of "rendering a fair an objective opinion without letting [his] personal prejudices override the need for judicial independence." Between the time of Mikva's confirmation in 1979 and 1982, the National Rifle Association filed suit against his judicial confirmation, arguing that his appointment violated the Constitution's ineligibility clause. Led by Senator James McClure (R-ID), an ally of Goldwater, the association's arguments were dismissed by a three-judge panel in the US

District Court for the District of Idaho. Mikva opined that he supported the per curiam, but his vote was unnecessary, and there is an absence of written communication from him to the other judges on this issue.

The Rapidity of Global Change

The United States' foreign policy was anything but clarified by Gasch's decision. Indeed, the nation's international affairs were in a seemingly insurmountable and exponentially growing state of crisis. One day before Gasch issued his decision, the State Department's special adviser to Secretary of State Cyrus Vance reported to the Senate that Soviet-US relations had deteriorated to a point that détente was in its death throes. The adviser cited growing Soviet influence in Rhodesia and Ethiopia, a crackdown on dissidents within the Soviet Union, and the Kremlin's claims that Carter's move to normalize relations with China included arming the Chinese military at the expense of peace. By the end of the week, the Soviet Union and South Yemen announced a "friendship pact," leading to concerns that the Soviet navy would have an operational port to disrupt maritime oil transportation, as well as a base to threaten North Yemen and Saudi Arabia. Given that the oil crisis was already wreaking havoc on the US and European economies, Soviet threats of oil disruption were serious enough to cause significant national security concerns. One day after Gasch issued his ruling, it was also reported that the numbers of Soviet advisers in Afghanistan had increased following a failed Afghan army mutiny against President Hafizulla Amin. By the end of October, US and Western European intelligence agencies reported that the elements of the Soviet military had moved into Afghanistan and established bases on the Iranian border.

During the week following Gasch's ruling, student protests against South Korea's dictatorial President Park erupted; in turn, Park issued curfews and arrest orders in a manner approximating martial law. On October 26, South Korea's intelligence chief killed Park, whose government responded by formally declaring martial law. In response, the thirty-eight thousand US military personnel stationed in South Korea were placed on alert. While Carter, along with the prime minister of Japan, stated that the murder of Park arose from a private argument and did not constitute a military coup, there were worries that communists in South Korea as well as the North Korean government would consider the upheaval an opportune time to stoke revolution.

On November 2, contrary to Carter's assessment, the interim South Korean government determined that the assassination of Park was part of an attempted coup. One day later, Secretary of State Vance arrived in Seoul to express support for South Korea's new government. Despite Vance's insistence that the United States favored a democratic form of government, he announced that "Korea's future must be decided by the Korean people themselves." Importantly, China's government publicly disavowed any intention to move into South Korea, and the North Korean military did not conduct any threatening movements against the South. By the end of November, South Korea's major political parties and its military leadership agreed to convene an assembly to replace the country's 1972 constitution that had created Park's dictatorial presidency. Importantly, at the time the Court of Appeals for the District of Columbia considered Carter's appeal, the Chinese government displayed rectitude toward a key US ally. Had the assassination of Park occurred two decades earlier, it was plausible that China and North Korea would have stoked an insurgency in South Korea.

The United States' foreign policy in South and Central America faced difficulties as well. In October, the governments of Bolivia and Chile threatened war over tin-mining claims in the midst of a meeting of the Organization of American States. One century earlier, Chile had defeated Bolivia in a war and seized territory that the Bolivian government now demanded be returned. The Organization of American States meeting was not concerned just with the Bolivia-Chile dispute, though Venezuela's president accused Carter of overreacting to Bolivia's threats; the conditions in Nicaragua and El Salvador also dominated discussions. But, in mid-November, Bolivian military officers attempted to overthrow their government. This was not the only attempted military coup in South and Central America. The Nicaraguan government announced that its police forces would summarily execute "counterrevolutionaries." While Nicaragua turned toward communism, a military junta deposed El Salvador's almost five-decade-old rightist government, which had attempted to prevent the spread of communism through means of terror and human rights abuses. A new government, led by two military officers and three civilians, promised agrarian reform and respect for human rights. This promise proved illusory in a very short period.

Between October 18 and November 30, Western European economic news was grim. The European Economic Community—the European Union's predecessor—announced that Britain's new prime minister, Margret Thatcher, demanded the reduction of Britain's payments and implied that Britain might leave that organization. At the same time, West German president Helmut Schmidt accused Britain of failing to sell North Sea oil at fair prices, and the French, British, and Italian governments accused each other of unfair agricultural subsidies. The European Economic Community, an outgrowth of the post–World War II coal and steel agreements between Belgium, Luxembourg, the Netherlands, France, and West Germany, was originally designed to reduce the possibility of another European war. However, it hardly resolved economic disputes. Added to Western Europe's difficulties was a growing and often caustic division within NATO over the costs of modernization and the placement of nuclear weapons in West Germany. Varying defense and economic policy divisions threatened to break NATO's solidarity at a time when the United States and Western Europe needed to show strength to the Soviet Union. The Chinese government, in an oblique manner, contributed to defusing dissension within NATO by stoking Soviet threats against West Germany. In late October, when Schmidt and China's foreign minister signed a trade agreement, China's ambassador to West Germany stressed the importance of European unity and a united Germany as a barrier against Soviet expansion. From the end of World War II through the collapse of communism in Europe, the Soviet Union opposed a unified Germany. For the first time, China, the second communist global power, joined with the United States and endorsed German unification. Brezhnev responded by warning that attempts to unify Germany would only be met with military confrontation from the Warsaw Pact.

While South Korea, Central and South America, Africa, Europe, and Afghanistan presented problems for US foreign policy, from the time of Gasch's ruling until the Supreme Court took up Goldwater's appeal, Iran dominated the news. On November 4, Iranian demonstrators swarmed the US embassy in Tehran and took fifty-two US citizens hostage. The next day, newspapers headlined that the Iranians demanded the United States return the Shah to Tehran in exchange for the release of the hostages. Yet, as the *Los Angeles Times*, *Washington Post*, *New York Times*, and almost every major news source reported that same day, Carter would not, under any circumstance, send the Shah back to Iran. Carter appeared to be in an untenable position. On November 16, Walter Cronkite on CBS news informed the nation that "no encouraging news" had come from Tehran, and even if the Shah were returned to Iran, there was no promise that the hostages would be freed. The possibility of military conflict with Iran seemed to grow daily. If a war with Iran occurred, Carter might need the powers inherent in his commander in chief capacity to order military strikes on Iran as well as work with allied nations to overthrow the revolutionary government.

On November 11, Carter announced that the Justice Department would investigate the visas of all Iranian students in the United States. There were slightly fewer than fifteen thousand Iranian nationals attending college in the United States. (The Shah had sent military officers to train in the United States as well, and Carter threatened to return them to Iran.) Prior to the Shah's ouster, some of the students, along with US citizens, had demonstrated against the Shah's dictatorial rule, and a cross section of media pundits presented the Iranians as a danger to the country. Senator S. I. Hayakawa (R-CA) introduced a bill to the Senate authorizing the government to arrest and deport Iranian nationals or hold them in detention. Hayakawa, who was born in Canada to parents of Japanese descent, witnessed Canadian and US citizens of Japanese descent interned in camps during World War I. Ironically, he now insisted that Carter reenact that internment toward foreign nationals. Other congressmen introduced measures to deport Iranian nationals who demonstrated, even legally, against the United States, as well as to expel Iranians from tax-supported colleges who likewise did so.

Several Iranian students filed suit in a receptive US District Court for the District of Columbia. Although Judge Joyce Hens Green would rule against Carter on December 5, after the Court of Appeals for the District of Columbia issued its decision on Carter's appeal against Gasch's decision, it became clear that Green at least considered the students' lawsuits meritorious when she denied summary judgment to the government and consolidated several of the students' claims into a single suit. That this occurred prior to the court of appeals announcing its decision on the

Mutual Defense Treaty's termination provides context for the appellate court's *Goldwater* decision occurring at a time of significant global crisis. Carter had appointed Green to the court the prior year, and like Gasch—albeit in a different matter—she determined that Carter had overreached his constitutional authority. By the end of December, the Court of Appeals for the District of Columbia would overturn Green, as it had overturned Gasch. Yet it cannot be overlooked that at the district court level, two judges in the nation's capital determined Carter had unconstitutionally acted in significant matter touching on both national security and foreign policy.

Although it was not argued in the appellate court, the Chinese government's actions in the Iran crisis contributed to ensuring that the Iranian Revolution remained contained in that country, and that Iran was without any powerful allies in the United Nations. On November 9, the Chinese ambassador to the United Nations voted in the Security Council in favor of a resolution for the freeing of the American hostages. The Chinese government had reasons, beyond developing trust with the United States, to make it known that it did not support the Iranian revolutionary government. In 1978, Khomeini openly spoke of his mistrust of China and exclaimed, "Our youth must know that China and Russia, like the United States and Britain, feed on the blood of our people." In another speech Khomeini declared that China had supported the Shah and "contaminated" Iranian culture. In early 1979, China negotiated the sale of its military hardware, including tanks and aircraft, to Iraq, which was shortly to be at war with Iran. In early November, Khomeini accused China of backing Israel over its Arab neighbors. On November 29, Carter noted in a press conference focused on the crisis in Iran that, in addition to strengthening NATO and confronting the Soviet Union, his foreign policy developed ties with China without alienating allied nations. In response to a reporter's question, Carter went so far as to suggest that China might be able to assert leverage in Iran to avoid war.

The Court Decides en Banc, per Curiam

In conference, Leventhal argued that while under Article IV of the US Constitution a treaty is the law of the land, treaties are listed apart from the normal laws because unlike the lawmaking process, which requires both houses of Congress to vote, treaty approval involves only the Senate. He then reasoned that if the Senate had wanted to make a treaty inviolate, it could have demanded it at the time of voting to approve it. Instead, the Mutual Defense Treaty had an exit clause listed as Article X. Leventhal concluded that the Senate had, in effect, enabled termination to occur in the manner Carter utilized. McGowan agreed with Leventhal as to the Senate enabling a president to rescind the Mutual Defense Treaty because of Article X, but he urged that the court not confer a broad authority on presidents to rescind treaties.

Although Wilkey did not disagree with Leventhal on this point, he countered that at no time had Carter argued that the particular treaty gave to the president a specified termination power. Instead, Wilkey reminded the court, Carter argued that a president's power was broad enough to terminate any treaty, and Wilkey could not agree with this position because it would recognize a vast constitutional power. In other words, while Wilkey would be willing to sign a decision resting on Article X, he would not agree to the court issuing a decision that added new a definition to the Constitution as Carter desired. Robinson added that just as presidents had the authority to determine when a foreign signatory nation breached the terms of a treaty or the authority to declare that a "fundamental change in circumstances" existed, thereby nullifying the treaty, a president's authority to rescind a treaty would be at its "zenith" if the treaty had an exit clause such as Article X. In effect, Robinson wanted to apply the model of presidential authority crafted by Justice Robert Jackson in *Youngstown Sheet and Tube v. Sawyer.* Wald agreed with Robinson on this point.

Wald was also concerned that the decision not state that a president had the constitutional authority to terminate a treaty in all instances where a treaty contained an exit clause. Rather, she wanted the decision to emphasize that in the absence of the Senate condemning a president's termination action, the courts would not inquire into a presidential act of terminating a treaty when the treaty contained an exit clause. She cautioned, "Anything beyond that involves us very controversially in defining the termination relationship between the two branches which has varied for two hundred years and may vary for another two hundred more which it immediately the subject of a new evolutionary turn." In other words, she concluded that the appellate court could not determine a matter of constitutional law broader than the confines of the Mutual Defense Treaty, particularly with the Senate's inaction, because doing so required the court to determine a political question outside of the judicial branch's authority.

Wright and Tamm would have rather reversed Gasch on the basis of Goldwater lacking standing to have the cause heard in federal court. This is not to say that Wright and Tamm wanted to disavow the concept of congressional standing. To the contrary, they worked to ensure that *Kennedy v. Sampson* remained the law of the circuit, if not the nation. They believed that Congress should be able to appeal to the federal courts for redress against the executive branch in certain narrow circumstances, such as a president's refusal to comply with the law, or a refusal to comply with Congress's investigative functions. "Undoubtedly [*Sampson*] will be an important tool in some future cases," Tamm penned to Wright. "I doubt whether we have any authority to overrule it." But neither Wright nor Tamm believed that *Sampson* applied to Goldwater's challenge because the Senate had not acted in opposition to the revocation of the treaty. Rather, to Wright and Tamm, the best that could be said about the Byrd Resolution was that the Senate expressed its disagreement with Carter's actions in a nebulous manner. Wright hinted that if more than six senators had signed on with Goldwater, he could determine Goldwater had standing. But, he cautioned, to recognize standing for less than 10 percent of the upper house would be to invite repeated suits against the government.

The en banc decision was written in per curiam format. A per curiam decision is a one that is issued in the name of a court, rather than a judge or a group of judges. While many, or most, appellate decisions list the authoring judge, a per curiam leaves the reader without the knowledge as to which judge wrote the decision. In their early history, per curiam decisions were short and designed so that the public would know of the absolute unanimity of the judges. By the mid-twentieth century, they had evolved to include decisions in which a judge dissented or concurred by name, while the rest of the court appeared to be steadfast in its agreement. By the time of *Goldwater*, the federal courts of appeal had departed from the idea that a per curiam required a showing of unanimity and instead adopted the per curiam model for causes that required a "rapid adjudication of cases requiring urgent resolution."

One example set by the Supreme Court in 1942 had to do with the appeals of captured German saboteurs at the height of World War II. (The Germans had sneaked into the United States with the design of bombing infrastructure critical to the war effort.) Consistent with the laws of war and the army's legal construct, several saboteurs were prosecuted and sentenced to death in a military trial as opposed to federal court. The defendant saboteurs appealed against the trial and sentence, which was to be quickly carried out, and the Court, in *Ex Parte Quirin*, issued a per curiam opinion denying to captured enemy combatants a court-based avenue to challenge detentions, trials, and sentences. The Court later issued a lengthier opinion, but not until after the executions had taken place. Likewise, in the Pentagon Papers case, the Court issued a per curiam opinion, through it contained six concurring opinions. It was for reasons of a perceived need for rapidity that Wright encouraged the appellate court to issue a per curiam opinion, even though he would ultimately concur, rather than join, with the majority.

While Wright pushed for an en banc hearing, he did not write the opinion, even though he set out to do so. On November 19, 1979, he forwarded his first draft to his fellow judges. The next day he urged the judges to reverse Gasch on the basis of standing and forgo delving into the substantive constitutional questions. "With great respect, I suggest that the court makes a great mistake if it goes beyond standing in deciding this important case," Wright urged his peers. "I submit that the attached opinion for Judge Tamm and me gives the reason why." Wright failed to convince his peers to overturn Gasch's decision on the basis of standing. McGowan countered Wright that Goldwater had standing in the case. This was because, unlike in *Edwards*, where the court determined that the Constitution specifically excluded the House of Representatives in treaty making, the Senate had a specified role in the approval of treaties. To Leventhal, the fact that Carter had not consulted with the Senate even though he earlier agreed to do so was one more reason standing existed.

It was McGowan who wrote the per curiam and finalized it after several circulations between Leventhal, Wald, Robinson, and Wilkey. The per curiam first examined the nature of the Mutual Defense Treaty in light of the Senate's consent for it. The treaty enabled either signatory nation to give a one-year notice of termination, and at no time did the Senate seek a reservation or amendment to include any requirement for senatorial advice or approval in the event a president acted to remove the United States from the treaty. The per curiam then noted that the treaty came into existence because of a threat from the People's Republic of China to Taiwan, and that the governments of both the People's Republic of China and Taiwan claimed to be the sole legitimate representative of China. The per curiam recognized that the international status of the People's Republic of China's had changed in the prior twenty-five years. In 1954, the Soviet Union and Eastern Bloc, several sub-Saharan countries, and India recognized China, whereas the North Atlantic Treaty Organization's member states, the Organization of American States, Japan, and South Korea recognized Taiwan as the legitimate representative of China. But the per curiam pointed out that by 1976, most of the world's governments and the United Nations recognized the People's Republic of China as "the one China." This placed the United States in the minority of states in the United Nations.

The per curiam next reviewed the Senate's prior actions regarding Taiwan and the People's Republic of China by noting that in September 1978, Senators Dole and Stone led the Senate to vote for a resolution arguing in favor of the executive branch consulting with Congress prior to renouncing the Mutual Defense Treaty. McGowan and the other per curiam judges acknowledged that Carter did not follow the spirit of the Dole-Stone Amendment, yet they found that the amendment was neither a demand nor a command on Carter. And, Congress had passed a bill enabling Taiwan to defend itself through military sales and weapons transfers. In regard to the Byrd Resolution, the judges recognized that the Senate had made a statement, but they expressed doubts as to whether it had created the basis for standing, let alone a justiciable question.

McGowan, in leading the per curiam, assumed, without providing much detail—Wright would call their decision "superficial—that Goldwater possessed standing for more than one reason. Because the Senate had a constitutional right to block the treaty termination with only one-third of the senators plus one voting against termination, Goldwater and the other legislators had standing before the district court because they were blocked from being able to vote by a majority of the Senate. In essence, the per curiam held that a reduction in senatorial effectiveness was not enough of a basis, but the disenfranchisement of a legislator, or actions causing a de facto disenfranchisement would enable standing. The per curiam then concluded that Carter had acted to make a meaningful vote on the treaty termination impossible. This resulted in the appellate court recognizing expanded legislative standing in foreign policy matters. Recognition of Goldwater's standing did not end the court's analysis as to why Gasch's ruling had to be overturned.

The per curiam disagreed with Gasch's constitutional interpretation that since the Senate had a role in the approval of treaties, it therefore had a correspondingly equal role in the termination of treaties. If this were true, they posited, it could also be true in regard to the dismissal of cabinet officers. But since the Court had already determined that the Constitution does not require senatorial approval for the dismissal of cabinet officers, it would require an untenable "expansion of the language of the Constitution by sequential linguistic projection." The per curiam also concluded that the supremacy clause did not provide any guidance on Congress's role in treaty termination. Because of the Constitution's silence on treaty termination, McGowan and the other judges believed they had to conclude that since treaties affect domestic law, withdrawal from a treaty necessarily implicated congressional authority, much as the termination of a domestic law would. However, they then determined that as a result of the unique nature of foreign policy and the inability to find a stated constitutional role for Congress in a treaty termination, the plain language of the treaty would have to serve as a guidepost. Since the Mutual Defense Treaty had a termination clause, the per curiam determined they were able to decide in favor of Carter. "The existence of Article X of the ROC treaty, permitting termination by either party on one year's notice, is an overarching factor in this case, which in effect enables all of the other considerations to be knit together," the per curiam concluded.

The per curiam decision was narrow in several respects. The judges limited their decision to the specific treaty under challenge and warned that had the withdrawal of another treaty with no exit clause been challenged, they could have reached a different result. In particular, they cautioned that the NATO treaty did not have the equivalent of an Article X exit clause. They also took pains to assure the legislative branch that they recognized Congress's constitutional role in foreign affairs, in particular, its power over appropriations. Of significance, the judges did not narrow the principle of legislative standing for future congressional challenges to executive branch action or inaction, and on this issue the concurring two judges agreed. Indeed, it is telling that both the per curiam and the concurrence sought to protect *Sampson* as a viable decision for future use.

Embedded in the per curiam decision is a commentary on executive authority in foreign policy, which is quite Palmerstonian in nature. The per curiam judges expressed doubts as to whether Taiwan was actually a country with which the United States could enter into a treaty. "The subtleties involved in maintaining amorphous relationships are often the very stuff of diplomacy, a field in which the President, and not Congress has responsibility under our Constitution," the per curiam opined. "The President makes a responsible claim that he has authority as chief executive to determine that there is no meaningful vitality to a mutual defense treaty when there is no recognized state." Following this comment, the per curiam expressed that the court was not presented with the question as to whether the authority to recognize a foreign state is without constitutional constraints.

As noted, Judges Wright and Tamm concurred with the per curiam's result but argued that it had been in error to decide the question of treaty revocation authority on narrow substantive grounds. Instead, they argued that the Constitution's limits on judicial review did not permit standing to parties who were "only generally and indistinguishably offended by act of the government." Moreover, they cautioned that granting individual members of Congress standing would place ordinary citizens into a lower class of persons before the courts. And they noted that while Congress had an interest in seeing the president act within his constitutional authorities, so too did all Americans.

Wright and Tam then argued that even assuming that if Carter had a duty to seek a two-thirds Senate vote or a majority of both houses, and the court were to accept that Carter's action prevented Congress from voting on the termination of a treaty, this would still not confer standing to Goldwater. Wright and Tamm took greater cognizance of the congressional debates over Carter's actions than the per curiam. For instance, they noted that the author of the Byrd Amendment explicitly conceded to the Senate that his resolution did not legally bind Carter to follow it. Moreover, they pointed out that the Senate never decided whether to approve Senator Church's proposed amendment or Goldwater's, which would have been important to the suit because the Byrd Resolution fell far short of a command to Carter. To Wright and Tamm, because the Senate had not actually passed a binding resolution, no senator could truly argue that Carter had impaired their vote. Finally, because the question over the authority to terminate a treaty had not been historically settled, the per curiam was in error to accept the definitive historic arguments of either Carter or Goldwater.

Wright and Tamm concluded their concurrence by arguing that since Congress had several constitutional authorities at its disposal, its members could pass a resolution objecting to termination and threaten to withhold funding from foreign policy programs. "A President is likely to pay heed to such disapproval, in which event no court need intervene," Wright observed. Finally, as in the per curiam, Wright placed into his concurrence a reassurance that treaties to which the United States is a party were also protected by popular opinion. "Were a President to attempt to unilaterally break a treaty vital to the interests of the nation, without sound reason and against the wishes of the great majority of citizens, congressional representatives, by any means they have already used or by those they may yet design, can ensure that the voice of that majority reaches the President," Wright concluded.

Although MacKinnon dissented from the per curiam, he agreed, in some measure, that Goldwater possessed standing and that the case did not present a nonjusticiable political question. In crafting his dissent, he expressed dismay at Gasch's use of Louis Henkin's work. MacKinnon had referenced Henkin in his dissent but for the purpose of pointing out that the per curiam, in citing to the noted scholar, had in fact engaged in creative editing to change the meaning of his work. Gasch, as noted, had cited to two of Henkin's articles. Ironically, perhaps, MacKinnon had relied heavily on Henkin in his dissent in *Edwards*, arguing that Carter could not "dispose" of the Panama Canal without first obtaining the House's consent. But after Gasch issued his second *Goldwater* ruling, Henkin authored another article in the *American Journal of International Law* in which he argued that Carter had the power to terminate minor treaties. Henkin conceded that had Carter, or a future president, attempted to rescind a treaty such as NATO, then this action would implicate the congressional power to "decide for war or peace." MacKinnon insisted in his communications—rather than in his dissent—that Henkin was of no further use to the courts. "It is interesting to note that even one of the most ardent supporters of the President's alleged right to terminate a treaty without the consent of Congress, Professor Henkin, cannot bear the thought that such power would be utilized to terminate important treaties such as NATO or SALT," MacKinnon claimed before arguing that in focusing on NATO, Henkin had undermined the utility of his previous work. This was because, MacKinnon insisted, "what is the Taiwan Mutual Defense Treaty if it isn't a treaty intended to threaten war, as a means of deterring aggression, implicating directly the Congressional War powers?"

Later, MacKinnon was angry after discovering that Henkin penned a letter to McGowan, lauding the per curiam, after the decision was published. Henkin had, in fact, noted that he agreed with the per curiam on the substantive issue of presidential authority but expressed unease with the court's treatment of standing. Dismay at the conduct of a professor was a minor matter to MacKinnon, however. He insisted that whatever minor differences he had with Gasch's ruling, he wanted the court to affirm it. MacKinnon then acknowledged that the Constitution did not, in its plain language, state the means to terminate treaties. Therefore, he insisted, treaty termination was an implied constitutional power. As a result, the necessary and proper clause—which he accused the majority of "avoiding like a plague"—enabled Congress to assume the authority to petition the courts on the very issue Goldwater raised. Then, MacKinnon issued a lengthy and sharp dissent against the per curiam. He accused the majority of permitting the executive branch's accretion of power while at the same time issuing a nonbinding decision. To MacKinnon, the merits were answerable in the legal history of the nation.

Article I of the Constitution has a clause, sometimes referred to as the "elastic clause," which states that Congress has the power "to make all Laws which shall be necessary and proper for carrying into Execution the foregoing Powers, and all other Powers vested by this Constitution in the Government of the United States, or in any Department or Officer thereof." The necessary and proper (or elastic) clause has enabled Congress to regulate commerce, legislate new create federal crimes, and permit the executive branch to run federal administrative programs that issue myriad regulations. In 1819, the Court unanimously determined, in *McCulloch v. Maryland*, that although the Constitution was silent on whether a second national bank was permissible, Congress had the implied power to charter such an enterprise as a matter of stabilizing currency values to protect the economy in response to an economic panic that same year. (The Panic of 1819 has been called the United States' first economic crisis.) MacKinnon, in large measure, rested his arguments on *McCulloch*. Since, as MacKinnon pointed out, the termination of a treaty implicated the repeal of laws, Congress had the implied power, as recognized in the clause, to prevent a presidential treaty termination. And, since Carter had never submitted the termination of the Mutual Defense Treaty to the full Congress, the termination could not take effect.

MacKinnon then turned to the nation's preconstitutional history to point out that the Articles of Confederation authorized Congress to enter into and to rescind treaties. He pointed out that the Court had, on prior occasions, noted that the experiences of the Constitution's framers prior to ratification could be used to interpret matters outside of the Constitution's plain language. That the Constitution's framers empowered the executive branch with Senate consent to enter into treaties, but were silent on treaty termination, to MacKinnon meant only that Congress had retained that authority. MacKinnon insisted, as had Goldwater, that Justice Iredell, in *Ware v. Hylton*, made it clear that a treaty could not be considered terminated until a foreign signatory broke with the United States, or Congress affirmatively acted. Thus, a reasonable—and unanswerable—question arose as to why Iredell would have written his seriatim opinion without objection from the other justices, if it were not the case that Congress had retained treaty termination authority. MacKinnon additionally asserted that Justice Joseph Story, in the 1821 *Amiable Isabella* decision, precluded a president terminating a treaty without the approval of Congress. He also appeared to place import in the Court's decision in *Van Der Weyde v. Ocean Transport Co.*, but as noted in the introduction to this book, in that instance the Court left the question of whether a president could unilaterally act for another time.

MacKinnon concluded his dissent by providing a recitation of instances in which a president terminated a treaty and Congress approved. Like Gasch, he concluded that the historic practice of treaty termination proved that a president had to submit the question of termination to Congress. In regard to Carter's assertion that there were instances in which a president acted without Congress, MacKinnon pointed out that Carter's reliance on these instances was flawed. For instance, Carter relied on President Madison's termination of the 1782 treaty with the Netherlands in 1815. But at that time, the Netherlands ceased to exist as an independent country, having been conquered by Napoleon. Likewise, President William McKinley's alleged termination of a trade treaty with Switzerland without Congress's approval actually occurred after Congress authorized him to negotiate trade reciprocity agreements. Calvin Coolidge terminated a treaty with Mexico, MacKinnon claimed, because "influential Congressmen" sought him out to do so. And, in 1933, President Franklin Roosevelt informed the League of Nations that the United States would withdraw from the 1927 Convention for the Abolition of Import and Export Prohibition and Restrictions, but the National Recovery Act empowered Roosevelt to embargo foreign goods and assert tariffs. "In almost 200 years of American history, these are the only instances that appellant has been able to dredge up to support his claim to absolute power," MacKinnon concluded before listing the greater numbers of instances when Congress had been a direct participant in treaty revocation. In the end, this historic study of treaty termination would prove to be a dead end despite its general historic accuracy.

MacKinnon's dissent was lengthy as a result of his intentional design. His dissent in the *Agee* passport revocation case was likewise long because he wanted to create a framework for the Court if it ultimately granted certiorari. Unlike his prediction in *Agee*, MacKinnon did not predict that the Court would adopt his *Goldwater* dissent as a matter of constitutional law. Rather, as he wrote to the aged former governor Harold Stassen and others: "I am satisfied that my argument on the merits is irrefutable. I had to get it out awfully fast. It is there for the future so that the majority opinion will not be unrefuted." When the Court determined to order Gasch to dismiss Goldwater's suit, this did not surprise MacKinnon at all. He assumed that at some point in the future, a president would try to terminate a more robust treaty, such as NATO, and a larger congressional alliance would challenge the president in the courts, making it likely that the Court would reconsider its treatment of the issue.

In the Eye of the Public

On December 1, 1979, the *Washington Post* reported on its front page that the court of appeals sided with Carter over Goldwater. The *New York Times* front-page headline read, "Appeal Court Backs Carter on Taiwan: Upholds His Abrogation of Treaty without Consent of Congress." The *Chicago Tribune*, *Philadelphia Inquirer*, and *San Francisco Chronicle* likewise placed the court's decision on their front pages. The *Tribune*, on its first page, reported that Goldwater claimed, "The framers of the Constitution would turn over in their graves at this ruling." The CBS evening news reported on the decision as well, calling it a victory for Carter. Republican presidential candidates Ronald Reagan and George H. W. Bush publicly backed Goldwater on appealing the issue to the Supreme Court. On December 3, the *Times* reported that Goldwater had filed an appeal to the Supreme Court. Goldwater reiterated his earlier warning that if Carter had the authority to withdraw the United States from the treaty with Taiwan, then NATO was at risk. But this article was on page 18 of the *Times*. Likewise, in a paragraph-length article on page 10, the *Chicago Tribune* reported that Goldwater had sought to appeal to the Supreme Court.

In the four days between the appellate court's decision and the time Goldwater filed his appeal for certiorari to the Court, the government of Pakistan reported that over 250,000 Afghan refugees had crossed the border into their country. The Soviet's military involvement in Afghanistan, even before the invasion, caused the displacement of hundreds of thousands of people and the deaths of thousands more. In response to the Soviet Union's aggression, the Senate Armed Services Committee announced that it opposed the proposed SALT II treaty that Carter had submitted for review. At any rate, the Soviet government expressed doubts as to the feasibility of a new arms treaty in light of the fact that NATO was considering the placement of intermediate-range ballistic missiles in Western Europe. Of course, the news of Iranian actions was devastating to the Carter administration. Khomeini threatened OPEC to wage an oil war against the United States or else face revolution in their countries, if not a stoppage of oil shipments on maritime waterways. He demanded that Carter, Nixon, and Lyndon Johnson be prosecuted in an international court for crimes against humanity. Since Johnson had died in 1974, one might wonder whether Khomeini meant Ford, but it was clear that in spite of his mistake, he meant to push the United States into a conflict. Evidencing his lack of reticence regarding a military conflict, he denounced the United Nations Security Council as "a tool of the United States." Perhaps because the Security Council could not agree on whether the use of military force against Iran was justifiable, military conflict was averted.

CHAPTER 5

In the Supreme Court

The Political Question Doctrine

On December 5, 1979, the *New York Times* placed the headline "Carter, without Fanfare, Declares He Is a Candidate for a Second Term" at the top of its front page. The same day, the Washington bureau chief for the *Los Angeles Times* characterized Carter as a besieged president. "As Carter officially announces his candidacy and launches his campaign for a second term he carries with him no heavier baggage than the economic ills that have developed during his administration, especially the 13.5% annual inflation—up dramatically from the 4.8% average of just three years ago," the bureau chief noted. "Critics are attacking his performance on almost every other issue as well, among them energy, defense, foreign policy, environment, civil rights, congressional relations, and his supervision of the White House staff." One day earlier, Carter was set to announce his reelection campaign only to learn that his newly appointed attorney general, Benjamin Civiletti, had ordered an investigation into the conduct of White House chief of staff Hamilton Jordan. Anonymous accusations that Jordan used cocaine at a party and cavorted with prostitutes became a part of the national news narrative. Although Civiletti quickly concluded that there was no evidence of Jordan breaking the law, the allegation was in the public's knowledge. In addition to the cabinet and staff shake-up the previous July, Carter upset senior members of his own party by asking Congress for significant defense budget increases despite promising not to do so during his 1976 presidential campaign. Carter had concluded that world affairs, in particular in regard to both Iran and increased Soviet aggression, necessitated a military increase.

Four days earlier, the *Washington Post* provided an equally dismal picture for Carter in reporting that he had originally intended to announce his reelection with the purchase of thirty minutes of prime-time television on Tuesday, December 4, from CBS, but had scaled back the purchase to five minutes. Even a five-minute purchase resulted in a widely reported legal controversy. Three of the major networks refused to sell airtime to Carter on "the grounds that it was too early in the election season." Carter, in turn, obtained a Federal Communications Commission (FCC) order requiring the networks to sell him airtime. Established in 1934, the FCC is an independent federal agency responsible for ensuring the fullest public access to radio, telephone, wire, television, and now internet communications. It also is responsible for ensuring that candidates for office have equal time to advance their causes. Of the seven FCC commissioners, the three republican appointees voted against the order and the four democrat appointees sided with Carter, but the three networks then successfully sued Carter in district court for a temporary "stay" against the enforcement of the FCC order. Ironically, on the same day the Court of Appeals for the District of Columbia in its en banc decision upheld Carter's action to terminate the Mutual Defense Treaty, a three-judge panel consisting of Roger Robb, Edward Tamm, and Malcolm Wilkey sided with the networks over Carter and the FCC; none of these three judges opposed Carter's actions regarding Taiwan.

On November 23, 1979, Admiral Stansfield Turner, the Central Intelligence Agency's director, had a questionable performance on National Public Radio. One of the reporters, Nina Totenberg, noted that while the agency had prevailed against one former agent who violated his employment contract and published an unauthorized book, the agency had several other employees who engaged in similar activity. Turner tried to distinguish between the one agent and the others, but his explanation fell flat. In response to reporter Peter Osnos, he also had to defend against the CIA failing to accurately predict how much oil Saudi Arabia could produce as well as defend against an accusation that the agency's misjudgment was designed to support the White House's conservation policy. Additionally, he tried to explain why intelligence had not uncovered the assassination plot against South Korea's president. After the murder of South Vietnamese president Ngo Diem in 1963, this was a touchy subject.

Most important, however, Turner claimed that the agency had not bungled in failing to predict the revolution in Iran or Khomeini's rapid ascension to power. He admitted that he earlier stated to the American Bar Association that "no one could predict that a seventy-eight-year-old quasi-senile fanatic would end up unifying the nation into a huge revolution." There was little success that he could claim for the agency in 1979, and his interview was not likely to give comfort to the nation. The interview did, however, capture that there was little predictability to the world.

The Political Question and the Courts

Carter was not the only party to the treaty termination issue pending before the nation's highest court to commit a public relations error. One day before the Supreme Court issued its decision to dismiss the suit against Carter, Goldwater announced that Taiwan was in a sound military position to defend itself against China. Speaking from Taipei, he proclaimed he "had great faith in Taiwan's military strength," adding that it would take China at least two decades to build the military power necessary to invade Taiwan. Goldwater noted that he had filed suit against Carter on the principle that the president had violated the Constitution, but he also claimed that Carter's actions meant that the United States was going to abandon an ally that was confronted by an aggressive behemoth with a notorious record of destroying liberty. While Goldwater's public speech in Taipei may have been made to bolster the morale of Taiwan's people or to assure them that the United States would protect the island regardless of the treaty abandonment, his timing was impolitic. If Taiwan was capable of defending itself, as Goldwater intimated, this took away some of the urgency associated with his appeal. The Taipei speech highlighted a fundamental problem with Goldwater's lawsuit: the case before the Court was both inherently and overtly political, which partly explained why several other Senate Republicans did not join with him.

Almost from the start of Carter's presidency, leading Republican legislators asserted standing to challenge the administration's foreign policy actions. In a sense, they acted similarly to Nixon's Democrat opponents in Congress during the Vietnam Conflict without heed to the fact that the courts often determined that the lack of standing or the political question doctrine prevented a judicial ruling. That is, even if granted standing, legislators in opposition to a president have to overcome the question of justiciability. Political questions that are constitutionally designed to be resolved between the two elected branches of government seldom can be adjudicated in the federal courts. In *Baker v. Carr*, a 1962 voting rights opinion that had nothing to do with treaties or international relations, the Court noted that in regard to foreign policy "there are sweeping statements to the effect that all questions touching foreign relations are political questions," and as a result, "resolution of such issues frequently turns on standards that defy judicial application, or involve the exercise of a discretion demonstrably committed to the executive or legislature." On the other hand, the Court also conceded that there may be unusual instances in the realm of foreign affairs in which the judiciary could determine a challenge against a president. Perhaps, because the justices in the *Baker* majority wanted to ensure that the political question doctrine remained important, they placed the observation about foreign policy into the decision to juxtapose it with the voting rights issues, where the doctrine did not apply to bar a decision.

In 1977, Senator Robert Dole—who had been Ford's vice presidential candidate the prior year—filed suit in the US District Court for the District of Kansas to prevent Carter from returning Hungarian cultural properties to that country. In seeking a preliminary injunction against Carter, Dole asserted that the return of medieval coronation regalia, including a crown bestowed by the Vatican to the Duke of Hungary in AD 1000, was an action tantamount to a breach of a treaty and therefore Carter had to seek the Senate's advice and consent. Between the time that the United States acquired the regalia and Carter's decision to return it, Hungary had fallen under communist domination. (In 1956, the Soviet Union and its communist allies within Hungary violently crushed a popular pro-democracy uprising.) Dole argued that because the former Hungarian government had given the United States the regalia for safekeeping in the closing days of World War II, a transfer of the properties to the new Hungarian government would be a violation of an understanding, tantamount to a treaty, between the former Hungarian government and the United States. The problem with Dole's argument was that the regalia was technically the property of the people of Hungary and not a government of Congress's choosing.

Judge Eugene O'Connor, a Nixon appointee, did not address the issue of standing, though in his decision he appeared to accept that a single senator had standing to seek redress on this issue. Rather, O'Connor found that Dole was unlikely to succeed on the merits of the suit because there was no treaty or statute prohibiting Carter's actions. Ironically, Dole had earlier lobbied the Nixon administration to appoint O'Connor to a federal judgeship. Because in order to obtain a preliminary injunction, the Federal Rules of Civil Procedure require the moving party to have "a reasonable likelihood of succeeding on their claim," O'Connor determined Dole could not get a court to reach the merits of his suit. On appeal, the Court of Appeals for the Tenth Circuit determined that Dole's claim was essentially a political question and therefore nonjusticiable in the federal courts. That court, moreover, held that matters of foreign policy "uniquely demand [a] single-voiced statement of the Government's views," and that voice had to be a president.

That Dole lost in the district court in Kansas as well as in the Court of Appeals for the Tenth Circuit might have led him not to join with Goldwater, though he certainly opposed Carter's action in recognizing China at Taiwan's expense. The experience of the sixty-two members of the House of Representatives who filed suit against the return of the Panama Canal served as a reminder to legislators of the difficulties in suing the executive branch. So too might have the unsuccessful efforts of Congressman Charles Diggs (D-MI), who argued that he had standing to have the federal courts order the executive branch to comply with a United Nations Security Council embargo of Rhodesia, influenced them not to join with Goldwater.

Diggs's efforts deserve attention as they further illustrate the difficulties in such suits. After separating from Great Britain in 1965, the Rhodesian government refused to recognize equal rights for the majority African population and established an apartheid-type government. In 1966, President Lyndon Johnson issued two executive orders enforcing the embargo, but in 1971 Congress voted in favor of a bill, known as the Byrd Amendment, to enable limited trade with Rhodesia. Yet Congress also determined that material critical to national security, such as chromium, could be exempt from the embargo if the only other source for the material was a communist country. In 1972, the Court of Appeals for the

District of Columbia determined that although the Byrd Amendment clearly violated the Security Council Resolution, the court was without authority to rule on the issue. In 1976, the same court determined that it had no authority to order the government to comply with the Security Council Resolution. Absent from either appellate court decision was a determination that Congressman Diggs lacked standing to seek redress in the federal courts. Finally, the experience of concerned citizens who argued that several members of Congress violated the Constitution's separation of powers doctrine in *Schlesinger v. Reservists Committee to Stop to the War*, only to receive a judicial answer that while the concerned citizens might be right, the judiciary could not resolve an issue that the Constitution intended for Congress to solve, might have caused senators to shy away from joining Goldwater.

The Continuing Downward Spiral of the World and the Court's Reaction: Strengthening the Presidency in Crisis Times

By the time the justices deliberated on Goldwater's suit, US foreign policy was further in crisis, not only in regard to Iran and South and Central America but also with Afghanistan and Pakistan. And, in times of crisis, the strength of the presidency is paramount to the nation's success in preserving its global position. On November 22, Americans woke to the news that for the second time in two months, a US embassy had been attacked. This time, antigovernment protesters in Pakistan stormed the US embassy in Islamabad, trapping over one hundred employees inside and burning the embassy to the ground. (The embassy personnel survived the fire by evacuating into a vault.) Pakistani military forces rescued the Americans but not before the protesters killed a US Marine embassy guard and two Pakistani guards. The protesters' embassy assault came after a Sunni Islamist attack on the Grand Mosque in Saudi Arabia the previous day. Saudi Arabia's Sunni Islamists were not aligned with the Shia in Iran, but they nonetheless called for cutting the United States off from Saudi oil in a manner similar to Khomeini's demands. In response, Saudi military forces stormed the Grand Mosque, killing over one hundred of the Islamists. Khomeini claimed that the Saudi assault was ordered by the United States and Israel, and he encouraged attacks on those nations' embassies worldwide. The Pakistani protesters, who initially were demonstrating against the United States' foreign policy in Cambodia, followed Khomeini's directions.

Carter had a poor relationship with Pakistan's leader Muhammad Zia-ul-Haq, a Pakistani army general who took power in 1978 after ousting the democratically elected Zulfikar Ali Bhutto in a military coup. Before the embassy storming, Zia rebuffed Carter's appeals not to execute Bhutto. Even after the House of Representatives, in a bipartisan vote, passed a resolution appealing to Zia to spare Bhutto's life, Zia ordered the execution to occur. The United States already had a complex relationship with Pakistan dating to that nation's independence in 1947. In his first year in office, President Dwight Eisenhower obtained permission to station military and CIA personnel on a Pakistani military base to conduct intelligence operations against the Soviet Union. In 1954, Eisenhower, with the Senate's confirmation, bound the United States to Pakistan in a Mutual Defense Assistance Agreement, much like Taiwan's. President Johnson had attempted an evenhanded foreign policy with both India and Pakistan during the 1965 India-Pakistan War, leading the Pakistani government to seek China as an ally. However, because the Soviet Union backed India, Pakistan's move toward China was not entirely in reaction to Johnson's policies. Nixon and Henry Kissinger sided with Pakistan in the 1971 India-Pakistan War. So, too, did China. Yet Pakistani military forces committed gross human rights violations in East Pakistan, including widespread murder and rape. And not only did India prevail militarily in the conflict but its military freed East Pakistan to become an independent Bangladesh. To Carter's ire, Zia's government pursued nuclear weapons. In spite of the problems attendant on supporting Pakistan, Zia's government also opposed the Soviet Union's military presence in Afghanistan, as well as the rise of Islamic extremists in the Near East and Iran.

Between the time the Court of Appeals for the District of Columbia issued its *Goldwater* decision and the Supreme Court deliberated on appeal, it was evident that Carter might reposition his administration's relationship with Zia's government. In late November, Vance and national security adviser Zbigniew Brzezinski reported that the Pakistani protesters who attacked the embassy were anti-Zia and favored Khomeini's regime. As a choice of evils, Zia was clearly preferable to Khomeini. Moreover, by December 13, the date the Court released its dismissal order on Goldwater's suit, thirty thousand Soviet military forces were mobilized on the Soviet-Afghan border. Thus, despite Zia's clear rejection of Carter's human rights focus, and because Pakistani foreign policy favored China and opposed both Khomeini and the Soviet Union, Zia could become an important ally. China's importance to containing Soviet aggression as well as helping to stem the spread of religious extremism was accentuated through the addition of Pakistan as an ally. Simply, there was no reasonable alternative to having Zia remain on the sidelines or be a pariah to the United States. While Carter had allies in Congress to support his volte-face with Pakistan, such as Clement Zablocki, others in his own party, including his intraparty opponent, Senator Edward Kennedy, had made it clear Pakistan should be barred from US aid. Once more, Carter needed space to maneuver against the Soviet Union as well to react to a rapidly deteriorating Near East, and once more, China offered a means to assist in both endeavors.

Sparks of dissent in Islamic majority nations seemed to explode against the United States. At the same time the embassy in Kabul was attacked, a Libyan demonstration outside of the US embassy in Tripoli turned violent. Libya's tyrannical leader, Muammar Gaddafi, and the Carter administration had had frosty relations since Carter assumed office. Indeed, ever since Gaddafi deposed King Idris in 1968 and ordered the US Air Force to depart from a base in Libya, relations between the two countries were poor. Gaddafi did not fit nicely into Carter's human rights policies. The Libyan leader was a tyrant who violently suppressed his own citizens when they dissented against his regime, and he supported international terrorism. Added to Carter's dislike of Gaddafi was the fact that Libyan military forces encroached on the African nation of Chad and also supported Idi Amin in Uganda. Carter had enabled a small increase of trade between the two countries, including the sale of four hundred trucks and two 747 aircraft to Libya in late 1978. On December 2, when Libyan demonstrators burned the embassy in Tripoli, Gaddafi, unlike Zia, appeared to celebrate the event. Carter sent a formal rebuke to Gaddafi, and while he acknowledged that the Libyan president had offered to mediate with Iran, he also accused him of withholding protection from the embassy. By the end of the month Carter listed Libya as a sponsor of international terrorism.

The antics of Carter's younger brother, Billy, did not help the administration. Several presidents have had to contend with errant family members, and Carter was no different in this respect. But, as 1979 ended, Billy Carter was in the news for allegedly consorting with Gaddafi. The younger Carter had traveled to Libya in September to participate in celebrations marking the tenth anniversary of the military coup against King Idris that had resulted in Gaddafi seizing power. Gaddafi denounced the peace agreement between Israel and Egypt, and the younger Carter appeared to approve of Gaddafi's statement. Indeed, Billy Carter, who would later be in the news for a scandal dubbed "Billygate," endorsed Gaddafi's anti-Semitism when he proclaimed "there are a lot more Arabs than Jews" to justify attempted equipment sales to Tripoli. Billy Carter was also seen in the presence of Yasser Arafat, leading President Carter to assure the United States that his younger brother had no role in the White House.

On December 7, Carter announced that if the Iranian government put any of the US citizens it held hostage on trial, he was prepared to order a full-scale embargo of Iranian commerce and would seek allies to join in it. The next day, Iran's foreign minister announced that an "international tribunal" would convene to uncover "the crimes of the United States Government in Iran." While Carter's position was short of a threat to use military force—indeed, he made it clear that he wanted to avoid bloodshed—he did not renounce the possibility of a military strike. Moreover, major newspapers and television news reported that Carter had not ruled out the use of military force against Iran. The Soviet government also unsuccessfully attempted to convince Khomeini that freeing the hostages was in the best interest of both Iran and the United States. However, on December 6, the main Soviet newspaper, *Pravda*, accused the Carter administration of using the Iranian crisis as a pretext to militarize the Near East, and Carter responded with a denunciation of the newspaper. Despite the Soviet effort to seek moderation within Iran, Soviet military forces continued to pour into Afghanistan. The Soviets also sent military advisers into Yemen to train that country's forces on their weaponry. The presence of Soviet forces along a major maritime route added to fears of Soviet expansion into the oil-producing nations of the Middle East and Near East. Neither the governments of the United States and the other NATO countries nor that of China wanted this expansion to occur.

The Iran crisis was problematic in other regions as well, including between the United States and its allies. On December 11, Secretary of State Vance excoriated the Japanese government for undercutting efforts to gain the release of hostages. "On a scale of one to fourteen, they'd get a one," Vance claimed. The Japanese foreign minister had cautioned against "haste" at the United Nations before expressing a reluctance to use economic coercion. In 1951, President Harry S. Truman gained the Senate's approval to enter into a defense treaty with Japan. Titled the Treaty of Mutual Cooperation and Security, the agreement with Japan allowed for the basing of US military forces to protect against a Chinese or Soviet invasion. There were occasional protests against US military forces in addition to a growing trade deficit with the importation of Japanese automobiles and other machinery that strained relations between the two governments. The Japanese government's reticence in regard to Iran was difficult for the US government to accept given the vast expenditures of US taxpayer money that went into defending Japan. Yet, beyond freezing Iranian funds in state banks, even Prime Minister Margaret Thatcher in the United Kingdom and President Valéry Giscard d'Estaing in France urged caution. The most Carter was able to obtain from Western Europe prior to the Court issuing *Goldwater* was a joint European Common Market statement insisting that all diplomatic personnel be protected and released.

In 1979, Iranian students in Southern California filed suit against the Justice Department in an effort to stop FBI interviews and potential deportations. More than a thousand Iranian students attended universities in Los Angeles and San Diego at that time and were subject to interrogations and detentions. While it was true that many of the students opposed the Shah, they also opposed Khomeini. Had they been sent home, they likely would have faced accusations of treason and imprisonment, if not death. Their attorneys publicly likened the Justice Department program to the internment of US citizens of Japanese descent during World War II. One of California's senators, the Republican S. I. Hayakawa, championed the constitutionality of reprising the internment as long as it did not include US citizens. He was not alone. Several politicians took cognizance of polls that indicated US citizens would tolerate mass deportations or internments, and then advocated for this to occur.

One of the only bright spots for Carter was that in a Tennessee straw poll, he bested his intraparty challenger, Senator Kennedy, by 83 percent to 14 percent. Yet it was clear that Carter's handling of Iran, rather than China, was emerging as the primary foreign policy challenge for his reelection. Between the release of the court of appeals decision and the Supreme Court's order to dismiss Goldwater's suit, Kennedy assailed Carter's foreign policies not only on Iran—he criticized Carter for permitting the Shah to enter the United States—but also for failing to hold the Chilean government to human rights standards, as well as being weak. Of the three leading Republican candidates, only John Connally—a onetime conservative Democrat who switched parties while serving as Nixon's Treasury secretary—refused to attack Carter on Iran as long as the hostages were in danger. In a Florida Republican straw poll taken in November, after Ronald Reagan, George Bush, and Connally spoke, Reagan emerged as the leader, exclaiming that if he were to become president "we're going to be so respected that never again will a dictator dare invade an American embassy." Connally and Bush echoed Reagan's words. But, in Florida, none of them openly criticized Carter's policy on China. In other venues, however, Reagan insisted that Carter had abandoned Taiwan out of expediency, and some of his Republican supporters compared the president to Neville Chamberlain, the British prime Minister who was the architect of an appeasement policy with Nazi Germany.

One means of understanding the Court's strengthening of the executive branch is to place *Goldwater* alongside contemporaneous judicial decisions directly implicating national security and foreign policy. The Carter administration had to contend with the possibility that intelligence personnel who opposed its Iran or Taiwan policies would take their arguments to the public. This was a reasonable fear, since the CIA itself had dedicated much of its resources to fighting the spread of communism and the recognition of China would not be universally embraced. General John Singlaub, who, it should be recalled, was at least subject to the Uniform Code of Military Justice and had criticized Carter over troop reductions in South Korea, could have faced a court-martial.

Civilians in the intelligence agencies and the military were not subject to court-martial jurisdiction or to a chain of command to the same degree as Singlaub and could go further in their criticisms of Carter. But some of their actions ran afoul of the law.

In the early 1970s, a small group of former intelligence agents, foreign policy employees, and White House personnel not only supplied the press with information embarrassing to presidential administrations but also wrote articles and books detailing the government's missteps, failures, and violations of law in Vietnam, in South and Central America, and even in the United States. Daniel Ellsberg was the most well known among the former analysts and agents who divulged information to the press. In addition to Ellsberg, Percy Fellwock, a twenty-five-year-old former National Security Agency analyst, gave an interview to *Ramparts* magazine, a left-leaning publication. He revealed to the public, for the first time, that the National Security Agency had a larger budget than the CIA and that his agency had surveilled US citizens. Like Ellsberg, Fellwock's reason for going public was to prevent another administration from committing the United States to an unnecessary war such as the Vietnam Conflict. "My experience with the United States government and its global mission has convinced me that the most dangerous threat to me, my family, and to world peace itself is the American military," he claimed to the *New York Times*.

In response to persons like Fellwock and Ellsberg, the Nixon, Ford, and Carter administrations pursued legal action against former intelligence employees, even when high-ranking government officials such as Henry Kissinger had engaged in misconduct and obtained legal coverage to do so. The Nixon administration's response to Ellsberg, including breaking into the office of his psychologist to find damaging information, is one example of the imbalanced enforcement of laws. None of the unlawful actors in the break-in faced criminal charges. Higher up in the Nixon administration, Kissinger convinced the FBI to wiretap the conversations of his National Security Council subordinates, including Morton Halperin—another instance of the disparity in treatment with senior officials. After being sued, Kissinger, Nixon, former attorney general John Mitchell, and H. R. Haldeman claimed qualified immunity. Kissinger ultimately apologized to Halperin but did not suffer in the courts.

Between 1970 and 1980, the federal courts issued three significant civil, rather than criminal, decisions that reduced the incentive for current and former government personnel to inform the public about governmental abuses and mismanagement. The federal judiciary did not narrow the ability of aggrieved federal employees to report misconduct to law enforcement or investigative agencies, but the justices disincentivized public releases. Prior to the Whistleblower Protection Act of 1989, civil servants could be removed from their employment after reporting misconduct. This is what Nixon tried to do with Arthur Ernest Fitzgerald. Three former intelligence agents, Victor Marchetti, Frank Snepp, and Philip Agee, had engaged in different activities. Marchetti, a former CIA agent, published a book that contained classified information in violation of his employment contract. Snepp published a book that contained no classified information but was nonetheless in violation of his CIA employment contract. Agee, on the other hand, endangered the lives of federal intelligence personnel around the world through the publication, in 1975, of his book *Inside the Company*. (Ford's administration was convinced that Agee was responsible for the murder of an agent in Athens named Richard Welch.)

Agee had worked for the CIA from 1957 to 1968 as an undercover operative in Mexico, Ecuador, and Uruguay and then resigned from the federal service to live in Europe and have his book published by a British press. Prior to the Court's *Goldwater* decision, the *New York Times* reported that Agee, from his new residence in Hamburg, West Germany, had communicated with the Iranian government. In response, the State Department revoked his passport in the hopes that West Germany would deport him. Although Agee's case would not be decided by the Court until after Reagan became president, it is noteworthy that after Agee left the United States, Secretary of State Vance stripped him of his passport and he filed suit before Goldwater filed his. Unlike Marchetti and Snepp, Agee's traverse through the courts had less to do with censorship or employment and more to do with the government's control over a citizen's movements abroad.

The legal environment of the first five years of the 1970s was characterized as a freeing of restraints against the class of speech that the executive branch asserted was detrimental to the safety of the nation. Put another way, during the Nixon administration, greater protections were given to speech against claims that the dissemination of government information would directly, or indirectly, harm national security. For instance, in 1971, the Court determined in *New York Times v. United States*, that the government had to overcome a heavy burden against any governmental system of prior restraint on expression, even over matters that the government claimed were secretive or essential to national security. This opinion arose from Ellsberg providing to the *New York Times* and the *Washington Post* a classified study on the origins and escalation of the United States' involvement in the Vietnam War. In response, Nixon sought a restraining order against both newspapers. He prevailed against the *New York Times* in district court and before the Court of Appeals for the Second Circuit, but lost to the *Washington Post* in district court and before the Court of Appeals for the District of Columbia. Ultimately, the administration failed to convince the Supreme Court that national security assertions alone could trounce freedom of the press.

Although the *New York Times* has been studied and analyzed for a variety of purposes, it is important to note that in issuing the decision, the Court enabled the press to report on national security policy misjudgments and agency infighting and to pressure the governmental toward greater transparency. While a free society may rightly prize a free press, it can also cause worry in the executive branch over legitimate national security and foreign policy decisions. This was not the executive branch's only worry. In *Gravel v. United States*, the Court found that the existence of a legislative privilege enabled a member of Congress to reveal classified information in Congress through the Constitution's speech and debate clause. This meant that a newspaper could publish a legislator's divulging of classified information. However, the federal judiciary enabled a means to prevent disclosure of classified information beyond traditional criminal prosecutions for offenders, and in 1979 the Court affirmed the application of constructive trusts—in effect, an embargo on remuneration for work—to national security leaks. As a result, if a government employee or contractor were to try to undermine Carter's determination to recognize the People's Republic of China and rescind the treaty with Taiwan, or weaken Carter's position with Iran, the judicial branch had given the administration a means to oppose such efforts short of criminal prosecution. There was some precedence for this leverage.

In 1972, the Court of Appeals for the Fourth Circuit determined that Frank Marchetti was bound by a prepublication agreement even after he left the agency. Marchetti served in the CIA for over a decade, including rising to become an assistant to the deputy director. But after leaving the agency in 1969, he published a novel as well as an article in *The Nation* in which he criticized the agency's policies. In contrast to Fellwock, Marchetti was not against the United States' involvement in Vietnam; indeed, he appears to have been a staunch conservative and anticommunist. Nixon obtained an injunction in court against Marchetti's future publications as well as stopping his work already with a publisher until it went through an agency prepublication review. Marchetti tried to rely on the *New York Times*, but the appellate court found a substantial difference between the executive branch trying to prevent a newspaper from publishing classified intelligence and a former employee's clear violation of an employment contract with the agency. In giving weight to the executive branch's argument that Marchetti's actions had the potential to undermine national security, the appellate court also determined that a ruling in the government's favor had to occur quickly in order to minimize the potential damage to national security that could ensue.

Marchetti's case drew Nixon's personal interest, although Nixon did not seek to retaliate against him as he had done against Fitzgerald. After disagreeing with national reporting on the Fourth Circuit's decision, the Nixon administration wrote to *Washington Post* reporter Katherine Graham that restrictions on federal employees already existed, such as the Hatch Act, which prevented civil servants from engaging in political activities. It was not, therefore, unreasonable to prevent national security and foreign policy leaks that could damage the nation's standing in the world. "In our view, the evidence established that if published the items in question would have a serious adverse impact on intelligence sources and methods," an administration official penned. "If such limitations can be imposed without the consent of the employee, how much more logical it is that the Government can expect compliance with every field of national security." Both the Court and the Ford and Carter administrations were to agree with this assessment.

The Court did not grant certiorari to Marchetti's appeal. However, the Fourth Circuit and the Supreme Court found further use for *Marchetti* in an appeal raised by Frank Snepp. The CIA employed Snepp from 1968 through 1976. Like Marchetti, at no time was he a part of the Carter administration, but the administration wanted to make an example out of him in the courts. A 1965 graduate of Columbia University, Snepp joined the agency as an analyst and an interrogator. From 1969 until the fall of Saigon in 1975, he worked in South Vietnam; the following year he resigned from the federal government in protest of the failure to evacuate hundreds of Vietnamese who aided the United States during the conflict and were now in Vietnamese prisons or had been executed. In 1977, Snepp published *Decent Interval*, a book that detailed the agency's failings in Vietnam. Shortly after, CIA director Stansfield Turner tried to have the Justice Department stop the book's publication on the basis that Snepp, like all agents, had signed in his employment contract a promise not to publish matters without agency approval and Snepp never obtained permission. Unlike in *Marchetti*, the agency also conceded that *Decent Interval* was unlikely to cause direct harm to the national security. On the other hand, Turner and former director William Colby both testified that while Snepp had not divulged classified evidence, he had violated the prepublication review agreement, and this imperiled the national security for other reasons—namely, both officials claimed that an inability to punish Snepp and others like him would result in foreign intelligence agencies becoming less likely to share classified information with the United States.

Both Snepp's book and the government's actions to punish him garnered national news coverage. He appeared on the widely watched CBS program *Sixty Minutes* in an interview conducted by Mike Wallace. Snepp claimed to Wallace that Kissinger had intentionally withheld important information from the South Vietnamese government during the 1972 Paris peace negotiations so that the cease-fire that resulted from the negotiations caught the Republic of Vietnam's government by surprise and unprepared to defend itself from North Vietnam as well as from the Viet Cong. Although Snepp had no personal knowledge of the intelligence failings in Iran, the timing of his book and public appearances placed the agency in the worst possible light. Turner, at Carter's direction and in response to the Senate and House investigations conducted during the Ford administration, had reduced the numbers of agents and clandestine operations. Carter's detractors claimed that as a result of his policies in shrinking the agency, the United States was wholly unprepared for the revolution in Iran. Indeed, the public was led to believe that the agency did not know Khomeini existed prior to his return to Tehran, with headlines such as the *Washington Post*'s from April 8, 1979, that read, "The Intelligence Community's Case against Turner: Stansfield Turner and the CIA." And, as early as February 1979, Turner conceded that his intelligence estimates for Iran were inadequate.

Even the public commentary on Snepp's case and appeal were problematic for the White House. On September 8, 1978, the *New York Times* reported that Judge Oren Lewis of the US District Court for the Eastern District of Virginia ruled that Snepp had to obtain the director's permission to publish and that Snepp had willfully violated his contract. Yet, the *Times* made it clear that Snepp had not endangered the country and the government's treatment of him appeared to be based on malice. Three months later, the *Times* headlined, "Ex-Official Suing to Block Move Barring Book on CIA Failures." On March 21, 1979, the *Washington Post* reported that the Court of Appeals for the Fourth Circuit determined that while Snepp had violated his employment contract, the district court had improperly punished him by imposing thousands of dollars in fines. Even the widest-circulating Canadian newspaper, the *Toronto Globe and Mail*, asked, in regard to the administration's handling of Snepp, "Why have things gone so wrong, from the viewpoint of civil liberties, in the Carter administration?"

But the district court had agreed with the government's argument that Snepp's employment contract was enforceable in the federal courts and with the remedies of preventing further publication as well as enabling the government take all the proceeds from the sale of *Decent Interval*. In essence, the district court enabled a constructive trust against Snepp. On appeal, the Fourth Circuit recognized that it could not stop the book publisher from printing and distributing Snepp's book; instead, it determined that Snepp could be held liable not only for compensatory damages but also punitive damages. Since Snepp could not discharge a debt to the federal government through bankruptcy, he now faced the possibility of owing a permanent financial debt to the government, which could be recouped through the garnishment of his income or property. Under the district court's remedy, the government would be able to recover for costs regardless of whether Snepp divulged classified information, and the appellate court's remedy would only be available if Snepp divulged classified information that caused harm to the agency. Both Snepp and the United States appealed the appellate court's decision, with the United States arguing for reimposing the district court's remedy, and Snepp arguing that he should be free to publish without any financial penalty.

At the same time the Court debated the merits of Goldwater's brief and Carter's response, it debated Snepp's case. On February 9, 1980, the Court, in a per curiam opinion authored by Justice Lewis Powell, who had long been involved in national security, issued *Snepp v. United States.* Initially only Powell wanted to grant certiorari, and he underscored what was at risk with the appeal. To Justice Harry Blackmun he penned, "My guess is that the government is nervous about this case as it would be quite disastrous if Snepp's cross-petition were granted and this Court went on to invalidate the secrecy agreement altogether . . . the CIA has taken a beating in recent years and its nervousness may be understandable." By the end of November, Powell convinced Chief Justice Warren Burger and Justices Blackmun, Byron White, and William Rehnquist that an oral argument or fuller consideration of Snepp's case would harm the government.

Justices William J. Brennan, Thurgood Marshall, John Paul Stevens, and Potter Stewart opposed any remedy that enabled the government to recover both economic and punitive damages. They also argued that while a constructive trust might be constitutional, it first had to be legislated in Congress before it could be enforced in the courts, and Congress had never specifically authorized this remedy. Powell initially found himself in dissent on the issue of a remedy in the absence of legislation. On November 16, 1979, he circulated his argument that the government had a constructive trust remedy available regardless of its nonexistence in statute. Powell explained to Blackmun that, after he conferred with former secretary of state Dean Rusk, he learned that a pending bill in Congress to modify the intelligence agencies' employment contracts to only require prepublication review for classified material "would damage even further the capacity of the CIA to function effectively in the national interest"; therefore, the Court had to make a statement that broad remedies could be applied regardless of the nature of the publication. In essence, Powell sought to preempt Congress in an act that can only be described as judicial activism.

Powell began his draft dissent by stressing the limited contractual nature of Snepp's appeal, which, when viewed through employment and contract law, was not a complaint restraint on freedom of speech. He then noted that Snepp's employment with the CIA was a position with "a high degree of public trust" and that Snepp had agreed to the agency's condition of employment requiring him to submit all potential publications to an agency review. Powell took exception to the appellate court's determination that the agency could only extend the prepublication review requirement to classified information, even though he accepted the government's apparent concession that Snepp had not, in fact, divulged sensitive information. To this end, he contended that the greater issue was that Snepp's actions had the potential to "be detrimental to [the nation's] national interests." Powell relied on Turner's testimony that intelligence agency's sources around the world had increasingly decided to cease cooperation with the United States. "If former agents may rely on their own judgment about what information is harmful," Powell argued "the intelligence agencies of friendly nations and the foreign agents recruited by the CIA cannot be assured of the secrecy upon which their cooperation depends."

Powell also recognized that conventional civil litigation subjected the government to open discovery of its evidence, which could prove more harmful to the national security than the publication of a book such as Snepp's. As a result, the enforcement of a contract through a constructive trust provided the best safeguard against the future actions of would-be Snepp imitators. A constructive trust enforcement would prevent Snepp, and other would-be writers, from receiving publication income without forcing the government to disclose classified or embarrassing information. On the other hand, Powell's draft dissent did not address instances where an intelligence agency employee freely divulged information to the public through the press.

Powell's argument evolved into a per curiam opinion, which Burger, Rehnquist, Blackmun, White, and Stewart ultimately joined. The transition into a per curiam occurred because Powell was able to sway Stewart and Blackmun away from viewing the appeal as a First Amendment issue to an employment contract issue. Stevens, along with Brennan and Marshall, dissented. They stressed that the purpose of the CIA's employment contract was never to censor its employees; rather, it was to ensure that classified information was not disclosed to the public. Because the government conceded that Snepp did not compromise the national security, Stevens argued, the Court had no authority to enforce a remedy that Congress had not expressly authorized. Moreover, Stevens stressed that Snepp's First Amendment right of free speech over nonclassified information had, by both the government and the Court, been "harshly restricted," and the majority enabled the government to "misuse its authority to delay the publication of a critical work or to persuade an author to modify the contents of his work beyond the demands of secrecy."

Former solicitor general and special prosecutor Archibald Cox penned in the *Harvard Law Review* that "Snepp's conduct aroused the scorn of a majority of Justices even though the use of the leak as an instrument of political conflict and its sanctification by the mass media have dulled some moral senses." Cox went on to criticize the *Snepp* decision for stifling a means for the population to know of their government's missteps and chastised the Court for its summary disposition of the appeal. He also juxtaposed the Court's decision in *Snepp* against *Hutchinson v. Proxmire*, a decision in which the Court permitted an aggrieved medical researcher to sue a US senator for libel. In *New York Times v. Sullivan*, in 1964, the Court determined that public officials could only prevail in a libel suit if they could prove actual malice instead of negligence. While the Court then, in 1979, strengthened the presidency in *Snepp* and *Goldwater*, the justices would not accord the same protections to members of Congress. *Hutchinson* arose from a medical researcher suing Senator William Proxmire (D-WI) for defamation after Proxmire accused the researcher of "fleecing" the nation's taxpayers. (Proxmire had issued "golden fleece" awards to scientific researchers who received federal grants for projects he deemed unworthy.) Cox finally argued that Snepp's attorneys should have been permitted to present a full argument to the Court so that the justices and the public could flesh out the issues raised in the appeal. Instead, the Court, as it would do in *Goldwater*, issued a decision without permitting oral argument. Cox was hardly alone in his criticisms of the Court not permitting full argument in Snepp's appeal. The *Washington Post*'s editorial board accused the Court of crafting a decision that would "help it plug its own leaks."

On October 30, 1979, the Court heard argument on an appeal titled *Vance v. Terrazas*. Although the decision would not be issued until January 15, 1980, like *Snepp*, it provides further context to the Court's strengthening the executive branch in crisis times. *Terrazas* arose from the government's denaturalizing a native-born citizen by utilizing the "preponderance of the evidence standard." It was true that Congress statutorily authorized the lower standard, but the Court did not always display deference to Congress's statutes on denaturalization. In 1958, the Court, in *Trop v Dulles*, rejected the government's position that citizenship could be stripped from military deserters in wartime, and in *Kennedy v. Mendoza-Martinez*, in 1963, the Court determined that a person who evaded the draft could likewise not be stripped of citizenship unless they declared they did not consider themselves a citizen. Indeed, in both cases the Court called US citizenship "one of the most valuable rights in the world today." In the sixteen years since *Mendoza-Martinez* and twenty-one years since *Trop*, global conditions had changed, as had much of the Court. (Indeed, only Brennan and Stewart were on the Court for both *Mendoza-Martinez* and *Terrazas*.) The "preponderance of the evidence" standard, typically used in civil trials such as tort cases and much easier to prove than the "beyond a reasonable doubt standard" used in criminal trials or the "clear and convincing standard" used in determining competency, was upheld by the justices. Justices Brennan, Marshall, and Stewart dissented, arguing in conference that the "preponderance of the evidence standard" was unfair to a litigant who fought to maintain the constitutional right of citizenship. *Terrazas* would make it easier to deport Iranian Americans or others who professed loyalty to the country of their birth.

The same day the justices heard argument on *Terrazas*, they also heard argument on *Kissinger v. Reporters Committee for Freedom of the Press*, an appeal against a lower court decision involving the extension of Freedom of Information Act disclosure requirements to former secretary of state Kissinger. The records in question would have fallen under the release requirements of the act had they been in the custody of the government. In this instance, the Court determined that although Kissinger may have wrongly removed correspondences from the State Department, once they were removed, the State Department was not obligated to retrieve them for public disclosure. During the Court's *Kissinger* deliberations, Justice Rehnquist insisted that the Court remain neutral and not assess whether Kissinger had broken the law in removing documents from the State Department. This decision, when viewed alongside *Snepp* and *Marchetti*, further illustrates the Court's role in strengthening the executive branch by creating shields against the disclosure of potentially embarrassing national security and foreign policy mishaps. That it occurred in the midst of the Iran and Soviet Union–Afghanistan crises, as well as in a period of economic woe, provides further context to *Goldwater's* contemporary importance.

Finally, there was the traverse of Arthur Ernest Fitzgerald's case through the courts, and the fact that the justices would later grant certiorari on Nixon's claim of presidential immunity. Fitzgerald had prevailed in the US District Court for the District of Columbia to force the Civil Service Commission to hold an open hearing into his efforts for reinstatement. The commission reinstated him, but he clearly suffered economic losses and public humiliation, and the Department of Defense had not reinstated him to his prior leadership position. When he tried to recover his full losses, the lower courts determined that he was time-barred from pursuing claims against governmental actors. However in the civil discovery process, he learned that the Nixon White House, including Nixon, had acted with personal malfeasance against him. The district court and appellate court then determined that because Fitzgerald had no reason to suspect White House officials who had hidden their malfeasance, he could pursue a lawsuit against them despite the statute of limitations. In the summer of 1978, the lawsuit named Richard Nixon, Alexander Butterfield, and Bryce Harlow, and it was inevitable that the Court would grant certiorari, even though the Court would not issue its opinion until 1982. After all, if a citizen could sue a president, it was possible that that the lawsuit could be used to upend a national security or foreign policy program. Given the widespread news reporting on Fitzgerald's suit against Nixon in 1979, as well as Nixon's public claims of immunity, it is hardly conceivable that the justices did not consider that they would take up the issue of presidential immunity from civil suits by the time they issued *Goldwater*.

Carter and the Supreme Court's Decision to Take Up the Issue

On the morning of December 13, Chief Justice Warren Burger informed the Court in a typewritten memo that the "case will come down as it appears in this attachment at 4 o'clock or soon thereafter as printing can be completed." Burger added in his personal handwriting, "subject to any contingencies." Justices Brennan, Stewart, and Marshall had experienced the type of "contingencies" that the chief justice referred to, including major public demonstrations and civic unrest against the Vietnam Conflict. In early May 1970, after President Nixon announced that thirty thousand of the nation's military forces along with a larger force of the army of the Republic of Vietnam crossed into Cambodia, the United States convulsed with antiwar demonstrations, making it difficult for the federal government to function in the nation's capital. The Iranian crisis did not result in major demonstrations that threatened the government, but it became public knowledge that the Department of Defense was considering a military strike. The justices knew this, and for reasons distinct from the summary disposition used in *Snepp*—mainly that maximum flexibility had to be accorded to the president on a political question—the majority was willing to speedily dispose of Goldwater's appeal. But, this was not because any of the justices had a particular affinity for Carter's insistence that a president had the sole authority to terminate a treaty. As in many presidential administrations, Carter's relationship to the Court defies a singular statement of "positive" or "negative." In at least one instance the justices were exasperated with the White House's conduct.

In 1977, Carter had tried to convince the Court to uphold university and college admissions programs that took race into account, even to the detriment of white applicants by filing an amicus brief. The University of California Davis School of Medicine had adopted an admissions system—often labeled as affirmative action—that denied entrance to Alan Bakke, a white Marine Corps veteran and NASA engineer, but accepted minority applicants with lower grade point averages and medical school aptitude test scores. Bakke's appeal made it to the Court after the California Supreme Court ruled against the university admissions system. Rather than remain quiet on this issue, Carter decided to file an amicus brief in favor of one of the sides in the case, but which side was initially unclear. Griffin Bell sided with Bakke and against affirmative action. However, Carter had obtained over 80 percent of the African American vote in 1976, and the leaders of the National Association for the Advancement of Colored People stressed to him that his attempts to balance the federal budget had deleterious effects on urban minorities. Carter opposed the Justice Department's first brief that argued admissions based on racial preferences violated the Constitution and insisted on involvement by the White House counsel in the amicus drafting process. Instead of a brief that sided with Bakke and denounced quotas as unconstitutional, Carter's administration forwarded a brief that opined quotas were unconstitutional, but racial considerations within affirmative action could be used to remedy past exclusions from higher education and therefore open doors to the economic advancement. Unlike amicus practice from other sources, the solicitor general is able to argue that the executive branch's amicus brief represents the best interests of the county, and generally the side that the Justice Department aligns with in an amicus brief prevails on appeal.

Laura Kalman, in her comprehensive book on the 1970s titled *Right Star Rising: A New Politics, 1974–1980*, noted "the extent of public interest in *Bakke*" was very broad. She also pointed out that Burger—who knew of the White House's role in changing the Justice Department's position—expressed to the solicitor general that "the entire Court was offended and displeased" by the White House's behavior. Ironically, the Court's plurality opinion enabled affirmative action to survive, though not systems of quotas, and the *Bakke* case served to further divide conservatives from liberals regarding the legality of Carter's actions within other areas of governance. It also may have led to some of the justices wondering whether Carter's claims of presidential authority were uniformly agreed on in the White House.

Carter's relationship with the justices, however, was not always uncooperative. Although Carter did not have the opportunity to nominate a justice to the Supreme Court, he turned to Burger for occasional advice. In 1977, Burger traveled to the Soviet Union and lectured on the US Constitution. While Burger was in Moscow, Premier Leonid Brezhnev "berated" him over the stalled Strategic Arms Limitations Talks II, and when Burger returned to the United States, he advised Carter on how to communicate with the premier. Thus, in the case of the chief justice, there is evidence of the Court working to strengthen the United States' position against the Soviet Union. Since one of Carter's rationales in seeking normalization was to counter the Soviet Union's apparent aggressions, Burger's advice to Carter and his siding with the plurality in

Goldwater evidences a desire to have Carter's foreign policy succeed as it applied to Soviet expansion.

Deliberations and Quick Decision: Standing and Justiciability

Three days after the court of appeals issued its decision, Goldwater petitioned the Supreme Court to conduct an expedited review. Just as Carter sought a quick decision at the appellate court, Goldwater's reasoning for this request was based on the fact that Carter had declared the Mutual Defense Treaty to be terminated on January 1, 1980. If the Court were to grant an expedited hearing, the solicitor general would have an abbreviated period in which to answer Goldwater's brief. There was a good reason for the solicitor general to not oppose an expedited hearing, beyond removing an impediment to an important foreign policy consideration as well as the possibility that the United States would find itself in a military conflict. In less than one year, the voters would determine whether Carter would be renominated as the Democratic Party's candidate for the presidency and then compete for the presidency against the Republican Party challenger, whoever the challenge might be. A judicial affirmance of presidential foreign policy authority could be favorable for Carter's reelection, or so it was believed, and a judicial rejection not only could add a difficulty to Carter's reelection prospects but also could confine future presidents. Blackmun and White found the push for an expedited review preposterous.

On December 7, 1979, the justices met in conference to discuss how to proceed on Goldwater's appeal. Burger began the Court's discussions by pointing out that Congress had never formally opposed Carter and therefore the justiciability of Goldwater's claim remained an open question on the basis of a lack of standing. While Burger doubted Goldwater possessed standing to proceed and agreed with Judges Wright and Tamm, he urged that the safest response was to deny Goldwater a full hearing on the basis of a lack of ripeness, because the Senate had yet to act against Carter. An issue is deemed not "ripe" when a controversy has yet to arise. Put another way, the federal judiciary, unlike its European counterparts, does not issue advisory opinions. Brennan argued to grant

Goldwater's appeal, but he intended to rule against the senator. Because the appellate court had overruled Gasch on the basis of the specific treaty rather than on a constitutional principle, Brennan believed that treaty termination could remain a contentious area between the legislative and executive branches, and this made it necessary for the Court to issue a substantive opinion. He insisted that the executive branch had the sole constitutional authority to terminate treaties and wanted the Court to make this clear. Stewart sought to vacate Gasch's ruling on the nonjusticiable political question doctrine and argued that Gasch should have dismissed Goldwater's appeal on this basis alone.

According to Powell's notes, when the justices met in conference to discuss how to proceed with Goldwater's appeal, there was a consensus among the majority that the Court should craft an order to the district court to dismiss the suit. But there was disagreement on the basis to do so. Burger sent out the first of several memorandums to the justices, insisting that Goldwater and the other signatories lacked standing to bring the claim to the courts in the first place. Together with Stevens, they presented a dismissal order that read, "Without intimating any view on whether the question presented is a non-justiciable political question, we hold that petitioners do not have standing to prosecute this action." However, Burger and Stevens did not persuade any of the other justices on the issue of standing. As of the morning of December 10, five of the justices, including Stevens, agreed that the suit presented a political question and was therefore not justiciable in the courts.

In the early evening of December 10, Burger circulated his notes of the justices' discussions on the merits of whether to consider the substantive constitutional issues raised by Goldwater. He also issued a short draft order to the district court to dismiss the original suit but assured the Court that he would be open to other avenues of disposing of the challenge to Carter's action. Blackmun responded that he intended to dissent, arguing that the Court's rush to dismiss Goldwater's suit created an unintended illusion that the senators had raised a meritless issue, when, in fact, there was a constitutional question to Carter's actions. That afternoon, Powell countered that while Burger had adopted the "Wright-Tamm" concurrence, he could not agree to a statement that denied that standing existed to members of Congress. Powell worried that doing so would weaken the ability of the legislative branch to confront a future wayward president in the courts. Instead, he recommended disposing of the suit on the basis of ripeness. To this end, he agreed with ordering the district court to dismiss the claim.

As of the next day, the Court still had not formulated an order on Goldwater's appeal. Stewart reminded Burger that unlike appeals that arose from a state supreme court, the justices had the authority to send the appeal back to the district court with an order to dismiss the suit. Stewart's advice to Burger also contained a statement that the justices might do so without explaining why. Implicit in Stewart's advice was that a dismissal order without an explanation might appear to the public as an act devoid of judicial neutrality. But, Stewart was not wedded to his own advice. "If Bill Rehnquist writes an explanation of why the case is non-justiciable, I shall likely join in such writing," he wrote. "If all five of us are inclined to do so, such a written explanation might well become a *per curiam*, and Lewis Powell's statement could still remain a concurrence in the order."

Rehnquist had, in fact, authored a proposed per curiam dismissing the suit based on the political question doctrine. While he was not convinced that standing existed in this instance, he also considered the ramifications of the Court denying standing to senators. To this end, Rehnquist penned that he was willing to assume, without ruling, that Goldwater possessed standing. Like Powell, Rehnquist did not want to close an avenue for congressional redress in the federal courts, and in crafting a dismissal on the basis of a nonjudicial political question doctrine, he at least preserved the notion that Goldwater had raised a legitimate constitutional challenge to Carter. He even posited in his memorandum to the Court that when the case came before Judge Gasch, it may have been justiciable, but subsequent events made it necessary to dismiss on the grounds he advanced.

In conference and in their private communications, both Rehnquist and Marshall took the strongest position against standing. Marshall argued "these senators have no more business to bring this suit than any citizen has" before concluding, "This is a purely political question and the petitioners want an advisory opinion." Marshall had no affinity for Goldwater's past political positions, which, if placed into law, would have perpetuated segregation. Rehnquist, though disagreeing with Marshall on his views of Goldwater, added that even if Congress had voted to retain the treaty, the Court "had no business getting into this political question." Stevens added to the conversation by calling Goldwater's appeal "a classic case of a political question with no judicially manageable standards."

Powell, as he had in *Bakke*, advanced a "middle position." He recognized that a majority of the Senate, or a majority of Congress as an entire body, could have disapproved of Carter's actions, and had this occurred, he argued, it would have made the outcome of the suit a different matter. If Carter ignored the legislative branch under such circumstances, then the federal courts could determine the issue over whether the executive branch possessed sole authority to terminate a treaty. "If Congress had taken a position," Powell reasoned, "there would be a genuine case or controversy." However, because neither the Senate acting alone nor Congress had affirmatively demanded Carter submit the revocation for their consent, "prudential reasons exist for the Court staying out of the argument." In contrast to the justices who wanted to avoid ruling on Goldwater's appeal, White countered that Goldwater possessed standing and that the issue of treaty revocation presented a genuine case or controversy. On the other hand, White opposed accelerating the Court's calendar because the treaty would survive an answer to the case. "If the president doesn't have power, his action on January 1 would become invalid," White concluded. Blackmun joined with White in arguing for standing and characterized the issue as "an extremely important case."

The Court's decision to dismiss Goldwater's suit, thereby negating the court of appeals and district court, was a fractured one, evidencing the justices' differing views on when, if ever, the judiciary should enter into the thicket of foreign policy. But it was clear that the Court did not want to solve a separation of powers quandary if it did not have to do so. Rehnquist's plurality statement joined by Burger, Stewart, and Stevens is, in reality, a lengthy denial of certiorari with an order to vacate the previous rulings. He began the opinion by arguing that Goldwater's legal arguments presented a nonjusticiable political question. In making his argument, Rehnquist relied on *Coleman v. Miller*, a 1939 opinion authored by Chief Justice Charles Evans Hughes that defined the political question doctrine. Rehnquist, perhaps in a nod to Stevens, also cited to *Dyer v Blair*, a three-judge panel decision of the US District Court for the

Northern District of Illinois. In that decision, authored in 1975 by Stevens, the three federal judges determined that the federal courts could not resolve how the state legislature would vote, in the midst of a dispute between state legislators, regarding the proposed Equal Rights Amendment for ratification to the Constitution.

Coleman arguably was a poor starting point as it arose from a domestic issue, albeit one of constitutional magnitude. (Powell would argue as much in his concurrence.) The Kansas state legislature sought a federal judicial declaration that the state senate's vote to ratify a child labor amendment was flawed and therefore invalid. In 1924, Congress passed a proposed amendment that would have enabled the legislative branch to regulate child labor. The proposed amendment arose in response to the Court earlier frustrating the federal government's attempts to regulate child labor In *Coleman*, the Court determined that Congress alone had the constitutional authority to determine how the states would ratify an amendment, and therefore the challenge of the disaffected Kansas state legislators represented a political question that could only be solved by the Congress. *Coleman* had nothing to do with foreign policy, though it is interesting that Rehnquist cited to an opinion resting on the authority of the legislative branch to explain why an appeal from federal legislators against a presidential foreign policy action also represented a political question.

Curtiss-Wright, as noted in the introduction to this book, possessed stronger precedential value to the disposition of Goldwater's suit than *Miller*. There was, however, a distinction between *Curtiss-Wright* and Goldwater's appeal. In 1934, Congress had specifically empowered Roosevelt to prohibit weapons sales to warring nations. In contrast, Carter acted without the express sanction of the Senate. Rehnquist did not note this distinction and, while perhaps he decided that the distinction was too insignificant to merit mention, there was a significant difference between the facts that gave rise to *Curtiss-Wright* and the situation involved in Goldwater's appeal.

Rehnquist also addressed Goldwater's contention that the Court had, in *Youngstown Sheet and Tube v. Sawyer*, limited the president's authority over foreign policy. But in that case, a steel manufacturing corporation contested the seizure of its domestic property by President Truman's administration. The seizure occurred during the Korean War when it appeared that the corporation and its unionized employees could not reach a collective bargaining agreement, and a strike would affect the war effort. In response to Goldwater's argument on presidential limitations, Rehnquist distinguished *Curtiss-Wright* as arising from a president's act that was purely external to the United States, from the seizure of corporate property within the United States during a crisis. In essence, Rehnquist determined that Carter's recognition of the People's Republic of China was more akin to *Curtiss-Wright* than *Youngstown Sheet and Tube*. Rehnquist's dismissal order eviscerated the court of appeals' narrow ruling that because of the manner in which the Mutual Defense Treaty was drafted and passed by Congress, Carter was within his delegated authority to act as he had. Instead, *Goldwater* left open the possibility that a future president could withdraw the United States from any treaty without congressional consent. This feature of the plurality troubled the justices who did not join with Rehnquist. Indeed, the plurality fashioned a statement that made it possible that no treaty was immune to a president's unitary renunciation.

Powell concurred with the plurality's result, but he disagreed that the confrontation between legislators and the president presented a nonjusticiable political question. Instead, he argued, the disagreement between the legislators and the executive branch was not ripe. He pointed out that the Court had previously determined, in *Buckley v. Valeo*, that even on challenges arising from the separation of powers, the judiciary had to wait until an issue was "ripe for judicial review." To Powell, Goldwater's appeal failed this test. Had a Senate majority demanded that Carter submit the issue of treaty revocation for Senate advice and Carter refused to do so, the Court would have had an obligation to determine the constitutional authority of Carter's refusal. As Powell concluded, "The judicial branch should not decide issues affecting the allocation of power between the President and Congress until the political branches reach a constitutional impasse."

Powell also recognized that only a fraction of the Senate had sought a judicial remedy, and if the Court were to act in favor of Goldwater, he believed that it would "encourage small groups or even individual Members of Congress to seek judicial resolution of the issues before the normal political process has the opportunity to resolve the conflict." Powell noted that although the Senate had a pending resolution requiring the executive branch to seek the Senate's advice and consent before undertaking a treaty revocation, there was nothing in the resolution that would have made such a requirement retroactive.

As to the political question doctrine, Powell argued that the particular disagreement between Goldwater and Carter was not nonjusticiable. Because of the Constitution's silence on treaty termination, Powell argued, Carter's claim that a president had the clear authority to rescind a treaty was reviewable under different circumstances. Powell also disagreed with the argument that there was "a lack of judicially discoverable and manageable standards for resolving" the appeal, and he countered that "normal principles of interpretation to the constitutional provisions at issue" would ultimately resolve the appeal. Among the many important features of Powell's concurrence was his insistence that even if the Court were to resolve the impasse between the Senate minority and the president, in this particular case the resolution would not redefine the president's "commander in chief" authorities. Nor, to Powell, would the Court's action impermissibly intrude into the authorities of the two political branches.

Blackmun authored one of the two dissents. Joined by White, Blackmun made it clear he believed that the treaty revocation issue was of significant constitutional importance and the Court should decide it after accepting formal briefs and oral argument. It was problematic, to Blackmun, that the Court denied Goldwater, in an echo of what had occurred in regard to Snepp's appeal, a full opportunity to argue his case. Brennan dissented from the plurality on the basis that the president had the constitutional authority to withdraw recognition of foreign governments. But he did not agree with the plurality's interpretation of the political question doctrine and, indeed, was against expanding the political question doctrine as the plurality appeared to have done. Instead, to Brennan, Goldwater's appeal failed because it asked the Court to redraw the allocations of power between the executive and legislative branches in regard to treaty revocation authority. "The issue of decision making authority must be resolved as a matter of constitutional law, not political discretion," he concluded. "Accordingly, it falls within the competence of the courts."

The Day After

On December 14, when the *New York Times* reported the Court's dismissal order with the headline "High Court Backs Carter on Ending Taiwan Pact: Two Different Rationales," it did so on page 13. The newspaper noted that only two justices voted to hear oral argument, and Brennan wanted to affirm the appellate court's decision. The comment on Brennan was not entirely correct, but the reporting on White and Blackmun insisting on oral argument was. So, too, was the reporting on the Court's two rationales; Rehnquist's and those of the four justices joining him who decided the issue was political and therefore not capable of resolution, and Powell's argument that the appeal was not "ripe for review." The *Times'* lack of excitement for the decision was matched by that of the *Washington Post,* which reported on page 5. The *Los Angeles Times* placed its reporting in its B section. On the *New York Times'* front page was a headline stating that Khomeini had approved of beginning trials over United States citizens for violations of international law. The CBS evening news barely reported on the Court's decision.

More prominently reported on December 14 was that the Japanese government finally agreed to reduce oil imports from Iran as a means for exerting pressure on Khomeini to release the embassy hostages. Also, Kennedy accused Carter of agreeing to drop his opposition to the construction of a new aircraft carrier to curry favor with Senator Jesse Helms (R-NC). Helms had sided with Goldwater and generally opposed Carter's foreign policies. Carter responded by accusing Kennedy of fabricating his information. Oddly, one day after the Court's ruling, the State Department placed restrictions on China's envoys and journalists in retaliation for limiting American journalists to Beijing. The *Los Angeles Times* placed this story on its front page, as did the other newspapers.

Two of the important features of the Court's decision appear to have eluded the news media. Senate majority leader Robert Byrd and his counterpart, minority leader Howard Baker, prevailed in the Court of Appeals for the District of Columbia because that court did not rule on standing or issue a sweeping decision on the nonjusticiable political question doctrine. In a sense, the appellate court's judges issued the decision that the majority of the Senate wanted. This could not be said about

Rehnquist's dismissal order. To be sure, the order intimated standing existed, but the Court's formulation of the political question doctrine was an answer Baker and Byrd dreaded. A second, and equally important, feature was that the Court's decision was not a wholesale loss for Goldwater and his fellow legislators. To the contrary, while the Court declined to rule on the constitutional parameters of treaty revocation, its decision reminded Congress that the elected legislators possessed unique powers to confront a president's foreign policies, such as defunding federal programs they disagreed with. More important, the decision informed Goldwater and his cosignatories that their arguments had constitutional merit, even though the federal judiciary could not take up the issue.

Because the Court placed treaty revocation in the political arena, there remain questions, particularly so in light of the presidency of Donald Trump: Can the intentional presidential breach of a treaty, or an unpopular treaty revocation, become the basis for a House impeachment, and removal through the Senate trial process? A related but broader question is: Can the foreign policy actions of a president that are undertaken for personal gain arise to the "high crimes and misdemeanors" standard required for a finding of guilt in an impeachment trial? And, if not, would the "high crimes and misdemeanor" standard be met if, while pushing for the foreign policy, a president intended the harassment of members of the national security community to prevent dissension from being made public? And, finally, did the Court, in some measure, inadvertently make it more difficult to answer any of these questions in the affirmative?

CHAPTER 6

Aftermath

Within days of the Court's decision, the leading Republican presidential candidates articulated their commitment to Taiwan's defense. Ronald Reagan, George H. W. Bush, Robert Dole, and John Connally promised they would militarily defend Taiwan if it became necessary. But their dedication to preserving Taiwan's sovereignty had limits. At a news event Reagan was asked whether he would accept Taiwanese support for his presidential campaign. Various lobbying organizations apparently offered Taiwanese money to candidates they believed would reverse Carter's policy. Reagan answered, "As President, I will not accept the interference of any foreign power in the process of safeguarding a vital American interest enshrined by law. To do otherwise would be a dereliction of my duty as President." Put another way, Reagan believed he would weaken the nation's sovereignty if his administration became beholden to another government, even to an important ally. The United States would defend Taiwan, Reagan insisted, because it was important for the future of democracy to do so. As recently as 2022, President Joseph Biden pronounced a similar commitment to Taiwan.

By the time the treaty termination was accomplished, there were more pressing matters confronting the United States. The Iranian hostage crisis continued without an end in sight. On April 24, 1980, the US military tried to conduct a hostage rescue. The forces involved never made it to Tehran. An aviation mishap that resulted in eight service members being killed and several others wounded led to the mission being aborted. Days before the mission, Secretary of State Cyrus Vance, who had helped craft the administration's policies with the People's Republic of China, notified Carter that he would resign from office. In his place, Carter selected Edmund Muskie (D-ME), a World War II veteran and a long-serving senator who had been Hubert Humphrey's running mate in 1968 and had unsuccessfully attempted to win the Democrat nomination in 1972. Muskie earlier served in the House of Representatives and was a two-term governor of Maine before being elected to the Senate in 1959. Carter hoped that Muskie would be able to gain legislative support for his policies toward the Soviet Union as well as the continuation of human rights as a tenet of foreign policy, and for the Chinese government to have confidence that the United States was a trustworthy partner in their new relationship.

Two days before Christmas 1979, the *New York Times* notified its readers, under a front-page headline, that the Soviet army had amassed three divisions of soldiers on the Afghanistan border. A Soviet division numbered close to ten thousand soldiers; thus, roughly thirty thousand front-line Soviet army forces were threatening to invade Afghanistan. What the *New York Times* did not, or rather could not, report was that some of the intelligence obtained on Soviet activities had come from China, as well as from US intelligence personnel operating in China with the Chinese government's permission. In spite of the CIA's knowledge of the Soviet presence on the Afghanistan border, as well as knowing that the Soviet army had already placed over five thousand advisers in Afghanistan, the agency's director, Stansfield Turner, publicly professed not to know of the Soviet government's intentions. These intentions became clear when, three days later, the thirty thousand Soviet troops entered Afghanistan and Hafizullah Amin, the leader of Afghanistan, was assassinated in a Soviet-engineered coup.

Although Premier Brezhnev denied complicity in the assassination of Amin, Carter accurately countered that the Soviet military had, indeed, been responsible for the act. In the midst of dozens of newspaper articles and evening news segments on Afghanistan and Iran, the *New York Times* ran an interesting front-page story on December 24 titled "Congress Broadens Its Influence in Foreign Policy." The article noted that within Congress, there was a lack of consensus as to whether an increased legislative role in foreign policy was justified in a time of several crises. Representatives of Carter's own party in the House were angry over the fact that when, in the prior year, Carter ordered a military airlift for the evacuation of Moroccan peacekeeping forces from Zaire after a hostile invasion, he did so without complying with the War Powers Act. Likewise, members of Congress objected to the sale of fighter aircraft to Egypt, Israel, and Saudi Arabia. But none of their objections made it into the federal courts. In response to the Soviet invasion into Afghanistan, the Senate Foreign Relations Committee informed Carter that it would not vote favorably on advancing the second the SALT II treaty for a full Senate vote, and Carter withdrew the treaty from the Senate, ending arms reductions limits with the Soviet Union.

Throughout the remainder of Carter's presidency, the Iran hostage crisis and the Soviet invasion of Afghanistan dominated foreign policy news. Carter increased defense spending and, indeed, began the means to build a larger conventional force through conscription should the need arise. This, too, proved contentious. On top of foreign crises, Americans had become weary of fuel shortages and price spikes, and job losses in the automobile, steel, and other manufacturing industries that only a decade earlier had been symbols of American economic might. Carter did not enter 1980 on an assured path to reelection.

The Aftermath of *Goldwater* in the Courts

Having decided *United States v. Snepp* at the beginning of 1980, the Court still had *Vance v. Agee* to determine. As a cosmetic feature reflecting a new secretary of state, the title of the appeal had changed from *Agee v. Vance* to *Agee v. Muskie* and now to *Haig v. Agee.* But the issue remained the same: How strong was the president in regard to controlling the men and women in the intelligence agencies? From 1957 to 1968, Phillip Agee had been a CIA employee. He resigned his position at the agency and moved to West Germany. Like Snepp, he was required to seek permission to publish or lecture on matters related to his agency service. Agee frequently traveled and gave lectures in which he purposefully disclosed classified information to the foreign public in the hopes that the executive branch's conduct in national security matters and foreign affairs would comport with his views of constitutional law and human rights.

On one occasion, Agee went so far as to advise Khomeini's government to negotiate the release of the hostages in exchange for the CIA providing access to its activities in Iran, with Agee volunteering to confirm to Khomeini the veracity of the agency's information. In response to Agee's activities, the State Department revoked his passport. This action did not strip Agee of citizenship, but it left him with two choices:

to return to the United States or try to gain citizenship elsewhere. The West German government, along with the governments of the other Western European countries, would not permit Agee to remain within their borders without a valid US passport. Agee feared that his return to the United States would result in a criminal prosecution, and he tried to preempt a prosecution with a judicial victory over the passport issue. Ultimately, Agee returned but was never convicted of a crime.

The Court, in a decision authored by Chief Justice Warren Burger, upheld the executive branch's authority to revoke or suspend a US citizen's passport if the citizen's conduct was detrimental to national security. In conference, Burger insisted that the First Amendment does not give a person the right to divulge national security, nor does it give a person the right to undermine the national security or foreign policy by advising foreign governments such as Khomeini's. Justice John Paul Stevens agreed that the right to foreign travel could be conditioned on the purpose of the travel, particularly if the purpose was to undermine the United States by divulging intelligence information. The majority recognized that it was, as a feature of domestic law in addition to the laws of other nations, illegal to travel abroad without a passport. They also recognized that in their prior decisions, the Court had made it clear that freedom of domestic travel is a right. Nonetheless, the justices held that while passport revocation curtailed international travel, any right to international travel was subordinate to "national security and foreign policy considerations." Brennan and Marshall dissented, arguing that just as the Constitution protects popular and unpopular speech, it also protects popular and unpopular travelers.

By 1979, the readiness of the nation's armed forces for a major conflict was in doubt, and the Senate Armed Services Committee, with Carter's support, began to examine the possibility of a new military draft. The All Volunteer Force—the name given to the military after President Nixon ended the draft in 1973—was considered a "hollow shell." Only 27 percent of recruits scored "above average" on the military's intelligence and aptitude tests. The military had become less of a mirror of US society than it had been during the draft. In NATO exercises, the army scored below its British, German, and Italian counterparts. While the United States maintained a nuclear force, there were questions as to whether a conventional war with Iran could be fought to a conclusion.

In his 1980 State of the Union address, Carter recommended a return to draft registration, which was rightly seen as a step toward conscription. In April of that year, Congress authorized Carter to enact Selective Service, and in June he did so. This required all males between the ages of eighteen and twenty-five to register for the draft. In *Rostker v. Goldberg*, the Court upheld the constitutionality of a male-only registration program. Because the Court had, on previous occasions, determined that a peacetime draft was constitutional, the issue in *Rostker* was limited to an equal protection challenge. That is, was a program that excluded women unconstitutional? Justices Byron White, William Brennan, and Thurgood Marshall dissented and found the administration's and Congress's reasons for excluding women a violation of the equal protection doctrine. The government went so far as to argue that the forced draft of women could "harm" the army. The government's position was interesting because the percentage of women in the armed forces had increased from the end of World War II from 1.1 percent to 6.2 percent, and Congress had approved it. In conference, Burger expressed support for the government's position, as did Justice William Rehnquist. White countered that because the armed forces had many positions staffed by women, the government's argument strained logic. In the end, Congress and the administration prevailed, and one may reasonably suspect they did so not only because of chauvinism but also because of the perils the nation faced and the fear of change. And, as the Court noted many years earlier in *Orloff v. Willoughby*, "judges are not tasked with running the Army."

By the time the Court issued *Rostker*, Reagan was president and the decision provided an avenue to enlarge the military through conscription, though this proved unneeded. The Court also issued *Dames & Moore v. Regan* which permitted Reagan to terminate legal proceedings against the government of Iran. Dames & Moore was a corporation and unlike the freed hostages, did not sue Khomeini's government. Rather, the corporation sued the Shah's government for a legitimate debt and the suit carried over to Iranian funds in United States banks. Under international law, Khomeini's government had a potential claim to these monies. Once Treasury Secretary Donald Regan, in accordance with the International Emergency Economic Powers Act moved to protect Iran's assets, the corporation sued the Treasury Department for recovery. The Court, in an eight to eight-to-one opinion, sided with the Reagan administration. The decision further expanded presidential authority in foreign policy, though, unlike in *Goldwater*, Congress had given broad statutory powers to the president to do so.

Although Ernest Fitzgerald had been reinstated to the air force, the fact that Nixon and two White House officials conspired to malign him remained in the news. As noted previously, Ford and Carter, and now Reagan, sided with Nixon on the issue of presidential immunity from civil suits. The Court, in *Nixon v. Fitzgerald*, an opinion authored by Justice Powell, determined that a president possesses immunity from civil suits arising out of presidential acts. White countered in his dissent that the Court distrusted the federal trial court to properly apply the Federal Rules of Civil Procedure to prevent frivolous suits. In other words, he insisted that the courts could be trusted on adjudicating civil claims of presidential wrongdoing, while accusing the majority of creating distrust in the courts. More important, he warned that the majority reverted the nation to the "king is above the law" concept found in eighteenth-century Europe. *Fitzgerald* is a powerful decision for shielding presidential misconduct, and unlike congressional immunity, which is rooted in the Constitution's language, the Constitution is silent on presidential immunity. It makes sense that presidential policies should not be halted by civil suits, although this type of immunity might encourage a president to commit tortious conduct.

The Supreme Court has not relied on *Goldwater* to a great degree, but this does not diminish the significance of the opinion. A brief recognition of *Goldwater*'s usage is worthy of note if for no other reason than understanding that the Court settled a pressing matter that since has given clarity to the elected branches of government. In 2012, the Court issued *Zivotofsky v. Clinton*, an opinion that arose from a challenge to the State Department's policies on the issuance of passports. (In 2015, the Court issued a further opinion titled *Zivotofsky v. Kerry*, which was referenced in the introduction to this book.) Congress had passed a law that permitted US citizens born in Jerusalem to have their place of birth listed as Israel on their US passport. While Congress enabled this to occur, the status of Jerusalem as Israel's capital has been a contentious political issue. When the United Nations voted to partition Britain's mandate in Palestine into a separate Israel and Palestine in 1947, Jerusalem was located in

Palestine. Through a series of armed conflicts, particularly the Six-Day War of 1967, the Israeli government claimed Jerusalem as its capital and Congress, in the Jerusalem Embassy Act of 1995, authorized a president to move the US embassy to that city. Binyamin Zivotofsky, a US citizen, was born in Jerusalem and sued the State Department when it refused to place Israel as his place of birth on his passport. His lawsuit bounced between the US District Court for the District of Columbia and the Court of Appeals for the District of Columbia, while the doctrines of standing and justiciability were considered. Ultimately the appellate court reasoned, in citing to Brennan's *Goldwater* dissent, that the president has the sole province to recognize foreign governments. (Of course, the issue in the Court during Goldwater's appeal was not recognition of the People's Republic of China but rather the power to terminate a treaty.)

The Court, in an opinion authored by Chief Justice John Roberts, concluded that Zivotofsky's suit was justiciable and remanded the case to the district court to determine the merits of Zivotofsky's claims. In their concurrence, Justices Sonya Sotomayor and Stephen Breyer quoted from Justice Powell's *Goldwater* concurrence that it "may be appropriate for courts to stay their hand in cases implicating delicate questions concerning the distribution of political authority between coordinate branches until a dispute is ripe, intractable, and incapable of resolution by the political process." After *Zivotofsky* was decided, President Donald Trump directed the US embassy to move from Tel Aviv to Jerusalem and to have passports marked in the manner Zivotofsky sought. Thus, the issue became moot.

The federal courts of appeal have cited to *Goldwater* for a variety of challenges to foreign policy and presidential authority. For instance, when Congressmen Theodore Weiss (D-NY) and Ronald Dellums (D-CA) aligned with peace organizations and British citizens to challenge the Reagan administration's placement of nuclear-armed cruise missiles in the United Kingdom (consistent with a NATO request), both a district court and the Court of Appeals for the Second Circuit determined, in citing to *Goldwater*, that the federal courts could not take up the suit. But the appellate court cited to Powell's concurrence, rather than the majority. In 1991, several Jamaican citizens being held in New York prisons sued to be transported to Jamaica to serve out their sentences. There are treaties and agreements between the United States and foreign governments that permit this to occur, but none in regard to Jamaica. The prisoners argued that they were deprived of a right that European nationals enjoyed. In response, a district court, in citing to *Goldwater*, concluded that foreign agreements were the sole province of the president and therefore nonjusticiable. In non–foreign policy decisions, the federal courts have cited to *Goldwater* over one hundred times, but none of the decisions rely solely on *Goldwater*, and it appears more as a means for drawing a distinction or explaining a general view on justiciability. Nonetheless, *Goldwater* is important beyond subsequent case law.

The Political Implications of *Goldwater v. Carter*

Shortly before the 1980 Winter Olympics began, a New York state trial judge ordered the city of Lake Placid to fly the Taiwanese flag. The International Olympic Committee had welcomed athletes from the People's Republic of China to participate in the Olympics, and the Carter administration celebrated their presence in the United States. The Olympic Committee tried to prevent the Taiwanese flag from being publicly displayed, but the Taiwanese also fielded a team, and the international organization tried to impose its flag decision on the city. To this end, Judge Norman Harvey, a former mayor of a nearby town, determined that issues of foreign policy had no bearing on how a visiting team would be honored by the city. This judicial act hardly made the news. Indeed, the major news items continued to be the hostage crisis with Iran, the Soviet invasion of Afghanistan, and Carter's announcement of a boycott of the 1980 Summer Olympics in Moscow. In all likelihood, the Olympics are remembered in the United States for its men's ice hockey team defeating the Soviet Union's team and winning the gold medal, and the flag dispute is largely forgotten.

On January 28, 1981, Alexander Haig delivered his first press briefing as secretary of state. He noted the United States' continuing commitment to South Korea as well as a heightened concern over international terrorism. In 1979, Haig had escaped an attempt on his life from terrorists while he commanded NATO's military forces. He reminded the news reporters that even the Soviet Union had been victimized by terrorism and that the Reagan administration opposed Muammar Gaddafi's invasion of Chad. Most of his discussion focused on the Soviet Union, particularly regarding Brezhnev's threats against Poland. After World War II, Poland had fallen under the "Iron Curtain," and its people suffered through a heavy-handed communist regime. Throughout the 1970s, however, there was an upwelling of social unrest, demanding greater freedoms; in response, the Soviet Union along with East Germany and other communist nations threatened a military invasion. "As you know, in early December, the North Atlantic Council of the NATO Alliance suggested in very clear language that any Soviet intervention in Poland would have the gravest consequence in the context of ongoing East-West relations, and that those consequences would be long-standing in time," Haig insisted. "I know of nothing today that would cause this Administration or this State Department to depart from the strong affirmation of that view." He went on to state, "It is clear that we have been witnessing an unprecedented—at least in character and scope—risk-taking on the part of the Soviet Union, not just in this hemisphere but in Africa as well." Not once did he mention China, and for good reason. The Chinese government condemned Soviet aggression against Poland, just as it had applauded the prospect of German unification. Carter's recognition of China and victory in the Supreme Court had made it more likely for this type of partnering to have occurred.

One measure of *Goldwater*'s importance is that it is not relied upon more; this may appear to be counterintuitive, but it is not. This is because *Goldwater* was, in effect, a dispositive judicial act that informed Congress and the president that the courts could not be used to adjudicate foreign policy disputes. Whether by design or not, the Court not only enabled Carter to proceed against the Soviet Union by withholding US participation in the 1980 Olympic Games but also further enabled Reagan to arm mujahideen rebels in Afghanistan without the worries of a challenge in the courts. Ultimately, the mujahideen achieved a remarkable military victory over the Soviet Union that contributed to the Soviet Union's dissolution. *Goldwater* may have also emboldened presidential administrations, including Reagan's, to skirt congressional limitations, such as the Boland Amendment, in the pursuit of foreign policy. In that instance, the Reagan administration supported clandestine operations to overthrow the communist Nicaraguan government as well as to support El Salvador's anticommunist regime.

Reagan, like Goldwater, was clearly unhappy with Carter's policy to disconnect Taiwan from the list of nations recognized by the United States. Yet, he did not just respect the Court's decision; it empowered his administration to conduct foreign policy without the fear of judicial review and, for that matter, has given authority to every administration since. Although he disagreed with Carter's decision to terminate the Mutual Defense Treaty, he did not campaign on a promise to restore Taiwan to its prior position. In August 1980, with the election three months out, Reagan promised to protect the integrity of Taiwan. This meant having a fully staffed embassy in Taipei and the sale of military equipment to Taiwan. Reagan did not publicly call the People's Republic of China a threat. Instead, he discussed the importance of Sino-US relations to his administration. "We have an obvious interest in developing our relationship with China—an interest that goes beyond trade and cultural ties," Reagan claimed. "It is an interest that is fundamental to a Reagan and Bush Administration. A dedication, a commitment to securing peace, for this and future generations." Five days after making that statement, Reagan once more tried to assure conservatives as well as the people of Taiwan that his administration would be dedicated to Taiwan's defense. "If the United States is to be a strong, reliable partner and friend, it requires that we listen carefully and consult with those who maintain friendly relations or alliances," he insisted.

Reagan's administration also undertook several steps to contain Iran; militarily confront Libya's dictator, Muammar Gaddafi; strengthen US military forces within NATO; and support insurgents in clandestine wars in Central America and in Afghanistan. Reagan was certainly a defense hawk and more willing than his predecessor to use military power across the globe. He was also willing to work with anticommunist dictators in a manner that Carter deplored as anti–human rights. But Reagan also had a sense of where presidential conduct in foreign policy had moral and ethical limits. As noted earlier, he believed it would be catastrophic to the United States' sovereignty for candidates to seek the aid of foreign governments in order to win elections.

Much has changed since *Goldwater*. While *Goldwater* did not directly address any constitutional area beyond treaty termination, it is helpful to recall Arthur Schlesinger's quote on the growth of presidential power. In his book *The Imperial Presidency*, he defined the term "imperial" as connoting when a president claimed to act on powers outside of the Constitution. On the third substantive page of his book, he argued that the Constitution withheld monarchal power from the president in the treaty-making process, and even in the power to involve the United States in a foreign war. *Goldwater* placed foreign policy back within the political arena. Its legacy is still felt in that arena.

It is important to recognize that legislators, unless they act with a majority voice, will have a more difficult time overcoming the hurdle of standing than Goldwater and his allies experienced. In 1997, the Court, in *Raines v. Byrd*, determined that individual members of Congress do not have special standing to challenge a law. *Raines* did not arise from a foreign policy action. Instead, Congress had passed a law, titled the Line Item Veto Act, that did not enable a president to veto particular spending measures but to "cancel" spending and tax measures after signing them into law. Six members of Congress challenged the law in the courts, arguing that it diluted their votes beyond what the Constitution permitted. While they had initial success at the district court, the Supreme Court held that their claims of an institutional injury were too "abstract and widely dispersed" to constitute an injury. Moreover, the Court noted that neither the House nor the Senate authorized their suit. Unless there is a unified legislative resolution authorizing a suit against the assertion of presidential power, *Raines* makes a legislative challenge to a presidential action such as Carter's being addressed by the courts much less likely.

On December 13, 2001, President George W. Bush notified the Russian government that he intended to remove the United States from the Anti-Ballistic Missile Treaty of 1972. The treaty, which had passed by a vote of eighty-eight to two, limited the number of missile defense systems the United States and the Soviet Union were permitted to possess. While a small number of Democrats in the Congress opposed Bush's determination to withdraw, a majority in Congress supported his decision. Dennis Kucinich (D-OH) and thirty-one other members of Congress tried to sue Bush in the US District Court for the District of Columbia on the basis that the withdrawal required congressional consent. Judge John D. Bates, in dismissing their suit, relied heavily on *Goldwater* to determine that the withdrawal was a political question. As an important point, he noted that *Goldwater* was a fractured ruling, and there was no "obviously binding holding." However, he then determined that Justice Rehnquist's plurality opinion was "instructive and compelling." As a result, in at least one court, Rehnquist's plurality is now viewed as binding.

On May 21, 2020, President Trump announced that the United States would withdraw from the Open Skies Treaty and insisted on the United States leaving the World Health Organization. Trump also withdrew the United States from the 1987 Intermediate Range Nuclear Forces Treaty. Originally signed into effect by Reagan and General Secretary Mikhail Gorbachev, the treaty was implemented to defuse tensions and accelerate peace and security for Europe. This time, a congressional majority disapproved of Trump's actions, but as the federal courts appear to offer no avenues of redress, the issue could only factor into elections and Congress's power of the purse.

The Trump administration provides the clearest illustration that Senator Goldwater's warning and that of Judge Gasch and Judge MacKinnon were neither illusory nor fanciful. Goldwater argued that a presidency corralled only by the threat of impeachment could remove the United States from NATO. On several occasions Trump spoke in a manner that at least was perceived as a threat to exit from NATO. He certainly threatened to act in a manner to reduce the effectiveness of the organization. Perhaps Goldwater did not envision that presidential immunity from misconduct in civil suits, or criminal charging as a result of prosecutorial discretion, would also enable a president to control the intelligence agencies through threats of criminal and civil prosecution of subordinates. And Goldwater likely did not foresee that a president might use a "bully pulpit" to have the lives of dedicated civil servants threatened by his loyal followers, or that a Congress would not have the strength to curtail such activities. Yet, during Trump's presidential tenure, threats against life and presidential harassment were directed at members of the national security community who uncovered that he tried to predicate favorable relations with Ukraine in exchange for that government's participation in sullying a potential competitor in an upcoming presidential election.

Further, it is likely that the Court did not envision a president using foreign policy for personal purposes such as the possibility that Trump's attempted partnering with Vladimir Putin might occur for reasons other than the best interests of the nation. In 2019, Senator Susan

Collins (R-ME) claimed Trump had "learned his lesson" after the first impeachment trial, in which the Senate acquitted the former president for his conduct involving Ukraine. Clearly, with revelations arising from congressional investigations after January 6, 2020, whatever "lesson" Trump learned did not involve conforming to the law or, for that matter, respecting the constitutional institutions of the government. Perhaps Donald Trump would have acted in the manner he did regardless of the Court's opinions. It is certainly possible that, with the shield of *Goldwater*, a future president will use foreign policy for personal reasons rather than in the best interests of national security or a commitment to protect democracy, and the only safeguard is Congress rather than the courts.

The issue of the Taiwanese flag at the 1980 Olympics is hardly remembered today. It is unlikely the machinations of the Trump administration will fall into this category at any time; indeed, his conduct will likely be embedded as a well-read chapter in the nation's history. With *Goldwater* enabling an insulated presidential foreign policy power, and being buttressed by contemporary opinions on control over civil servants, presidential immunity from civil suits, and the authority to stop civil suits between nongovernmental parties that might, in the judgment of a malfeasant president, hamper foreign policy and national security, the power recognized in *Goldwater* provides a stamp of possibility for a repeat occurrence of the Ukraine debacle of 2018–2019. But, it also enables a well-meaning president to act decisively in foreign affairs without much fear from the courts. Prime Minister Winston Churchill, who, like Carter and Goldwater, had Palmerstonian attributes, once quipped that "democracy is the worst form of government—except for all the others that have been tried." In *Goldwater*, the Court placed the burden of deciding presidential conduct in the broader foreign policy realm wholly within the political, rather than legal, arena, which means that it falls to elected legislators and the electorate itself—that is, citizens who both desire to vote and are permitted to do so—to decide whether a president is acting in the best constitutional interests of the nation.

CHRONOLOGY

August 21, 1927	Chinese Civil War between Kuomintang (Nationalist) government and Chinese Communist Party
July 7, 1937	Empire of Japan began invasion of Republic of China; Chinese Civil War temporarily ceased during the course of World War II
April 25, 1941	US government and the Nationalist forces under Chiang Kai-shek enter into an agreement through which US loans and equipment support the war against Japan
December 8, 1941	US government declares war on Japan and becomes formal ally of China
August 9, 1945	Soviet Union enters into the war against Japan and occupies Manchuria; Soviet military arms Chinese Communist Party forces for continuation of war against Japan
August 30, 1945	Small-scale clashes resume between Kuomintang (Nationalist) government and Chinese Communist Party
September 9, 1945	Japanese forces in China formally surrender to Chiang Kai-shek
July 20, 1946	Chiang Kai-shek commands a military offensive into communist-held areas in North China
October 1, 1949	After a succession of military defeats, Chiang Kai-shek's surviving forces retreat to Taiwan and establish the Republic of China
June 25, 1950	Korean War begins
November 8, 1952	Barry Goldwater elected US senator for Arizona
July 27, 1953	Armistice of warring nations in Korean War concluded
December 2, 1954	United States and Republic of China enter into the Mutual Defense Treaty
February 9, 1955	US Senate votes in favor of treaty ratification
November 1, 1955	Vietnam War (Second Indochina War) begins
August 23, 1958	Second Taiwan Strait Crisis: President Eisenhower orders the US military to protect Taiwan if invasion by communist Chinese occurs
August 10, 1964	Gulf of Tonkin Resolution: enlargement of US military forces in Vietnam
February 28, 1972	President Richard M. Nixon begins the process of normalization with the People's Republic of China

	but assures the Republic of China that the Mutual Defense Treaty remains intact
January 27, 1973	Paris Peace Accords: United States' formal role in Vietnam War ceases
April 30, 1975	Vietnam War ends with the communist victory over South Vietnam (Republic of Vietnam)
January 20, 1977	James Earl Carter becomes the thirty-ninth president of the United States
September 7, 1977	Panama Canal Treaty signed with the Panamanian government; congressional conservatives unsuccessfully try to stop the canal transfer in the federal courts
January 7, 1978	Iranian Revolution begins
December 15, 1978	President Carter announces normalization with the People's Republic of China and termination of the Mutual Defense Treaty with the Republic of China
December 16, 1978	Senator Goldwater announces he will file suit against President Carter in the US District Court for the District of Columbia
February 11, 1979	Ayatollah Ruhollah Khomeini and Shia religious leaders in control of Iran
June 6, 1979	Judge Oliver Gasch hears arguments between Goldwater et al. and President Carter over the treaty termination; Gasch initially decides against Goldwater
June 7, 1979	US Senate passes resolution stating that the Senate believes a vote on treaty revocation is required by the Constitution
September 11, 1979	Prime minister of Afghanistan assassinated and Soviet invasion appears imminent
October 17, 1979	Judge Oliver Gasch rules in favor of Goldwater et al. and determines that President Carter's actions, if taken, would violate the US Constitution
November 4, 1979	US embassy personnel taken hostage in Tehran, Iran
November 13, 1979	US Court of Appeals for the District of Columbia hears arguments challenging Gasch's decision
November 30, 1979	Court of appeals reverses Gasch, but the per curiam (majority) determines their decision only on the specific treaty, and not on a general constitutional principle
December 13, 1979	US Supreme Court, without oral argument, dismisses Goldwater et al.'s suit and orders Gasch to vacate decision

BIBLIOGRAPHIC ESSAY

This project originated at Arizona State University's Distinctive Collections Library in 2017. This is an important point. Much of this book is based on primary source material such as the correspondences of the principal actors, rather than secondary sources such as books and articles. But it began there because I was researching Barry Goldwater's role in the attempted impeachment of Justice William O. Douglas in 1970. Because of library renovations, in the four times I visited, the Barry Goldwater Papers had three different homes: the main campus library; the library annex in Mesa, Arizona; and the Music Library. This is a huge collection, and as a result of beginning my research there, when I later conducted research in the Strom Thurmond Papers at Clemson University, the Carl Curtis Papers at the Nebraska State Historical Society, and the Paul Laxalt Papers at the University of Nevada, as well as other congressional collections, I often discovered redundancy insofar as evidence of the political reasons for joining with Goldwater. But this redundancy illuminated an important character of Goldwater and his congressional allies: they believed that abandoning Taiwan endangered democracy in the long term to the point that they excoriated those who argued that opening China to business investment would help bring the United States out of an economic slump. Certainly, they had little affinity for Carter and often derided his "human rights" focus as being "soft." They were livid over his grant of amnesty to those who evaded the draft during the Vietnam War as much as they were angered over the Panama Canal Treaty. And they were often reactionary. In regard to the legislators opposing Carter, though, there was a genuineness to their opposition to him in the federal courts.

I also conducted research in the Senator Frank Church Papers at Boise State University's Special Collections and Archives. Like the Goldwater Papers, this collection is a treasure trove for scholars of the 1960s and 1970s. Finally, I visited the James Earl Carter Library at Georgia Southwestern State University and reviewed dozens of memorandums, but because I wanted to concentrate on the legislative-judicial relationship, much of this research served the important step of providing context for how the Carter administration planned to respond to Goldwater. Before noting the location and importance of judicial and other collections, I must mention three other presidential libraries where I conducted research: the Richard Nixon, Gerald Ford, and Ronald Reagan libraries, which are administered by the National Archives and Records Administration. All three of these libraries provided useful context to this project.

Judge Oliver Gasch's papers are located at the Georgetown University School of Law Library. The two largest portions of his collection are the trials of Robert "Bobby" Baker and various matters related to the Watergate scandal. Yet there is enough material in the collection related to *Goldwater v. Carter* to help one understand Gasch's reasoning and how he shaped his two decisions. The papers of Judges Harold Leventhal, J. Skelly Wright, and Carl McGowan are located in the Library of Congress Manuscript Reading Room. I made extensive use of these three collections. I also utilized the papers of Judge Charles Fahy at the Library of Congress and the papers of Judge David Lionel Bazelon at the University of Pennsylvania. One appellate court judge's collection bears an important distinction: the George MacKinnon Papers at the Minnesota Historical Society. MacKinnon fascinates me because he had been portrayed as a political hack by one of the other judges on the appellate court, but his letters have an intelligence to them that makes clear he was a deeply thoughtful man.

The Harry A. Blackmun Papers at the Library of Congress Manuscript Reading Room are immeasurably helpful to any legal history scholar studying the 1970s and 1980s. This collection is well preserved and sizable, including correspondence with other justices, clerks, politicians, and the public. I relied on it as I did the collections of Justice William Brennan, Justice Thurgood Marshall, Justice Byron White, and Justice John Paul Stevens. The papers of Chief Justice Warren Burger are not yet open to the public. The William Hubbs Rehnquist Papers are available to the public at the Hoover Institution's library at Stanford University. By the time I examined his papers, I discovered a redundancy with those in the Library of Congress. As helpful as the Blackmun, Brennan, and Marshall collections are, however, the Lewis Powell Papers at the Washington and Lee Law School in Lexington, Virginia, are a treasure trove. I twice visited the library, but the entire collection is now digitized and available online, allowing scholars to conduct research from afar.

In terms of other collections that I have cited to, the Alan Cranston

Papers at the University of California Berkeley, Bancroft Library, the Robert Byrd Papers at the Robert C. Byrd Center at Shepherd University in West Virginia, and the Howard Baker Papers at the University of Tennessee were helpful to this project in several ways. Two aspects of them are important to highlight: first, they describe the views and reactions of other senators, including the majority of the legislators who wanted a "middle-ground" approach; second, because these senators, along with Frank Church, had served in Congress, their collections provide insight into the evolving views of US foreign policy, communism, China, and the Soviet Union. This is true in regard to the papers of Senator Abe Ribicoff, Senator Robert Alphonso Taft Jr., Senator Edwin Brooke, and Congresswoman Patsy Mink at the Library of Congress, as well as the papers of Congressman Gilbert Gude at the George Washington University Special Collections Library.

Other legislative collections that proved helpful to this project include the Joseph M. Montoya Papers at the University of New Mexico; the David L. Boren Collection and Carl Albert Collection at the University of Oklahoma; and the Francis McNamara Papers, Joel L. Fisher Papers, and William Lloyd Scott Papers at the George Mason University Special Collections Research Center. The Michel Oksenberg Papers at the University of Michigan's Bentley Historical Library, as well as the Herbert A. Philbrick Papers and William A. Rusher Papers at the Library of Congress, proved very helpful in understanding opposition to the recognition of China. Philbrick and Rusher were staunch anticommunists who corresponded with several of the legislators who aligned with Goldwater. I also quoted from the papers of Clinton Presba Anderson, Robert Taft, Tom Connally, Averell Harriman, and Emanuel Celler, all at the Library of Congress, as a matter of background. None of these men were in government at the time Carter announced his decision. Taft, Connally, and Celler had passed away by the time Goldwater filed suit. The Mary McGrory Papers, the George Lardner Papers, and the Anthony Lewis Papers at the Library of Congress were also helpful. Finally, as a matter of original source material, a great deal can be learned from the treaty termination hearings held on April 9–11, 1979, before the Senate Foreign Relations Committee.

For Carter's decisional processes, I have already noted that I conducted research at the James Earl Carter Presidential Library, but the

Walter Mondale Papers at the Minnesota Historical Society provide important data as well. As another important voice, Carter's national security adviser, Zbigniew Kazimierz Brzezinski published *Power and Principle: Memoirs of the National Security Advisor* (New York: Farrar, Straus & Giroux, 1983). I also recommend Brian J. Auten, *Carter's Conversion: The Hindering of American Defense Policy* (Columbia: University of Missouri Press, 2008), and Stuart E. Eizenstat, *President Carter: The White House Years* (New York: Thomas Dunne Books, 2018). Of course, Carter published his White House diary, which is a critical part of any study on his presidency; it is, not unexpectedly, titled *White House Diary* (New York: Farrar, Straus & Giroux, 2010). He also published *Keeping the Faith: Memoirs of a President* (Little Rock: University of Arkansas Press, 1982), and this too is helpful to understanding his views on China, communism, and imperialism.

Several secondary sources were helpful to accomplishing this book. Excellent overviews of the "Carter years" can be found in Edward Berkowitz, *Something Happened: A Political and Cultural Overview of the Seventies* (New York: Columbia University Press, 2006); Patrick Anderson, *Electing Jimmy Carter: The Campaign of 1976* (Baton Rouge: Louisiana State University Press, 1994); Carl Biven, *Jimmy Carter's Economy: Politics in an Age of Limits* (Chapel Hill: University of North Carolina Press, 2002); Matthew J. Ouiment, *The Rise and Fall of the Brezhnev Doctrine in Soviet Foreign Policy* (Chapel Hill: University of North Carolina Press, 2003); and Thomas J. Borstelmann, *The 1970s: A New Global History from Civil Rights to Economic Inequality* (Princeton, NJ: Princeton University Press, 2012). However, in my estimation, two books in particular rise above the others: Laura Kalman, *Right Star Rising: A New Politics, 1974–1980* (New York: W. W. Norton, 2010), and Daniel J. Sargent, *A Superpower Transformed: The Remaking of American Foreign Relations in the 1970s* (London: Oxford University Press, 2015). While neither of these books highlights Goldwater's efforts in the federal courts, both provide an unequaled context to the changing world of the later 1970s.

In terms of the history of Sino-US relations as well as relations between Taiwan and the United States, I made use of the following books, all of which I recommend. All the contributors to *Dangerous Strait: The U.S.-China-Taiwan Crisis* (New York: Columbia University Press, 2005), edited by Nancy Bernkopf Tucker, produced helpful essays. For the initial US commitment to Taiwan, I relied on Robert Accinelli's *Crisis and Commitment: United States Policy toward Taiwan, 1950–1955* (Chapel Hill: University of North Carolina Press, 1996). For further examination of the Taiwan Relations Act, I recommend David Lee's *The Making of the Taiwan Relations Act: Twenty Years in Retrospect* (New York: Oxford University Press, 2000). Most recently, Hsiao-ting Lin has published *Taiwan, the United States, and the Hidden History of the Cold War in Asia: Divided Allies* (New York: Routledge, 2022). I recommend this work, and while because of timing I did not make use of it in my own writing here, it was the final work I used to check the accuracy of this book.

On the congressional participants, readers who desire to understand the transformation of conservatism in the 1970s and the "Old Guard's" role in that transformation, should examine the following: Nadine Cohodas, *Strom Thurmond and the Politics of Southern Change* (Atlanta: Mercer University Press, 1993); Joseph Crespino, *Strom Thurmond's America* (New York: Hill & Wang, 2012); Ernest B. Ferguson, *Hard Right: The Rise of Jesse Helms* (New York: W. W. Norton, 1986); David W. Reinhard, *The Republican Right since 1945* (Lexington: University Press of Kentucky, 1983); and William C. Kasthaus, *Dapper Dan Flood: The Controversial Life of a Congressional Power Broker* (University Park: Penn State University Press, 2010). Finally, for background, James Lee Annis, *Howard Baker: Conciliator in an Age of Crisis* (Knoxville: University of Tennessee Press, 2007), is most helpful in understanding how Senate Republicans were diverse in their views on Carter's foreign policies. One source that is worthy to research but difficult to find is John M. Ashbrook's *No Left Turns: A Handbook for Conservatives Based on the Writings of John M. Ashbrook* (Fairfield, OH: Hamilton Hobby, 1986). Other books that provided background included Raymond L. Garthoff's *Détente and Confrontation: American-Soviet Relations from Nixon to Reagan* (Washington, DC: Brookings Institution Press, 1994), and Richard Vetterli and Brad Hainsworth's *The Lion's Den: The Story of Senator Hatch* (Springville, UT: Cedar Fort, 1994).

In regard to the Burger Court, the following books provide varying context: Tinsley E. Yarbrough, *The Burger Court: Justices, Rulings, and Legacy* (Santa Barbara, CA: ABC-CLIO, 2000); and Bernard Schwartz, *The Ascent of Pragmatism: The Burger Court in Action* (Menlo Park, CA: Addison-Wesley, 1990). On individual justices, see Mark V. Tushnet, *Making Constitutional Law, Thurgood Marshall and the Supreme Court, 1961–1991* (New

York: Oxford University Press, 1997); Earl Maltz, *The Chief Justiceship of Warren Burger, 1969–1986* (Columbia: University of South Carolina Press, 2000); Howard Ball, *Defiant Life: Thurgood Marshall and the Persistence of Racism in America* (New York: Crown, 1998); and John Calvin Jeffries, *Justice Lewis F. Powell* (New York: Fordham University Press, 2001). Of course, John R. Vile's edited book *Great American Judges* (Santa Barbara, CA: ABC-CLIO, 2003) is an excellent source for judicial biography as well as being a springboard for further research.

Finally, I utilized more newspaper research in this book than I have in previous books. Because of the rapidity of global change in the period 1978–1980, it is impossible for a historian to include all the nuanced events that, if not directly affecting judicial judgments, certainly contextualize them. To that end, the *New York Times*, *Christian Science Monitor*, *Washington Post*, *Chicago Tribune*, *Wall Street Journal*, and *Los Angeles Times* enable a scholar to understand the rapidity of crisis from the time of Carter's normalization announcement through the Court's dismissal of Goldwater's suit. The *Arizona Republic* must be noted as it captured Goldwater's statements in a manner that the other major newspapers did not. Other regional newspapers were helpful as well.

INDEX